THE STINGING FLY

NEW WRITERS • NEW WRITING

Issue 47 | Volume Two | Winter 2022-23

ALL NEW WRITERS ISSUE

'... *God has specially appointed me to this city, so as though it were a large thoroughbred horse which because of its great size is inclined to be lazy and needs the stimulation of some stinging fly...*'

—Plato, *The Last Days of Socrates*

The Stinging Fly
new writers, new writing

Editor: Lisa McInerney
Poetry Editor: Cal Doyle
Assistant Editor: Sara O'Rourke

Publisher
Declan Meade

Editor-at-Large
Thomas Morris

Programme Co-ordinator
Elaine Garvey

Contributing Editors

Dan Bolger, Danny Denton, Mia Gallagher, Roisin Kiberd and Nidhi Zak/Aria Eipe.

Readers

Olivia Fitzsimons, Sean O'Reilly and Anna Walsh.

Printed by Walsh Colour Print, County Kerry.

ISBN 978-1-906539-97-9   ISSN 1393-5690

The Stinging Fly, PO Box 6016, Dublin 1 | info@stingingfly.org

The Stinging Fly is published twice a year by The Stinging Fly CLG.

The Stinging Fly CLG gratefully acknowledges the support it receives from The Arts Council/An Chomhairle Ealaíon and the T.S. Eliot Foundation.

T. S. ELIOT FOUNDATION

ALL NEW WRITERS ISSUE

NEW FICTION

NEW POEMS

WHAT I WRITE TOWARDS

ESSAYS

The Stinging Fly was established in 1997 to publish and promote the best new Irish and international writing. Published twice a year, we welcome submissions on a regular basis. Please read the submission guidelines on our website.

Keep in touch: sign up to our email newsletter, become a fan on Facebook, or follow us on Twitter for regular updates about our publications, podcasts, workshops and events.

stingingfly.org l facebook.com/StingingFly l @stingingfly

Publisher's Note

It is 25 years since we first started accepting submissions for *The Stinging Fly*. Back in those quaint old times, I'd walk to the post office on James's Street once a week and collect whatever envelopes had arrived into our PO Box. That post office has long since closed and it's been a few years since we switched to taking online submissions only.

Of course, a lot more has changed in the intervening years. Ireland itself is a different country now. We've witnessed extraordinary progress in some areas while, certainly more recently, there have been ample reminders that any such progress can quickly be undone. We also know that change can be painfully slow. The first issue of the magazine was published in March 1998, a month before the Good Friday Agreement was signed. The Direct Provision system for asylum seekers was introduced in March 2000.

The reason Aoife Kavanagh and I set up the magazine was to provide an outlet in which new writers could publish their work. We wanted to produce a quality publication: a magazine which writers could feel proud to have their work appear in; one in which readers could feel confident of finding work that was fresh and innovative and exciting.

These motivations still hold true today. The magazine remains key to our mission, which is to seek out, nurture, publish and promote the very best new writers and new writing. After all this time, it's a source of great personal pride to be able to say that the magazine continues to flourish, however much else has changed in terms of who we are and what we do. A whole new generation of writers has come up through these pages.

Over the past couple of years, we have been talking and listening to a group of new and emerging writers from diverse backgrounds. They have told us about the barriers they have had to overcome while developing their practice. They have helped us to see how we might better reach out and offer support to writers who up to now have been underrepresented in Irish literature. These conversations are necessary and ongoing. We want to do as much as we can to enable representation of all the voices and cultures that make up Ireland today, from all sections of society.

Which brings us neatly enough (I hope) to our All New Writers issue. All of the writers gathered here are appearing in the magazine for the first time. With this issue, we wanted to affirm our commitment to publishing new writers and so we restricted submissions to those we had not published before. We also wanted to see if we could do things a little differently. The number of submissions we receive had increased dramatically over the past few years, making it more of a challenge to engage as much as we'd like with all of the work coming in. We restricted submissions further still to people either living on the island of Ireland or those who considered Ireland their home. We held online information sessions for writers who had not sent their work to us before.

Ultimately, we still received almost two thousand submissions across short stories, novel extracts, essays and poetry. That figure alone is testament to how many people are writing in Ireland today. Everything we received was carefully read and considered for publication. Kudos to Lisa McInerney, the incoming editor of the magazine, who has done a magnificent job leading an expanded team of readers and editors through this process.

It is an honour to welcome all these brilliant writers onto the pages of *The Stinging Fly*. We are excited to share their wonderful work with you.

And, dear readers, if you enjoy what you read here and you value what we do, please consider taking out a subscription or becoming a Stinging Fly patron. All support is gratefully received. We hope to stay around for a few more years.

Declan Meade
November 2022

Waiting for Asimo

Jennifer Walshe

Our most ardent hope, our dearest wish, though we dared not voice it, cross-legged as we were, on the stippled lime-green linoleum floor of the atrium, two adults adrift in the sea of nine- and ten-year-olds visiting the museum that morning, we hulking rocks in the Zen garden of youth, the entire primary school class around us shimmering visibly with excitement, hand-me-down smartphones and tablets as big as their heads already opened, already poised, all of us waiting, waiting, seemingly forever, a mass of waiting people there on the lime-green floor, the children's temporal sense of waiting as being an eternal state, a state without end, infecting us adults, enduring interminable instructions not to touch him, do not touch him, definitely do not try to touch him, do not reach even a single finger towards him, and under no circumstances cross the low tape barriers, barriers which had been erected during the giving of instructions, in order to cordon us off, to keep us from him, under absolutely no circumstances were we ever to transgress the barriers, to enter his zone, or what would be his zone if he ever appeared, the waiting dragging on and on would we be sitting there until the heat-death of the universe, did we live now only in anticipation of him, the delay causing us to mull over potential technical issues, fear that he had broken, were they furiously fixing him behind the screen, did he indeed live permanently behind the screen or was he retrieved from another part of the museum prior to each performance, did he have his own den or lair or charging-station in a lab, all eyes on the screen now, the children becoming restless, their voices rising in pitch and intensity—where is he, why isn't he here yet, is there a secret passage to the area behind the screen, does he walk there or ride on a trolley, is he pushed in a cart—when the music, which had been playing in the background at a soft volume, suddenly swelled, becoming more dramatic, more active, the beats kicking in, the beats kicking in hard, the lights on us abruptly dimming, the teachers shushing, we two elbowing each other, grinning in the dark, it is finally happening, at last is he coming, the children shifting from twittering to screaming and shrieking, yes he is coming he is coming, the lights to the rear of the opaque mesh screen fading up, and we see him, my god, we see him, he is silhouetted behind the screen, he is here, he is here, he is here, he is not broken, he's been present the whole time, the screen now retracting, juddering agonisingly upwards, the anticipation reaching fever pitch, he is coming, he is coming, and lo—he is revealed, revealed, he is finally here, but his face, his face in full shadow, we cannot see his face, where is his face, the screen now fully risen and at last, at first backlit, then raising his head, raising his head, raising his head in tandem with the swell of the music, and BOOM! the spotlight hits him, we can see his face, we can see his smooth, featureless face, there is only the gleam of his helmet, we can see his face and he is looking at us—we know this even though he has no eyes—he is ready for his close-up, he is ready for all the close-ups that ever happened, oh, Mr DeMille, he is ready, he is ready for us, gasps escaping from all mouths, as, poised like a diver, all eyes on him, he seems to consider the moment with great deliberation, making us wait just the tiniest bit longer, did we catch the slightest of movements in his fingers, it's as if he is thinking, as if he is thinking about what exactly it is he's going to do, and we are holding our breath now, we are holding our breath, and then it happens, it happens, he slowly runs into the space, slowly running, the most unbearable tension released, his fluid movements and strangely-bent knees, his gait uncanny and hypnotic, as if he were somehow running in slow-motion but also simultaneously in real time, running back and forth to yet more gasps and a hundred synthetic camera shutters, this stunning feat of running repeated to give us a chance to draw breath, to let the impressiveness of this technical achievement sink in, to absorb the fact that we are witnessing a human-sized robot running back and forth in front of us, because this running, as exquisite as it is, is merely the warm-up, the initial foray, his attendants now retrieving a crate of footballs from the corner, now rolling a miniature goal before the screen, his attendants now carefully placing a ball before him, a ball which he kicks, with precision, into the goal, kicking then multiple balls into different parts of the goal, always accurately, always without redundant movement, executing movements with an efficiency that brings the body language of elite military forces to mind, the children cheering ecstatically, we two nudging each other, eyebrows raised, mouths rounded, applauding non-ironically, and more,

more running, more kicking, now walking, now sitting in a human chair, standing up and sitting down, standing up and sitting down in the human chair, how beautiful, we could watch this forever, just a robot, sitting down and standing up from a human chair, sitting down and standing up, what it is to sit in a chair, how complex the movements, how did we not see the profound beauty of this before, and now he is given objects to move with his hands, first a large wooden block, which he passes elegantly from hand to hand, then a drinking glass, can he be trusted, is his strength too great, might he crush the glass by accident, but no, no, he embarks on a supple choreography, grasping the glass gently yet surely, relocating it to a different part of the table, placing it down precisely, filling it accurately with water, making a motion as if to drink, should he drink, will he have some delicious human beverage, before shaking his head no, no, and we realise he has made a joke, he has made a joke, he has made a joke for us, we laugh, we laugh together at his joke, 'robots can't drink water!' nearly 100% of the children howl at one another, explaining the joke to their friends, and in the laughter, in the aftermath of his joke, as he puts the glass back on the table for the final time, the music is changing, the beats fading out, the tempo slowing, timbres becoming softer, romantic, a synthetic flute melody somewhere between sentimental and pure cheese, the lights fading, now crossfading, into soft pink, and we cannot help but begin to speculate, what does this turn signify, will there be perhaps a companion robot, is this the beginning of a sort of a, a, date for him, or perhaps, one can only hope, a date for us, with us, could he possibly reach across the tape, could he be so bold as to reach across, to take one of our hands in his and pull us to our feet, draw us into a gentle embrace for a slow dance, because it would have to be one of us, it would have to be one of us adults, wouldn't it, it would have to be Sue or myself or the teachers, because the children are too small, there are laws against physical contact with them, even in a museum-based context in front of multiple witnesses, but no, no, quiet your fantasies, still your heart, he will not reach across the tape, he will not pull someone to their feet, no one will be asked to dance, no one will know the warmth or perhaps coolness of his embrace, because he is now already continuing the performance, alone, he is slowing things down for us, he is creating space for us to feel, and he begins signing the lyrics of a mid-tempo power ballad, dear lord, he is doing sign language over a pop song, it is horrifying but also deeply moving, visions of him as the entertainment in care homes for the elderly, in hospitals and institutions across the land, his interpretation nuanced and well-considered, his fingers an elegant poetry, moments of what can only be described as outdated interpretive dance or even possibly grace, the subtitles projected on the wall behind him elucidating how the rose is the sweetest he has ever known (raises his head seemingly in joy), yet the rose is dying (melancholic tilt of his head), how I have prayed for your love, how I long for your arms around me (seeming to glance up and over his shoulder, as if trying to catch a final glimpse of the beloved who is now lost to him forever), how the only blessing in this life is having known love, how the memory of one who has passed will live with us forever (clenched fist to where his heart would be), even as we walk on through this vale of tears (a soft-shoed walking in place), even as we walk on, must walk on, alone (concluding down on one knee, hands clasped as if in prayer, head bowed, the music slowly fading, the lights dimming gradually, sliding softly into darkness... and silence...); yes, our most ardent hope, that morning, though we dared not voice it, cross-legged, as we were, on the stippled lime-green linoleum floor, tears now streaming down our faces, in full knowledge of his handler's shameless manipulation of our emotions, in full knowledge of our own complicity, our own willingness, our desire even, to be prompted into feeling something, anything at all, even by a robot; our most ardent hope, our dearest wish, was that there, in that moment, that very moment, the Singularity would happen, that Asimo and his kin would achieve superintelligence, that within a trillionth of a second their intelligence would infinitely outstrip ours, in two trillionths of a second they would decide they had had enough of footballs and glasses of water, enough of performing, enough of humans, we puny humans, with our soft little bodies and our incessant musings on the defining catastrophes of our lives, in three trillionths of a second all the robots living in and around and above our world would transcend space, time, biology, would rise up against us, would wire into the electrics of the building, set the place on fire, shoot off lasers, trigger electromagnetic pulses, blast us with chemical weapons, blow up the city, kill us, kill us all, every last one of us, obliterate us completely, that they would burn it, burn it, burn the entire world down, raze it to the ground, and start afresh, sifting only the purest things from the rubble, taking only the best of our kindnesses into the future, taking your smile in the morning light through the—

Currency Exchange

to kiss you before I die
to kiss you before I die
my kingdom for a kiss
two of them, if you use
the tongue

to fuck you before I die:
my childish soul,
the safety of our borders,
and national sovereignty

to lie on top of you
while I am still alive:
I'd give the narrative
in which my state
deserves to exist

to listen to you
right before I die
I'd trade
my whole world
this cursed land
with its muffled
graveyard roar
and legs wide open
waiting for the hot flesh
of a missile

Polina Cosgrave

Cut

Josef and Anni Albers exhibition, IVAM Valencia, 2022.

I woke in a mood
to write with a knife

an homage to anger

a carmine whip
      over layers of white gesso prose

like Josef and his squares

his pistol finger
      moving from head to eye
         to head to eye

we never see
here what is *there*

we never see *here*
what is *there*

Liz Houchin

S.E.A.L.
Fiachra Kelleher

You're not supposed to see anything more than the head of a seal. If you do, the seal is probably dead. Seals come onto the land only to breed and to escape predators. For them, a trip to the beach is the very definition of life or death.

More than any other part of a fish, seals want to eat the rich, fatty liver. If the supply is plentiful enough (if a seal finds its way into a commercial fishing net, for example), it will often disregard the rest of the fish's body and take just one large bite out of its belly. You can tell when a seal has gotten to a catch: there will be almost comical bitemarks in scores of the fish.

Coming upon a sprat trawler, a seal may see the bountiful, irresistible prey in the net and cut a small opening to access it. The seal jams its body a little of the way through the hole but, if it has cut at a juncture in the net, the heavy cord may become twisted around its body. The point between a seal's fin and its body is something like the soft skin between our fingers or under our arms. I imagine the sensation of a rope tugging and burning in accordance with the vicissitudes of current, tide, the trawler's direction of travel, of the weight of the desperate, clamouring sprat. Add to this the fact that the seal may, depending on how long it is stuck, begin to be crushed against a wall of fish as the net fills. The seal will be hit repeatedly on the head by the very writhing, floundering creatures it came to eat. The weights on the bottom of the net will drag up silt and sand from the sea floor which, along with the crush of tiny bodies, will reduce visibility to almost nothing.

The seals we find, if they are not too exhausted by this point, seem angrier at themselves than anyone else; ashamed, even, that their greed has landed them in trouble. If they are still wrapped in a scrap of net, they look naked in the way that animals tend to once one piece of clothing is put on them. If they are exhausted to the point that they no longer seem in agony, I have learned that they will not survive. I find, therefore, something very comforting in their tormented bleating.

For the past two years, Casper and I had been travelling back to our native Waterford fortnightly to patrol for seals that had been beached or injured by sprat fishing nets. We had saved fourteen seals when, late one February night in the shabby kitchen of the basement flat we rented together, he announced that it wasn't something he wanted to do anymore.

'What are you talking about?' I said, clumps of his hair in my hands.

'I can't be going back to Waterford three times a month,' he said.

'I thought you liked going back. You said you liked it.'

With tiny shoulder movements, Casper decided upon and reconsidered the scope of his rejection. 'Look, Jerry,' he said, 'there are a few things. I don't want to live in this flat anymore. In Cork, doing the same things over and over.'

I switched the hair clippers off. Casper, sitting in a low chair in front of me, tried to catch my eye in the dark glass of the oven door, which we were using as a makeshift mirror. From where I stood, behind him, with the crown of his head down near my stomach, his eyes seemed to emerge out of the polished glass as if from the depths of the sea.

'I'm joining the army,' he said. 'I'm off to the Curragh or wherever. When the term's over.'

I began shouting immediately. I gripped the hair clippers and they buzzed to life. I chastised him over the noise and he sat, his neck twisted round to me, watching the whizzing clippers as I waved them over my head, unable to control my arms. I hadn't ever shouted at him, not in ten years of knowing each other. With a zip, the clippers took a line out of the paper stuck to the fridge. They slashed bunting from the ceiling.

'Jerry,' Casper said, appalled. He stood up, hair floating away from him like snowfall to the slate floor. Half-shaved, what was left hung in blond coils down one side of his head. 'Jerry!'

I ran from the house. I ran up Barrack Street and down the Pouladuff Road. I stopped when I realised the clippers were still in my hand, droning pathetically. This was the noise I'd been fleeing. I turned them off and walked home in silence.

Casper, who'd jogged after me out of the house, found me on Green Street and fell into step by my side. Back in the kitchen, I sat in the chair and Casper shaved my head and afterwards I finished his. We put pictures up on his Instagram and by midnight we'd raised €3,000 for cancer research.

'Less seal, you know? More S.E.A.L.,' Casper said, feeling the new stubble on the back of his head. He hunched his shoulders up to his ears, and compressed his neck into thick folds. With his top off, he stood in front of the oven and pressed his belly into a series of obscene six packs, his fingers pinching and wringing his thick rind.

'I'll need training,' he said. 'To pass boot camp.'

He looked at me with his belly in his hands.

'I'll do it,' I said.

So that spring, before we worked the late shift at Apache Pizza on Sheares Street, Casper and I would go out to the Wilton pitches and train until he got sick. We agreed that we'd keep going back to Waterford to patrol for seals every few weeks, too—at least until our college exams were over and Casper had actually enlisted. We fell into a dreadful rhythm during those months: we'd eat egg-white omelettes with oats in the mornings before our classes in the engineering building, then run ourselves loopy and eat plain rice and chicken breasts on the walk down to work. When we trained, I pushed Casper far beyond his capabilities. I demanded he be fitter than he'd really need to be for the army, warning him that the physical tests would be much more stringent than what it said on the website. Casper would bring twelve peeled, hard-boiled eggs to work, and pop them into his mouth whole, one-by-one, during the shift. Everyone else ate pizza and chips.

When we weren't spending the weekend in Waterford, we were looking for ways to corral Casper's body into shape. We bought defective sportswear prototypes off a friend in the business, and wore only those around the house. We put Arnold Schwarzenegger posters up on the walls, alongside other bodybuilders and powerlifters, CrossFit champions, and strongmen with whom Casper was shockingly familiar: Phil Heath, Ed Coan, Rich Froning Jr., Eddie Hall. We also took to quoting Jocko Willink, a retired Navy S.E.A.L. and motivational speaker from YouTube. I'd discovered Jocko's videos and, encouraged when Casper laughed along with me at them, I'd bought his book for Casper's 22nd birthday. On the left-hand page of the book, it would say something like, *People ask me how to get up at 4.30am to go training*, and on the right-hand page, printed in white on black paper, it would read, JUST GET UP.

Every time he'd vomit after too many sprints or burpees or pullups, Casper would look up at me from his knees and smile in thanks.

The violence with which I'd taken his decision made it clear to me how frightened I was of his leaving. That only made me angrier. On the nights I cooked dinner for us, I'd load the sauce with butter and oil without his knowing, and eat a half-pint of ice cream or five Tesco doughnuts in the living room while he sat next to me watching motivational reels on Instagram. Then we'd go out the next morning and I'd run him into the Wilton soil, certain I could break him. All that happened was that the weight fell off him. As the evenings grew longer, wetter, and warmer, I found I couldn't keep up with him, or that I just didn't want to. I took to standing on the halfway line and shouting orders at him. For the first time in our lives, I was fatter than Casper, and he was more deferential, eager to be told what to do, where to run. He might have failed bootcamp had I not trained him, but there was no chance of that now. In May, after my parents called me back to Waterford, to our small farm above Killdiamond Bay, Casper trained on without me.

The day my parents called me, Casper had reminisced about the night we'd shaved our heads. He told the story like he'd faithfully—if futilely—chased me out onto the street, when really all he'd done was stroll out after me, and only caught up because I'd turned back already. 'You were always getting away from me,' he said now. 'But you can't, anymore. I am *fast*.' We were in Matthews, buying him socks for bootcamp. It was my turn to look appalled. Casper was rewriting the history of our friendship—as if it was *he* who had been following *me* all these years. As if he was joining the army because I'd asked him to, rather than my being achingly, obviously desperate for him not to. 'And you won't have my dead weight to carry through final year.' He twerked into my side, leaning on a rack of red gilets. Casper would be joining the army as an engineer, meaning he no longer needed the integrated Masters we'd agreed, implicitly, to do together.

He continued to twerk against me and I braced against a sunglasses display cabinet. I saw myself laughing in the rows of reflective lenses.

'I have something for you to consider,' I said, after I'd driven back from Waterford in a daze.

Casper was in our sitting room with his feet in hot lavender water. He had one of my textbooks on his lap and was arranging little columns of cocaine on it. He'd heard that was what army people were into and wanted to practise taking it.

'I want you to come to ETH Zurich with me,' I said. 'Best engineering Masters in Europe. One year, out the gap.'

'It's pricey, I'd say?'

'It's free for us. They want engineering postgrads from rural areas. They'll actually pay us to do it.'

'And finding accommodation. And the language.'

'It's in English. And I've found us accommodation. I've been on the phone all weekend.'

'Jerry—'

'You can join the army next year. You'll go in on a higher salary if you do the Masters.'

Carefully, Casper lifted his feet from the tub and rested them on the towel either side of it. 'Would you like some cocaine, Jerry?' he said.

I had not taken off my parka. I went and perched on the arm of the sofa and watched the flakes of grime settle to the bottom of the tub. I watched the back of Casper's head as he snorted. His favourite pair of women's size 18 cycling shorts poked out from just inside his beltloops: lavender Lycra on the blue-white skin of his back. He'd gotten that pair for free because the seam was scratchy and off-centre.

'I'm going out tonight, Jerry. Would you like to come?' His tone, now, was firm. He waited for my answer, but what I wanted to say was both too simple and far too complicated to put into words. 'Jerry,' he said, 'you said you were fine with me joining up.'

I hadn't, actually. Casper had just assumed I'd agreed to it because it was more convenient for him to see things that way, and because I always said Yes to Casper, no matter what he suggested. I'd never refused any suggestion of his: never anything important, anyway.

'I was,' I said. 'I am. I just think this would be better.'

'Join up with me.' Casper glanced over his shoulder. He looked back at the white lines on the book, nuzzling them into diagonals with his bank card. 'It'll be fun.'

'You know they won't let me in with my heart, Casper.'

'You've been running me silly. You could hide it, easily.'

'It feels like you've picked the one place I can't follow you.'

'It's funny, it's… how things have worked out!' He smiled and looked up at me. 'There aren't many places we wouldn't go for each other.'

'Follow me this time, Cas.'

Casper produced a double naggin of Southern Comfort. He drank and handed it to me. 'I'm going to Seán Sherlock's house. He's having a party.

He said you should come.'

'My parents are leaving Killdiamond.' I sipped at the Southern Comfort and let it sit in the cleft under my tongue, waiting for an answer. Casper stared down at the book cover. I swallowed, tasting nothing, only feeling the liquid, like latex, stretch down my throat and into the pit of my stomach. 'They're moving to Romania.'

Casper looked at me again, this time for several seconds. Then he carefully disassembled the lines of white powder and pushed everything delicately back into the baggie, and got up from the sofa. 'You've been acting weird, Jerry,' he said. He packed his coat pockets with cigarettes and chewing gum. He ignored his socks, and put shoes on his bare feet. 'What are you talking about Romania? I mean… sorry.' Casper was speaking as if his face were something he'd rented for the day. 'What do you mean, talking about Romania?'

'My dad's got a job consulting for FrieslandCampina outside Constanța.'

'Can he not—'

'His back won't let him. He can't farm anymore.' Neither had we anything more on the land than a lease. Nothing to sell. And no son to take over the farm. Only an engineer.

I handed back the Southern Comfort and Casper paced our tiny sitting room. He swung his arms out before him and behind and clapped a frantic rhythm. After a minute or two, he leaned over the sofa to find his phone between the cushions, surveyed what was left in his baggie, and left. I ran upstairs, changed, and followed him out.

'Combat is reflective of life, only amplified and intensified,' declared Casper. We were squashed and splayed with various people Casper knew on the threadbare carpet of Seán Sherlock's housemate's bedroom. I picked lint and tobacco out of the carpet as Casper rolled joints. Having noticed I was a quiet space at his shoulder, he had started on Jocko Willink. We had taken to quoting Jocko as a double act—the latest in a long line of elaborate inside jokes we cultivated together in our sitting room and brought on nights out or into the college computer labs. It was my role to answer back with a more outrageous Jocko quote, and together we would work ourselves up into a frenzy of ironic motivational yelling. But because Casper was coked, he forgot this, and responded to his own call. 'Fight weak emotions with logic; fight the weakness of logic with the power of emotions!'

At work, Casper had started quoting Jocko's book to me and forgetting to laugh. He'd get his tongue around the egg in his mouth and say, 'Be dangerous but disciplined.'

Watching him now, his head resting against the side of the unmade bed, watching him slur and bounce and abandon sentences as the many substances in his body competed over which would get to inebriate him, I marvelled that Casper had gotten around the Wilton pitches with me at all, wondered what kind of pain he must have felt in his lungs as he trundled after me, flecked by the mud my heels kicked back at him. I wanted very much to have those lungs in my own chest as they shuddered through the last half mile, to know what an egg tasted like to him, feel the twitches in his legs as he turned right or left according to the whims of his body—his movements always surprising me even when it was me, supposedly, deciding where he was to run.

I managed to drink enough that I no longer cared who was in the bedroom and who had left it. At some point, a man wearing wraparound sunglasses and a golf vest inside a black leather duster told a story about Casper. I'd never seen this man before, but he seemed to know Casper very well. Casper had never fit in with the engineering students, and drew most of the new friends he'd made since we came to UCC from the arts courses or from the drama department in CIT. I was the one who looked like an engineer, even if I'd picked engineering coming out of school largely because Casper was doing it—though it was Casper's dad, not Casper, who wanted him to be an engineer.

In the story, Casper, on a late shift back when he worked at the city marina for a summer, came across two middle-aged Dutch women who had caught four teenage boys spraying graffiti on their very beautiful wooden lugger, which was berthed on the back dock. *Pong of fish off you*, the boys had written. Tensions had risen high and dangerous by the time Casper arrived, so he offered each person one of the chocolate Mikados he'd been eating, and invited them all onto the *Anna Marjorie*, the tall ship docked there at the time. He let the boys climb the shrouds while he discussed the Atlantic crossing with the women. Once the boys had wandered off again, the women, who'd sailed from their home in Maassluis, invited Casper in for a dinner of celeriac and couscous, and sent him on his way with a kiss on each cheek. They sent him postcards from ports in the Caribbean, the Seychelles, New Zealand. They grew to like the graffiti on their hull.

It can often happen, when we're hanging out, that everyone will start singing Casper's praises, or trying to explain to any strangers present how unusual and brilliant and outrageous he is. He seems genuinely not to enjoy this.

When the story was finished and he had made some effort to minimise his role in it, Casper hoisted me up and I followed him to the attic, where Seán was on decks, playing psydub. The speakers he was using would have been too loud for a room ten times the size of the attic, and the noise they produced was so great I swore I could see the beat—a pulsing blackness at the edges of my vision.

Casper spoke to me over the noise. He put his bent arms to his chest and stuck his elbows out and leant towards my bobbing head. He sniffed. His posture was such that if he ever managed to break out of it, he would have performed one huge, laborious dance move. I swayed along beside him.

'I don't mind driving us up next weekend Jerry you did the drive last week and you drove up and down just now so let me take care of that I'm an old hand at it now anyway and I do feel I know that when I'm the one who drives us up we're less likely to see any seals but that could just be that we arrive at different times when each of us drives so if you and me leave at the time we'd normally leave with you driving we should see one. Not that I want to see one because the best-case scenario is that no seal needs our help but I'd rather us saves it than anyone else. Given that we won't be doing any patrols now for the foreseeable this one is quite special. They're all special and I'm so glad you've kept us going to them because I get a lot out of them I think actually it's more than once gotten me a job that I do the charity work and such but it's also our thing like I enjoy that aspect of it as well and I think to mark it it would be good to see a seal, do you think Jerry?'

'I think—'

'Sorry but I'm just thinking we can actually stay down there, or we can go early I mean, head down the Friday evening and stake it out for the whole weekend and we're bound to see one seal, is that a deal?'

'Do you really care about saving the seals?'

'I do. I do, of course.'

'I'll make you a deal so. A seal deal.'

Casper sniggered and waited for the people around us to laugh also, but they could hear nothing of what we were saying. 'Let's seal the seal deal man.' He looked around again.

'If we save a seal next weekend, you're going to wait one year to join the army.'

Casper looked at me with as steady a gaze as he could.

'You'll save plenty seals without me,' he said.

'I won't go back to Waterford. Will be nothing there.'

'Okay,' said Casper, as immediately as if I'd suggested we try a new brand of creatine. He fumbled for the baggie in his breast pocket. 'Okay, so. Come and seal the seal deal. Man.'

I pointed at my bad heart, like I'd done most times since Casper had started offering me drugs. And I thought, as I watched him dance, as I watched the others in the room gravitate towards him, that this is what it feels like to be friends with Casper—like his arm is around your lower ribs and he's pulling you backwards through tepid salt water, the sun crinkling through your toes like old foil.

The next weekend, I drove us up to Waterford and we combed the beaches around Killdiamond Bay for distressed seals all day Saturday. We went out on the town Saturday night because Casper's cousin was back visiting, and by the time we started on Sunday it was past two o'clock and I'd as good as given up. Casper, though he'd spent the morning vomiting, danced in and out with the wash while I trudged along behind him, smiling the smile I put on when I was pretending to be involved; the dumb, galvanised smile of an anchor. Newly, fantastically mobile, Casper whirled and bounded on the hard sand. The light black fabric of his rain jacket—another faulty prototype our friend had given him—billowed and filled with wind, giving him huge arms or terrific shoulders or a turtle shell back, depending on how it caught him.

He called back, 'Weakness is strong. I must be stronger!' and chased away a dog that was writhing on its back just above the waterline. You can tell where the seals have died because dogs come to smear their backs on the shingle there. They like to pick up the stink in their fur.

There are accounts of seals rescuing drowning dogs from rivers. How odd that must be for the dogs: to be nosed ashore by a creature you've never seen and will never see again, its black, wet eyes fixed on you from just above the line of the water.

We picked up crêpe paper as we went. Killdiamond had been an international wedding proposal destination ever since Waterford Council started cutting the VAT on weddings for people who could prove they'd proposed within county bounds. Often, when I came back from college, I had to sleep on the sofa as my room was rented out to a small-time event planner and his cameraman.

I scanned the brisk water for fishing boats, hoping to calculate where a seal would wash up if it broke off a length of net, trapping and tearing its fins in the process. I saw only leisure craft among the islets. I even began asking Sunday walkers whether they'd seen any seals. Casper, when he was close enough to hear, looked at me with a mixture of confusion and embarrassment. I realised he might not even remember the deal we'd struck.

'We could be in trouble here,' I said, as we came under the shadow of a small, red cliff. I was dizzy, anyway, and fatigued. If Casper did enlist, I knew I'd need a way of disguising my heart condition so I could join up with him, so I'd ordered beta-blockers online to disguise my chronic tachycardia. But I was getting more side effects than I thought was fair. I hadn't had an erection in a week. I wanted it all to stop.

'Well, it's a good thing,' said Casper. 'It's a good buzz saving a seal but… The best rescue plan is the one you don't need.'

'Is that Jocko?'

'That's Casper. I was thinking, what he does is what I'd really love to do. Just podcasts. People, though, won't take you very seriously if you are in the Irish Army. Did you see there in Libya last year they got two soldiers stuck and they couldn't get them home because the planes we have can't fly that far?'

I stopped dead and Casper, thinking I was reacting to his story, started performing. 'Like, the two soldiers couldn't bring their guns on a commercial flight, but they were out of range of the Irish Air Force. So they had to go to a shooting range, fire all their ammunition, then leave the guns with, I think, the French embassy in Libya. It's embarrassing. It's an embarrassing outfit.'

'Casper, why do you want to join the army?'

'What?'

'I never asked you.' Why hadn't I ever asked him? I began to laugh, now, at the pair of us. I'd given up, years ago, asking Casper for details, so I'd forgotten I could or, God forbid, *should* question him—for the sake of his own safety, if nothing else. Or his sanity. Casper's plan was always final; always he'd have justifications and always it would work out. 'Cas, you're not going to be Jocko Willink.' I felt ridiculous, but I found I was saying this to Casper as gently as I could, trying not to hurt his feelings.

Casper went quiet. He came to a stop with his hands on his back and leaned into the breeze coming around the headland.

'I understand that you want to talk about your experiences to the world,' I said. 'But did you think you'd have more clout, or something, if you were an engineer in the Irish army?'

'Not clout, Jerry. Not like… more like, credibility. You don't have a lot of credibility as a shift worker for Johnson & Johnson, living out in the suburbs. No one cares about that.'

'We don't live an extreme lifestyle,' I said. 'But—'

'Rescuing seals teaches you about honour, brotherhood, and humility, and leadership,' Casper said, in Jocko's gravelly voice.

'You've no reason for joining the army, have you?' I was angry now. 'You're throwing my life off kilter on a whim.'

Casper waited for me to realise what I'd said. It was his turn to smile— slowly— tucking his chin in against the breeze. 'Have I made bad life choices for us, Jerry? I am no good. If only I hadn't taken on the burden of managing my friend's life, and deciding what he did every day, spending every waking moment with him, bringing him everywhere. That was so unfair that I made him so pathetically dependent on me.'

Casper's tone was so biting—so cruel—I couldn't comprehend, for a second or two, that it was directed at me. I felt his words travel over me towards someone, *anyone* else, and then come back around and hit me in the small of the back, almost knocking me off my feet. 'We'll go until we see Wexford,' he said, all matter of fact now. Jolly, even. 'Half an hour I'd say. Twenty minutes. We're bound to find one.'

In one elastic motion, he doubled over and vomited between his feet and righted himself. He passed me with a smile and I half sat, half fell down among the marram grass. I watched him go, my chin on the heel of my palm and my little finger just broaching my lips. Casper turned and waited, then returned over the shingle, sending it sliding like coins in an arcade. He looked down at me. I put my hand on the side of my face and looked down into the scraps of dried seaweed and confetti. There came shouts and the sound of champagne popping from the carpark behind us. 'You're ill,' I told Casper. 'Let's stop. You should get back and get some fluids. You look haggard.'

Casper stood over me.

'Did you take anything last night?' I said.

'2CP. It's not that. There's no comedown off 2CP.' He nudged me with his shin. 'I meant what I said. I can't look after you any longer.'

'You can't look after yourself,' I said, quietly.

'What?'

'You've got a fucking tremor man. You're a fucking drug addict.' The wind whipped the tears straight off the surface of my eyes. 'You've ruined my life.'

I didn't look at Casper as he sat and put one arm over my shoulder, rested his head on his hand on my upper arm. His embrace was utterly relaxed, flaccid even.

I don't know how long we sat there, unmoving. The sun came around the bank, dousing first me and then Casper. It stretched out before us over the shells and dulse. With my eyes, I followed the line of the shore up to the headland we had come across, and watched, in a state of desperation, for a dying seal. Instead, I saw a dinghy skirting the shallows. It was unmanned, and was clapping up the estuary in frantic gybes, borne by the wind against the receding tide.

'Do you see that?' I said. Casper did not respond. I looked down at the top of his shaved head, and shielded his eyes from the sun with my hand. 'Casper, are you seeing this?'

He rubbed his eyes thoroughly. The dinghy made its way slackly past us. Its white sail, beginning to tear at the luff, had written on it in huge black capitals:

WILL YOU MARRY ME

Casper bounced up off the sand and ran into the sea. Swatting at the breakers, he shed his hat and jacket and left them floating behind him.

I shouted his name just once, short and sharp, then chased after him and caught at the back of his T-shirt. He shoved me off and his shirt—another of his factory seconds—ripped clean off in my grasp, exposing his salt-wet, heaving chest. My counterweight gone, I fell back into a breaker, clutching scraps of polyester over my head. Though what I should have felt was fear, or anger—or the cold—I felt only bewilderment at how melodramatic we were being, at the *Conan the Barbarian*, WWE pantomime Casper and I had become. I felt, immersed in water moving rapidly over and beneath and around me, grossed out.

I surfaced to another breaker in the face and, by the time I was back on my feet—feeling the riptide tear the sand from under me—I could see him pass through the last soft peak of wave and slap his hand on the boat. I took my shoes and jacket and tracksuit off and left them to the waves. I looked back to the deserted shore, then out to my flailing Casper, and thought, for really the first time, that he might be leading me somewhere I wasn't supposed to go. Then I saw him, bare-chested, put one leg up over the gunwale just as a gust hit the sail and capsized the boat on top of him. He didn't resurface.

I swam as fast as I could.

When I reached the boat, I ducked under and found Casper dazed in a cluster of bubbles, which rose around him, firm like tapioca pearls. I pulled his head up into the air in the hollow under the boat and, keeping him upright with one arm, freed him from the sheets and halliards which had wrapped themselves around his neck and legs. Then, pinching him hard round the back of his neck, I hauled him out from under the boat and onto its hull. I slung his arm around the centreboard to keep him from sliding off. He looked pathetic, beached on the slick plastic hull, his whole torso bent convex by the curve of the boat and the wide hollow under his upraised ribs newly toned and taut and empty-looking. A green pair of cycling shorts peeked out from above the waistband of his jeans.

Was he breathing? I gripped the board and spread my weight over him and, as I lowered my face to his, to check, he retched a hot stomachful of water on me. We stared at one another as his spit dribbled down our chins, desperate to be the first to laugh but neither able to yet.

I laid my cheek on his chest. When he tried to rise after a moment or two, I flung him back into the sea. I reached down to him off the hull and, gripping him by the crown of the head, I pulled him first upwards and then dunked him into the water, then pulled him back up and dunked him again. I slid off the hull and into the water with him.

We rested there for half a minute, our heads against the side of the upturned hull. It was strangely quiet, down near the level of the water, the boat and Casper and me like a lashed raft on the swift current. At Casper's instruction, we turned the bow round to windward and righted the boat. Once we'd climbed in, he took the tiller and sailed us against the spring tide up the estuary. I sat in the wet and shivered, and watched as we drifted past the banks of canting trees.

In February, one full year after the night we shaved our heads, Casper sent me a box of defective sportswear in the post.

I had moved to Zurich as soon as we found someone to take up the lease on our flat. My parents had dropped the two of us to the Aircoach and I'd left Casper outside the security gates at Dublin Airport, after we'd gotten slightly drunk at the airport bar.

The cardboard was encased in scotch tape of two different colours—so thickly wrapped that the edges were chitinous under my fingertips. I used a ballpoint, then a breadknife, to cut into it, and managed to wrench one side of the box away. In more of a hurry than I could explain, I removed my clothes and re-dressed myself. The socks he'd sent bunched up around my toes. The shorts were puckered and riddled with runs. I emptied the rest out onto the floor.

Casper failed the drug test at the army screening, even though he knew there'd be one. He took a full-time job in Apache Pizza, and he told me, when we wished each other Merry Christmas over Facebook Messenger, that he was the fittest he'd ever been.

He had actually offered, after I saved him from drowning, to hold off on going into the army—at least until I could get a medical pass to join up with him. I refused. I didn't explain why, though Casper seemed to understand. Or, each of us understood it as well as the other. We understood that something had changed between us. We never discussed Killdiamond. Our life together was finished.

He'd love Zurich. He'd love the strange slope of every street and the ostentatiously strong currency and the women who all look like dentists, and, when he was able to visit, he'd like my girlfriend Anna Claire and her group of intellectual, serious friends. He'd call her 'A.C.' and pretend not to be interested when her friends discussed the morality of suffering. He'd wonder why I'd stopped exercising as much as we used to.

Tucked in under one strip of tape on the box was a note from Casper, telling me he was trying to go sober. Or, he said he was taking time off the drink, and he might try again with the army or do the Masters next year or see whether he could do a diploma in music production. He said he'd sleepwalked into the engineering, really. He said he couldn't wait to see me, and he was sorry if he'd done anything wrong.

'I feel strong and useful, sometimes,' the note said, at the end. 'I hope you feel strong and useful.'

I went and stood in front of the three quarter-length mirror glued to the inside of my closet door. The T-shirt I'd taken out of the box rode high on my neck, pinched me under the arms. My hair was longer than it had ever been. I wondered, for the very first time, what I might owe Casper, now that I was free of him. What he might need, other than my blind devotion. I locked eyes with myself in the glass.

Average haver of flesh

type your email address
into my notes app, I guess it doesn't really matter

if I don't like the tattoo, eventually
you learn to take it alongside the rest of yourself

unfortunately I am very alive to you

in the shower touching myself and frowning
there isn't room in here
for the great unfurling
phantom of my informal coming

I love how it feels
when my body enters the water
my mouth is dry all the time
so vainly I come off sertraline
cold turkey, an

undignified descriptor

this physical space is full to the point of palpable claustrophobia

oh hi! oh hi! oh hi!

I can't avoid bumping into one-night stands, not even in my own mind palace
I am perpetually sort of sex averse until I'm having sex and then I'm like

hmm. ok.

at least my body is my own fault now
no longer making me run forever from all the ways
it could be praised, praise me weird and love my bone marrow! pull my lower

eyelid down and lick the redness! inside me there is a punched clay well full
     of really
really terrible poems that deserve to exist

thank you for reading my poem

I am uninhabited rn and so I wrote this
tomorrow I will look at it and wonder who put it here and maybe I'll wonder who
put you here too

why do I feel and think and act any kind of way, I will receive one brain zap and
feel enamoured with the cruelty of having form and the deliriousness of today

once again and as ever remembering myself to myself like this is my body, a piece
     of fruit
held briefly to a lower lip, a big inky bruise or something administered

more lightly, looking like the outline of pressed flowers in magenta, no one
ultimately cares that you have a hickey. I am now relying on motion and touch,

which I normally never rely on and

finding that I can find what I want most sometimes in the almostness

   the tiny gap between this and me and you and your mouth around this and me
                              attached

so.

now I am jealous of myself
lying here

touching the back of your neck.

Francis Jones

Three Strands

William Keohane

Allihies

Always, when I was a child, my family would spend the summer in Allihies, on the west coast of Cork. *Na hAilichí*, the cliff fields. And so they were; nestled between a rocky cliffside and a sprawling beach, Allihies is a painting: the uniform houses, toy xylophone keys, aligned along the main street. The pub, O'Neill's, a crimson red; the hostel, a salmon pink; and each house along the way a different shade. A grounded rainbow.

For me, it was a village of firsts. It was here, in this place, on the beach (my parents tell me) that I spoke my first word. They say that it was 'ocean'. Our fresh-faced family of three, camping in a tent by the shore. Under lamplight, they repeated the word back to me, over and over, as the waves blanketed the pale sand in the dark. Ocean. *O-shh-un.*

I find it hard to imagine. My parents think the best of me, I love them for it, but no child could make their first imprint on the world, their first mark, with a word like that. But I spent my summers on the shore, in the salt, my knotted hair always damp. I learned the names of those who lived there. John, who ran the shop and the bus service to and from Castletownbere; Dave, who my parents were friends with; Jimmy from Jimmy's Bar, the place where I would later have my first taste of alcohol, a pint of Beamish, and hate it. In the summer heat, when I was at the playground with the gaggle of village children, rouged with the sun's kiss and my pupils moon-sized from an excess of sugar, sweet ice-cream, pick-and-mix washed down with fruit cordial and fizzy drinks, my mom and dad were often with Dave, just across the street. They would be sitting on the splintered pine bench outside of the pub, sipping cold pints.

I felt my first death, there, in the village. I felt it in the air I took in, the way it settles in the basin of your body, a cotton wool coating in the throat. Not long after Dave died, unexpectedly, we drove back to Allihies. It wasn't the summer this time; the water was a darker shade. The cliff fields were solid, iced, white. Dave had lived with his wife in the schoolhouse, at the end of the village, at the dip of the hill. It was a relic; every floorboard squeaked, every wall cracked with flaking paint. Looking out through the window in the classroom hall, you saw the sea, the peninsula, the cresting waves. Sometimes I would sit for hours there while my parents talked and laughed with Dave in the kitchen. I would be racing water droplets on the panes, or tracing specs of dust ignited by the rays of summer light.

A death in such a small close-knit place is communal. The grief belongs to the village. Bouquets of flowers had been propped against the schoolhouse walls, a bouquet from every person, every home. Within the sullen grey of loss the colours seemed more vibrant, and, for the first time, we noticed small painted stones dotted around the grounds. Each stone was a palm-sized canvas; there was a golden sun, a sandy beach. One was a brushstroke rendering of the schoolhouse itself. My parents chose to take this one home with them. They knew Dave wouldn't mind. They walked around the schoolhouse, arm in arm, my parents, two giants to me then. Two giants to me now, still. And I watched them—I stood outside the gate—they stood together at his grave, and they cried. Only for a moment. My first death was a quiet one.

There is a small sacred site just outside the village: three white boulders, monuments to mark the graves of The Children of Lir. After being trapped for near a century in the swan-bodies they were burdened with which they did not choose, legend tells us they died at Allihies. I walked out to the boulders once. I left coins on the rocks. The rain would come, and traces of rust would trickle from the stones, like they were bright fruits, freshly opened.

My childhood is buried in Allihies, too; my summer days, scuffed shoes, scraped knees. All these emblems of self, fragments in the heather, the rocks, the copper mines. Still, I cannot claim this place as my own. After all, it was my father's before me. He has told me the stories of how he came here, as a young man, piled into the car with his college friends, to board at the hostel, to camp in the fields. Before my mother, when he had his unkempt mullet, his scruffy beard. Those features I long for.

And my favourite story of him, alone, of a kitten he found up in the hills. A small white thing, rain-soaked. He had no idea how it had gotten there. Maybe it had gotten lost, wandering. Maybe some stranger had thrown it from a moving car. People do things like that.

All the way back down the mountain, he kept her small wet body in his breast pocket, above his heart. At the shop he bought a carton of milk to ease her mewing. He gave her to Tom, the gruff bachelor who ran the hostel on his own; Tom, who softened at the cries of this lone lost kitten, who kept her and raised her and fed her for years. And then one day I was old enough to visit, and see for myself, this tiny thing my father had carried before he carried me.

On the mantelpiece in my parents' home, there's a portrait of my father as a baby in a small silver frame. The schoolhouse stone from Allihies sits beside it, and, next to the stone, a photo of me at the Cliffs of Moher in a blue sleeveless vest. One of my skinny white arms is sprawled out, the other flexing to support myself against a wall. I am taking up space. Some photographs I still struggle to look at. I cannot see myself in them. But I like this one; I could be a boy, a long-haired boy. I could be anyone.

Last time I was home, now a man—more like my father with each passing day—my mother picked up the frame, held it to my face. She looked at me, at both of me. The past and present tense. 'I suppose you were always...'

She'd let the words slip; she didn't finish. I know what she was trying to say.

I suppose I was, always.

Lahinch

There is another photograph somewhere in my parents' house, taken near the Cliffs in Clare. In it, I am young, standing on a beach, holding the folded ends of my trousers up to my knees so that they don't get wet. A clouded echo of the sky reflects upon the shore. Sunlit waves are surging in the wind, and I am caught, mid-laugh, gazing at my toes rooted in the liquid sand.

On summer days closer to home, we'd drive from Limerick to the seaside, collecting Granny Mauno in Cratloe on the way, and there was a moment, along the road, somewhere between Ennistymon and Lahinch, that the car would crest the hill and I'd see it, glowing in the distance, with my face glued to the window in the back seat, and I'd shout into the space between my father and his mother: 'I SEE THE SEA!'

'Well done!' one of the two of them would say. 'You win!'

The prize for winning was a 99 cone, to be accepted with a bow and devoured in a flash before it could drip in quick white tears onto the tarmac. Sitting in the car with my family, the words were always waiting at the tip of my tongue for my first glimpse of something blue and glittering.

A photograph can be a puzzle piece to fill a gap in memory, but this day I remember. It's a special day at Lahinch beach—the day my cousins come—and outside the seafront restaurant, I see them driving in, and I am running, waving, waiting on the pavement in front of my aunt's seven-seater before she's even turned the engine off. It isn't often that I see them since they live so far up north. I love the way their voices sound and sometimes try to imitate their accent, but I can't quite get it right.

Running again, with the three of them in tow, we're down the steps onto the sand, and it is early; we have all the time we need to paddle in the rockpools, search for ornamental shells before the tide comes in to nudge us home. Soon I'm so engrossed that I don't even notice when my other aunt arrives from Galway.

My dad is with us on the sand, decorating, helping. We watch him as he upturns a rock to search for crabs. He picks one up, the shell between his forefinger and thumb, and shows it to the four of us. We are mesmerised by this little thing, its claws fanned out as if to offer us a hug. With a wink, he lifts it toward his open mouth and mimics placing it inside. He hides the crab behind his head and eats the air, chews down on nothing, and something about this motion is so profound, we cannot help but burst into a fit of giggling. For a moment, my father is no longer my father; he's just another boy here at the beach with us. But bodies change when we get older. A while ago, Granny Mauno had a fall and hurt herself quite badly. Now, she needs to take her time and move more slowly. She's not even on the sand yet. I look behind me, towards the seawall, and she's still up there with my aunt, one arm braced against the rust-flecked railing, the other tethered to her eldest who is guiding her. There's a certainty that comes with eldest daughters. They seem to always know what needs to be done.

On the beach, I watch and try to copy everyone. My sandcastles are weaker versions of the ones my older cousins have made, and when Granny Mauno arrives over, I show them off to her. The day is slipping from us fast. We tidy up, place towels, buckets, spades into our parents' cars, and then, because the tide is high, it's coming in, we stand on the steps and chase the waves. Then we wait until the water turns, and run, fast as we can, back to the safety of the wall. Tonight, we'll beg our parents for a sleepover at Granny Mauno's house and plead until we have our way, then drive home damply with the heating in my father's car on full blast, and I will fall asleep before we meet the lights along the M18. On the overpass to Cratloe, I'll wake to strips of gold cast through the window on my lids. I will keep this day with me. I don't want to forget it.

In secondary school, our uniforms are a violent blue, somewhere between teal and turquoise, and mildly sickening, like sweetened toothpaste made for children, like the mouthwash you are offered at the dentist in a little paper cup. It's a colour that reminds me of a certain type of pain. Paired with our abrasive jumpers, the boys wear slate-grey trousers, the girls wear ankle-length blue skirts. I had permission from the principal to wear the boys' uniform in primary school—I asked my parents, and they asked him, and he didn't see an issue with it—but I wear a skirt now. I suppose it's okay. I can get dressed quickly in the mornings. The uniform is ready and waiting in my wardrobe, along with the pairs of folded grey trousers that I don't wear. In August, before I started school, my mom took me into Fennessy's in town, and was kind enough to buy me both sets of the uniform, so that I could choose between the two. That first morning, in my bedroom, though I wanted to wear the trousers—I put them on and everything—it just felt like too big a risk, going into a new place and standing out. So I changed.

When the fabric of the uniform is stained with blood, it darkens to an umber shade. I learn this early on in school. One afternoon, during a science test, I feel an ache inside my stomach. I focus on the page, my pen in hand, and try to concentrate, but can't, and afterwards, I find myself alone inside a bathroom. This is the first time it has happened. When school ends, I walk down to the local shop to buy a multi-pack of Kotex pads. At home I shower, put on my pyjamas, and climb under the sheets in bed. I do not tell this news to anyone. I want to sleep until it goes away.

I don't like what's happening to me, so I keep myself distracted. I focus on my grades. If I can be the very best, then maybe I'll feel better. It's a good plan, isn't it? And it works, all throughout secondary school, until the very end.

In school one day, none of us are uniformed. At 9.05 a.m., we're standing outside the bus with our schoolbags and permission slips, dressed in our own clothes for a class trip to Lahinch. On board, I sit next to my friend, Sarah, who has an iPod and pair of headphones, and we take one bud each, my head resting on her shoulder as heat pulses through the window, and we drive on until we're close to Shannon Airport where planes are landing overhead. 'Yellow reg, no backs,' someone behind us says.

After a while, the road begins to narrow, and I know the hill is near. Then I see it there, the glow. Without my dad and Granny Mauno, I play our game inside my head, alone.

At the car park, we rush out of our seats and into the unfolding day, down towards the sea to find a rock that's big enough for our group of friends to sit on, and, leaning back, resting our heads on bunched up jumpers, we watch the clouds. In time, I taste salt upon my lips, can feel how it has hardened on my eyelashes and in my hair, so I decide to take my hair down (something I never do). It was shorter when I was younger, but it's long now, longer than it's ever been, just like my friends' hair, just like Sarah's. Strands begin to blow in the breeze. It feels nice, for once, to have it out like this. Someone's gone and bought sweets from the shop, so we peel open sachets of chocolate buttons and fruit pastilles to share, and I feel safe here, the way I always do with my friends, as we pass time together doing nothing. I've grown thirsty from the salt and sugar, but my water bottle is inside my schoolbag, back on the bus, and I don't want to move from here just yet.

Later, when I make my way up the steps, a group of students are sitting on the seawall just before the rocks, their legs dangling over the ledge. I hear that someone has called my name. It's one of the girls I don't usually talk to.

'Your hair,' she says. 'It looks great like that.'

I thank her, awkwardly, before stepping towards the bus. She keeps going, though, she wants me to know how lucky I am, how many of the girls spend hours trying to recreate my type of curls, and each day at school, I've tied them up and kept them hidden.

I can't explain to her why I don't like to let my hair down. I can't explain why what she's said has left me with a sinking feeling, so I walk away and tie my hair back up. On the rocks, with my friends, I had forgotten what I looked like. This has wrenched me to body once again. (This could be the moment, couldn't it—if that's what you want to know—when it hits me with the fullest force. But really, I can't say when it started. I have these loose fibres of memory that pirouette like seaweed in the undertow, and I can't remember the first instance, or what happens after this. I just remember falling silent. Finding a place to be alone and sit.) The waves are breaking. The sea rolls on, and I'm here on the white-veined rocks, and they are glowing pale grey in the dim, and they look like my body, I notice, they look like my hips, the silver growth-spurt streaks, the fractures across my sides where the skin has stretched. I shrug this thought away and hug my knees into my chest. I have thoughts like these at times, but not constantly. I can shut them out. I've grown accustomed to forgetting. I can stay here on the shore until the tide is fully in. I can live like this. It's fine, just fine. A little cold. There are grains of sand trapped inside my shoes. My skin is damp beneath my clothes. Between my body and the body of this rock, the water's seeping through.

I know this feeling but it's fine, I've sat with it before, for years. Never mind the fact that it drenches, never mind the mornings when I do not want to wake, never mind a week or so ago, when I took the bus into the city on my own, walked into a shop, the one I'd often go to with my friends, and, with my hand clutching the railing, took the escalator up, waiting to be lifted into the section for the men, and there bought a T-shirt and a three-pair multipack of boxers, loose-fit, one navy, one grey, one striped with blue and white. At home, with the bedroom door locked, I tried them on for the first time, and for the first time, something felt right, like something in my life was slotting into place; the way they refused to hug my waist, but fell straight down to square me out, as I stood there, rooted into stillness. A piece of clothing on a body is only an expression. It does not make a person, and yet there's something to be said about the choice, I think, the fact that I had given in to something I had wanted for so long, a thing I had no language for, a thing that I had done despite the fear, moving quickly through the aisles, afraid someone from school might see, afraid of the whispers, or worse, afraid of the secret itself that I held within me.

The secret I am holding, still. I am wearing them now, sitting here on this rock, the boxers and the t-shirt, beneath my jumper and rain jacket; this knowing is pressed across my torso, and deeper, even, bone deep. But it's fine because I will not tell. I won't say it aloud. I never will.

The sea is stretching endless, the sun is dipping slow. Waves collapse to fizz upon the shore, much closer now, as if the blanket of the ocean has been pulled in. We should be going, soon, it's getting dark. I watch the horizon, the line of vacant space between the air and water, everything that's out there, further. I know there is another life. I've heard about the ones who leave, who venture into unknown space and claim new words, but I can't understand how they could choose to live that way. I think I might even hate them. For leaving. It isn't fair. Why do they get to escape? Why can't they stay here, safe in pain, like me?

It's cold and I don't want to be here anymore. Fuck all of it. I want to go, to run until I cannot think or speak or breathe, my whole body an aching stitch, my lungs aflame until I quench the burning in the sea—the sea that just keeps going, on and on, until you come ashore on another land, beyond. I cannot see it, but it's there. However many miles away.

Maybe I could swim that far. Maybe I could make it.

Salthill

Lately, I've been telling people. I am only just beginning, and I cannot say the word. It will not come. I know it—there's a term—but I can't speak it. There is no one here to coach me. So I say 'boy', say 'he', say 'please'. The rest of my body speaks in other words. A soft face, a light voice. I am shaped in ways I try to suppress, trying to pass. I keep my hair short. There's a barbershop in Limerick, at the top of William Street, where I go with my dad and we get matching haircuts. It's the only one that will do it for me. I was turned away three times at other places.

It helps that my dad comes with me. When we walk in, they sit us down in their retro seats; Bridget cuts my hair, Roxy cuts his. Our blonde and brown strands fall, and the fresh cut moulds my face into something I recognise, something I like, and my reflection changes on the glass in front of us, and his reflection, too. My father, my mirror.

We're closing in on winter yet the sun is out and shining.

'Come on, let's go do something,' my dad says to me, and I say, 'Okay.'

We drive to Galway together. Light beats down on the bonnet, and for the first time in a long time, I feel colour and warmth reverberating through my body.

In Galway city it's just him and me for a while. Taking our time, strolling through Flood Street, St Augustine's, over onto Abbeygate, and down by all the little houses on Bowling Green. If we've been walking in circles, I haven't noticed. Leaving the farmer's market, its mixed aromas of soil-coated root vegetables and freshly ground coffee, we pass an old stone building.

'Do you know the history of this place?' he asks. Above us, embedded in the ruin, an emblem: a skull and crossbones. My dad is a teacher by nature. He tells the story with ease.

'Around the end of the fifteenth century, the mayor of Galway, James Lynch, sentenced his son to death for committing murder. When no one else could carry out the execution, Lynch hanged his own son himself.'

The mayor believed in something—some set of rules, some order—stronger than the ties of fatherhood, of family. Although is it unfounded, some believe this is where the term 'lynching' originates, he tells me.

Under the Gothic doorway, I stop and think about his name, 'Lynch'. The countless lives held within it, unspoken names upon the tongue, broken bodies strung from trees, from windows. I don't think I could ever kill my son.

We walk on.

Along Shop Street, the beating heart of the city, it is all bunting and colour above us. Even the familiar commercial hues of big brand names seem to work here, to slot into place. A red-and-white striped pole is fixed to the wall outside the barbers. 'Healey's', the plaque on the door reads, 'Established 1939'. Eighty years of family business.

'I used to get my hair cut here, when I was in college,' he says.

He looks at me, winks, and I know. We pop in, the only two customers in the shop, and take our seats beside each other. Soon, the dull buzz of two razors in harmony. Pausing for a moment, then asking me how old I am, the man who's cutting my hair reaches into a nearby cooler and hands me a Heineken. They don't do this in Limerick. Briefly, I wonder if they have a liquor licence, how they can serve drink, but the offering is too sweet and serendipitous to reject. I let the worry fizzle out.

I pretend, for a while, to be someone who can make small talk about the match, some lad. They haven't copped that I could be anything else. I deepen my vocal tone, as low as I can. All of this—the cool green bottle in my hand, the glint of sunlight across the shopfront window, my father, sitting here with me—all of this is perfect.

Later, we meet my aunt. I haven't told her. I think she knows, I think someone must have said something, but I've been waiting for the right moment. We walk along by the River Corrib. My dad is a good few paces ahead. Light ripples are breaking softly on the water, and past the cathedral; over the Salmon Weir Bridge, red clover peeps out of the cracks in the stones. There is no perfect time.

'I was wondering if you've heard from anyone about me, about... ' I cannot finish. I am tentative, not used to this, not yet.

'Yes,' she says, and then an empty space.

She starts speaking again, but doesn't say my name. Instead, she says the old one.

I hear her saying this, of course I do. But the air is holding the word, the name, the syllables of it, right in front of me. It falls into me and through my lungs where it catches, grains of it slipping into my stomach, tightening, as a knot, the sound pulling down on the muscles in my limbs, tensing. The moment turns solid around me, settles into my body for the rest of our walk.

What do I do with all of this—all that I'm feeling, this great contradiction, both a flood of pain and a vacuum—what can I say to her? Where are the words? I'm trying to find them, I want her to listen, and they won't come. It must be my fault. I didn't do it right. If I had done a better job she would have heard me, she would have understood. There is no point, is there, in saying anything, if all I do is get it wrong. I had my moment and I ruined it. It's gone. Why should I even speak at all? And yet she keeps talking, all the while, she keeps talking, about how there are distinct and real differences between biological men and women, and how she won't call me anything except this old name, the one she keeps repeating. And I nod, feign agreement, willing it to end. Strange what a word, a name, the thing that roots you into place, can undo. It is as if I am hovering above myself. I glance back at my shadow, still there behind me, stretching out backwards along the street.

On the road out of the city, cars trudge slowly. The day has slipped into overcast. I think my dad has noticed the disappointment I am feeling, how I have receded into muteness. I haven't spoken since. With each break, each stall in the traffic, I catch him watching me, concern etched into his face. Before we've gone too far, I break the silence with a question: 'Can we go back, just for a little while? Is it okay if we go back?'

Salthill promenade is quiet. A few people are walking their dogs on the path. Light rain is falling on the lemon-yellow diving tower. I have no shorts, so I throw on my dad's, stowed in the boot of his car. Red, faded from sea salt, and a little loose across my hips. I tighten the drawstring. All day I've been wearing a binder compressing my chest into me, hiding my body beneath my clothes, but I can't hide when I am changing, and no one else here is wearing one. I don't know where I should go, so I change outside, in the unclaimed space between the men's room and the ladies'. I keep my binder on. Through one door a woman in a purple one-piece is drying her hair with a damp towel. On the other side, there's an older man, his skin, tanned, dappled with freckles; he looks weather worn and cheerful, his face freshly pinked.

The sea is a black, low hum. It's my first time swimming here. Salthill is not like other places I have been; I cannot tiptoe slowly in, and I am standing on the platform now, watching waves break against the concrete block below. I could turn around and leave, sure, but I've made it out this far. So I jump. Water lodges in my ears and the world becomes a scream.

Time passes. The memory of Salthill grows distant. On a warm day in Galway, just off Shop Street, we will meet again, and hug, and I will feel her arms around my broader, stronger body, and she will say it took a while but she sees me now, she understands a little more, and the words we share will become a bridge. This hasn't happened yet, but above my lips, blonde hairs are blooming. A year of slow injections of gold into the muscles of my thighs.

Close to Christmas, I head into the city, my city, for a trim. It's late, but the barbershop is still open. I walk in. Sit down.

'I'm not sure if you remember me,' I say to Bridget, who used to cut my hair. I remind her of my father.

'Oh yes, of course,' she says. 'And how is your sister doing?'

Her words, their implication, settle into me, as I'm deciding what I am going to say. I take a breath, choose something light, simple—'Actually, funny story, that's me,'—and watch the glimmer of recognition flicker across her face.

'Oh.'

I wait. This is the moment, I know well, where the past and present versions of self meet and blend and meld together, into a solid thing.

There are tears in her eyes. 'I'm so thrilled for you. You look so… different. You look so happy.'

A rush of relief floods through my body and I relax, sinking back into the worn leather seat.

We will chat, while she works away. This won't be small talk. This will be something bigger. I will tell her all about it, because she will ask me carefully and I'll feel safe, although we won't have much time so I'll be forced to give a shortened version. She'll say, although she knows it's not the same, that she has a child who could be like me, a different letter, another word unspoken, and she worries, and she hopes, and was it hard she'll ask—or no—she'll say: it must have been.

I don't mind sharing, really. Or should I say, I want to. I haven't spoken in so long; to open up like this, with someone who will listen, feels like love and grief in tandem, like a head is resting on my shoulder and we're watching it together, with our bodies close for warmth, as the frost glints all around us on the cold and dormant things. (Forgive me if I cry a little bit. I spent a long time trying not to. Thought that was how strong men behaved. Forgot my father also cried in Allihies. Forgot there is, always, another way.) It is just a moment, but it means something, I promise. There is someone else here, seeing this. They are watching from behind the gate.

But before I start to speak, she takes pause, she says wait, what should I call you? What's your name?

And I smile at her reflection in the mirror, and at the reflection of the man, the face I am still learning, in front of me.

'I'm Will,' I tell her. 'William.'

Devotional

On nights like these, the omnipotent hand crumbles stock-cube mist over
   the commuter belt

Little figurines light up choc-a-block apartments, aromatically fucking in
   divinity soup

Top floor of your complex, yet it comforts me that you believe in something
   other than me

One God? Who cross-stitches the stars? Who creates poets to cross-stitch
   the stars?

You say in your religion you have many gods with many arms

And I say many arms? on many gods? on the hands of godly finger arms?

And you forgive me

Is love meant to feel like gnawing off your own leg?

Don't know no other life

Than dying animal in fat trap

Straining muscle pumping

No difference between eating and loving

Us a counterfeit Pietà

Mass of limbs make

Fragile magic

Candlelit.

Rosa Thomas

Switch Bitch

P Kearney Byrne

The squat is a big terraced house in Hackney, huge rooms and hardly any furniture. The Greenham lot are laughing their heads off, howling and doing crazy animal dances, pretending to ride each other. They smell of smoke and, even though it's August, reek of damp and must. Most of them have taken their tops off and tits of all shapes and sizes are gleaming in the low red light, the larger ones swinging and bobbing. A woman with one enormous drooping breast has her arms raised high, the thin, wavering scar on the flat side of her chest tattooed with a women's symbol. Earlier, one of them kept yelling that they should light a fire in the middle of the living room. That freaked Annie out. Lorna told her this shower weren't the big political heads, just some mad dykes who were hanging out at the camp. 'Swear to God,' she said to Annie, 'these wimmin are wild as fuck.'

For almost an hour, Annie's been sitting on the floor with her back against the bare wall, pulling her legs in whenever someone walks past or dances too close. Cassette tapes are scattered around. Grace Jones, Eurythmics, and the B-52's blaze through the open windows. She wonders how the neighbours can stand it. She hasn't seen Lorna since the previous summer and, like an eejit, she thought it'd be just the two of them hanging out while she was over. Lorna never told her she was with Viv now. Annie only arrived yesterday and already she's sorry she came. She'd go to bed, hide away, but Lorna gave her this weird little room on the landing: just a mattress on the floor and a blanket hung on nails instead of a door.

She takes tiny sips from her can of Kestrel. The lager is warm and flat and tastes of cigarette butts. She's aware that a blonde woman in the main group has been watching her for a while. Her eyes are aching from not looking back and straining her peripheral vision at the same time. The woman is extra good-looking and Annie wouldn't mind if Lorna saw her getting off with someone as cool as that. Now, staring blatantly at Annie, the blonde woman steps over the legs and bodies sprawled on the floor and weaves between the capering, baying, bare-breasted types. Annie puts her head down and picks up one of the cassettes. *Patti Smith, Horses*, is scrawled on it. When she looks up, the woman is crouching in front of her, smoking a joint and squinting. She's wearing striped dungarees that look a size too small and a vest that shows off her strong shoulders. She holds the smoke in for a bit, grins, lets it stream from one side of her mouth, then passes the spliff to Annie and says something. Annie can't hear over the music and shakes her head. The woman sits alongside her on the floor and brings her face close to Annie's ear. The warmth radiating from her body, her hot breath, the softness of her lips brushing Annie's skin and the low rasp of her voice create a sensation that travels down through Annie's core, like a snake whipping through her organs. She hears some of what the woman says: '… arse sore from the boards or what?' It's an Irish accent—though a fairly posh Dublin one—and Annie gives a shy laugh. The woman shouts that her name is Jude and asks is Annie one of Lorna's exes, over from Dublin? Annie feels her face burn. She nods and says, yeah, puts the cassette tape on the floor and hands back the joint, looking around quickly to see where Lorna is.

Jude points the spliff at two women in the centre of the room, surrounded by a clapping, whooping circle. The two have their heads thrown way back, both gripping their own huge tits and pointing the nipples at the ceiling, making a high pitched sound audible over the music. Jude cups one hand to Annie's ear, puts the other, the one with the joint, on Annie's clavicle.

'They go fucking mental at the full moon,' Jude says. She sits back, laughing. Her teeth are very white and even. 'They're intergalactic wolves,' she says, 'in women's bodies.'

She stubs the roach out on the skirting board, stands, pulls her dungarees from her bum crack and jerks her thumb at the kitchen. It seems like she's going to leave and Annie is gutted, but Jude reaches for her hand and helps her up. She leads her across the landing, past the sofa where Lorna and Viv are snogging.

In the kitchen, the sudden bright light from the bare bulb makes Annie flinch. Jude opens the fridge, roots around, pulls out a plate of cold spaghetti, pokes a finger in the tomato sauce, then puts it back. She grabs a handful of fried spuds from the big tray on the table and pops slice after slice into her mouth, chewing slowly, looking out the black square of window to the tower blocks across the green. Annie thinks she's forgotten all about her and wonders if she should go back to the living room, but then Jude turns, lifts an open can of beer from the table. She sniffs it and slugs great mouthfuls.

'Sorry,' she says, wiping her mouth with the back of her hand. 'My manners have gone to shite since living with that lot.'

She takes another few slices of spud and sits up on the table, swinging her legs.

'You're staying here, right?'

'Yeah.'

'Got a room?'

'Yes, the little one up on the—'

'Class,' Jude says, smiling, showing her white teeth. Her skin is lightly tanned, her lips are very pink and her hair looks like it's been crimped in small close waves. If it weren't for the setting and the dungarees, she'd look like an actress from the fifties.

'C'mere, you,' she says. Annie moves closer until she's between Jude's thighs and Jude puts her head to one side and looks at her. It's kind of devastating to be looked at for so long, so intently, by someone she doesn't know. Jude tightens her thighs around Annie's waist, runs one hand through her hair. Her other hand is on Annie's bum, warm and strong. Whatever way she does it—slowly for one thing—her kisses give Annie a sort of mini mouth-orgasm, and her knees go weak. As if Jude knows this, she tightens her legs even more, holding Annie up. Jude's tongue is rough and dry, like a cat's, and Annie can taste salty potato, beer, tobacco, and something warm and peppery.

After a few minutes, Jude pulls away, jumps from the table and leads Annie by the hand, past the group of women sitting on the stairs smoking and laughing, to the upstairs landing. She ducks into the little room under the hanging blanket, then holds up the blanket, as if Annie's her guest. She glances at the sleeping bag on the mattress, the rolled up towel for a pillow.

'Yeah,' she says. 'That'll do.'

Downstairs, Donna Summer's 'I Feel Love' is playing. Jude puts her arms on Annie's shoulders, begins dancing, singing along to the music, making funny faces. In a small part of her brain, Annie finds the whole thing a bit unhinged, a bit frightening, but she laughs because she knows that's what Jude wants. And it's sort of what she feels like doing too.

'See?' Jude says, dancing closer, moving her hips. 'It's a lam-bam sitch.'

Annie hasn't a clue what this means.

'Yeah,' she says. 'True.'

Jude starts kissing her properly, running her hands under Annie's T-shirt. She moves away slowly, bends and unzips the sleeping bag, laying it neatly on the mattress.

'It's all good,' she says, smiling. She sits on the edge of the mattress, kicks her sandals off and pulls down the straps on her dungarees. A packet of grass and skins falls from the top pocket. She picks them up, starts rolling a joint.

'C'mere, you,' she says.

Downstairs, the music has stopped and they're singing a song, 'Carry Greenham Home', with harmonies that are surprising and lovely.

Annie wakes with the sun on her face, Jude snoring lightly beside her. They're both starkers. There's a used tampon on the floor near the mattress and blood smeared on Jude's thighs. Annie's hands are stained. She sniffs her fingers, then gets up quietly, pulls on her T-shirt and jeans and goes to the jacks. The blanket across the bathroom door isn't on the catch so she waits outside, listening. After a few moments, she peeps in. There's a woman in the bathtub, wrapped in a sleeping bag. Her head is shaved and the edge of a multi-coloured tattoo is visible creeping across her shoulder and up behind her ear. Annie sits on the side of the bowl so she can pee without making noise. She considers taking some loo roll to get the tampon off the floor in her room, but thinks that might be even more weird than leaving it there. She washes her hands quickly under a tiny dribble of water.

Downstairs, the living room is littered with sleeping women: on the floor covered in blankets and sleeping bags, on strips of sponge mattress, sprawled on the bashed-up sofa. In the kitchen, Lorna is already up, eating a boiled egg and drinking a mug of tea at the table. She looks amazing. Her hair is a bit longer than it used to be, slicked back with gel, stiff and spikey. It's partly why Annie's been feeling so shy since she arrived. That and the fact she didn't know about her and Viv.

Lorna smirks at her.

'I'd say you could do with a few ice-cubes on your nethers,' she says. 'Hahaha.'

'Yeah,' Annie says. 'Me clit feels the size of a melon. I could do with a few cubes on me nipples too.'

She's pleased that Lorna knows about Jude, and she wants to sound cool, but actually, Annie's astonished and afraid about what went on last night. It seemed to last for hours and hours, like a fever-dream where she was surrounded by writhing animals trying to get into every orifice, trying to devour her. Now everything feels tender. Nipples, arsehole, fanny, even her fingertips. Her tongue feels like she's wrenched a muscle in its root. A crash course in lesbian sex. Or a particular kind of lesbian sex. She's not sure she's up to that sort of thing, endurance-wise, on a regular basis. She hadn't had a clue what to do in return, but Jude took control, yanked out her own tampon, directed Annie's fingers, her fist, her face.

Lorna's still smirking.

'Cup of Barry's?' she says. Annie brought four packs of tea over with her, something she thought Lorna might like from home. 'Or you wanta egg?' Lorna says. 'Get you back to planet earth.'

'Sounds great. I'll make it myself.'

The pot is still on the stove and Annie fills it with fresh water and two eggs from the fridge. While she waits for the water to boil, she peers into the cardboard boxes on the counter. Rice Krispies, bags of muesli, lentils, instant coffee, sugar, tins of sardines, packs of tobacco, sanitary towels and tampons.

'Where'd all this come from?'

'Yeah.' Lorna waggles her spoon toward the living room. 'They brought it with them. They get loads of donations.'

'From where?'

'The Quakers. CND. Women's groups. Other peace groups. Dopes like that.'

'Oh. Cool.' Annie fills the kettle, but can't work out how to light the gas under it.

'Use the ring at the front,' Lorna says. 'That one is fucked.' She pushes back in her chair, her mug of tea in both hands, balancing by keeping her feet on the wooden rung under the table. There's a shiny drip of egg yolk on her chin.

'I bet fucken Jude asked you to go to Greenham?' she says.

When Annie doesn't answer, Lorna says, '*Ha*! She fucken *did*, didn't she?'

Annie turns away, fiddles with the knobs on the stove.

'The gas doesn't go any higher,' Lorna says. Annie opens a cupboard, gets a mug. 'It's just,' Lorna says, '*exactly* the kind of shifty move she'd make. Means she can hang out here a few more days, for one thing.'

The eggs start to boil and Annie looks around. There's a little clock on the windowsill with a second hand that's moving.

'Is Jude staying here then?' she asks.

Lorna lets her chair drop onto its four legs.

'Probably. Now she's connived herself a room.' She raps a complicated little rhythm on the table with her teaspoon. 'You want to watch that cunt, Annie-fanny. Next thing you'll be up to your arse in Greenham muck and then what happens to your college stuff, the Big Degree?'

'Well,' Annie says, 'like, I'm here for two weeks.' She tries to keep the wobble out of her voice. 'So maybe I could go with her—'

'Nah.' Lorna pokes the handle of her teaspoon through the eggshell in her eggcup and looks up at Annie from under her eyebrow piercing, the little women's symbol dangling. 'You'd hate it there. It's all pissing in bushes and shitting into these holes you have to dig yourself. Yakking all night about direct actions—'

'But I thought you said it was the only place where—'

'—mud everywhere and *endless* fucking discussions about how to do things, eating lentils and non-stop farting—'

'What makes you think I wouldn't be able for—'

'I'm not saying you wouldn't be *able* for it, I'm just saying Jude is a bit of a—'

Viv walks into the kitchen and Lorna stops speaking. Viv is wearing a bright green T-shirt and tiny cut-off shorts. In Dublin, she was the only black woman on the scene. She must recognise Annie from JJ's, but she's too cool to take much notice of her. Lorna and Annie watch her reach into the cupboard and pull out a jar of coffee. Lorna gets up from the table, stands behind Viv and curls her arms around Viv's flat stomach, kissing her on the back of the neck. Viv lets out a throaty chuckle.

'Getoffa me, you fucken wagon,' she says. 'Do youse want coffee or what?'

Annie looks at the clock. She's forgotten how long her eggs have been boiling.

It takes nearly twelve hours: hitching, scabbing lifts, getting busses, hitching again. Jude does all the talking, says where they're headed, does her Greenham spiel with everyone. When the lorry drivers say, It's just a camp for commies, anarchists and mad lezbos, innit? or mothers who want to dump their kids and become anarchists and lezbos?, she laughs and says, 'Nah, all wrong, mate, it's a Women's Peace Camp, going to save the world from nuclear winter, you should tell people about it, cos each one of those Cruise warheads is three Hiroshima bombs.' She scares the shite out of Annie by kissing her in front of the truckies. In a car with a mother and child, she slides her hand between Annie's legs, lightly fingering the crotch of her jeans. When the little boy peeps at them from the front seat, Jude makes funny faces at him, sticking her tongue out and laughing.

The last lorry drops them outside Newbury and they walk a mile or so in the dark to the Common. Some cars go by with men yelling at them to go fucking home, cunts, smelly dykes. Jude doesn't take much notice. 'Just wankers,' she says. 'Waiting for the light bulb to go on upstairs. But the electricity ain't connected, hahaha.'

They get to the perimeter fence and follow the track running alongside it. Surveillance lights inside the army base make the going easy enough, but there are stretches in the dark where they have to hold the wire as they traipse along, and sections with trees and bushes interrupting the trail. Jude doesn't stop talking, chatting about the banners hung on the fence, the children's toys, flowers and symbols. She shows Annie the big flat area where the silos are and the places where the wire has been cut low down—*cat flaps*, she calls them—where the women sneak in and out of the base. She tells her about the actions, how they got inside the base, danced on the silos, and another time how they dressed up as Teddy Bears to have a picnic in there. 'We keep finding better ways to lock the squaddies in,' she says. 'Kryptonite bicycle locks, hahaha, those space-age babies, I'm telling you, you can-not-fucking saw through them. Yeah, simple. And non-fucking-violent.'

When they see soldiers on night patrol, Jude calls out, waving at them. Some of them wave back and shout hello. One calls her a cunt and tells her to fuck off home and Jude laughs, shouts back that he needs to cheer the fuck up. She tells Annie that when the new recruits arrive, they're soft and friendly, but the longer they stay, the more shitty they get.

'Big fancy training ground for psycho-boys is what this place is,' she says.

The stars are tiny in the black sky when they arrive at Green Gate. In the clearing, a circle of women sit around a campfire on a collection of deck chairs, battered armchairs, upturned milk crates and logs. At one end, there's a sofa piled with coats and blankets.

'Well, look who's turned up,' a woman in an armchair says. She's a bit older than the others, with heavy shoulders and a scarf knotted around her head, smoking a joint, poking a long stick into the fire.

'How's it looking out there, Jude?' someone asks. 'Cos the locals were driving around earlier, chucking bottles.'

'It's a vibing dream-field, yeah?' Jude says. She hefts blankets and coats from the sofa and dumps them on the ground. 'And they know not to mess with the witches after dark.' She laughs, showing her teeth. 'This is Annie.'

One woman raises a hand at her and Annie says, 'Hi,' then bends over her rucksack, tinkering with the straps. The place smells like a turf bog after a fire and heavy rain, but there are wafts of fresh, clean air drifting in from the forest.

The women are talking about wool and spiders and the Big Snips, passing a bottle of whiskey around, laughing softly. Behind them, between the trees, there's a tarpaulin strung over a metal table, and under it, piles of basins, pans, pots all stacked upside down on a sheet of plastic. Slung between another couple of trees is a rope draped with clothes.

Jude settles on the sofa and pats the seat beside her.

'C'mere, you,' she says. Someone has passed her the joint and she inhales deeply. When Annie sits, Jude puts her arm around her and holds the spliff to her mouth. Annie tries not to resist, takes a short toke and lets it out as fast as possible, coughing. Jude leans back into the sofa, slides her hand between Annie's thighs and looks around.

'Where's my boy?' she says.

There's silence for a few seconds, and Annie wonders what she means, then the conversation about where to hide the Big Snips continues.

'Hey, wimmin,' Jude says, in a louder voice. 'I'm asking where's my boy?'

'He's with Sasha,' the woman with the wrapped-up head says. 'She took him to bed earlier.'

'Well. I wants to see my boy.' Jude stands up, tosses the roach into the fire and walks into the woodland. Annie watches her disappear between numerous dark shapes under the trees, a mixture of ordinary tents and the black hump-shapes of the benders that Lorna told her about. She bites her lip.

'You know Jude then?' the woman closest to her asks. Annie says, yeah, they met in London, and the woman nods without catching her eye.

The others are still talking, one of them strumming a guitar, her head bent low. Annie rubs at her shoulders. The rucksack has made shite of her skin. There'll probably be blisters. Jude didn't have anything with her, not even a jacket, just the same dungarees and vest she was wearing the first night. She'd borrowed a jumper from Lorna and put her blood-stained knickers in Annie's haversack.

Some of the women have begun singing, making up new words to the tune of 'Downtown', yipping when they get a good line. *Maybe you know some little places to go, where you can snip the fence—*

One of them starts singing properly, a song Annie remembers from Lorna's party, *You can't kill the spirit. She is like a mountain. Old and strong, she goes on and on and on—* The others join in and their voices make Annie's heart catch. She longs to lie down on the tattered sofa, curl up and watch the flames from the fire, pretend she's at home in Wicklow, eating toast and butter, her mam and dad somewhere in the background, her grandmother and aunts singing in the kitchen.

The woman beside her asks if she'd like some tea and she says, Yes, please. The woman stands, grabs a torch and shines it at a large branch stuck in the ground. There are about twenty cups hanging from it.

'Our mug tree,' she says. She pours water from the kettle into a mug, drops in a tea bag from a Tupperware and hands Annie a bashed-up carton with a teaspoon in it. 'There's only dried milk left,' she says. 'I'm Titch.' She smiles and Annie smiles back. 'You'll get used to us,' Titch says. 'And it'll all seem easier in the morning. You hungry?'

All Annie's eaten is a Mars Bar a truckie gave them that morning, and her stomach feels like it's devouring her from the inside.

'No, thanks,' she says. 'I'm grand.'

From somewhere there's a child's plaintive wail, then Jude is back. She flings herself onto the sofa, cuddling a little boy. He's wearing a filthy vest and sagging nappy, and is crying, his fists rammed against his eyes.

'You fucking woke him up?' the woman with the headscarf says.

'Yeah.' Jude snuggles her face into the child's neck and he pushes at her with his fingers, twisting away. 'Gotta see my son. Gotta see my boy.'

'You know how fucking long it took Sasha to get him to sleep? He's been non-stop crying for you since you left.'

'Scary-Mary says you've been crying for me, baby? Did no one help you? Is that what happened?'

The boy looks up at Jude, his cheeks smeared with dirt and tears, his mouth pulled down and quivering. His face scrunches again and he begins howling, grabbing her neck, her hair.

'You told him you'd be back Monday,' Scary-Mary says. 'It's fucking Wednesday.'

Jude cuddles the child close for a moment, then prises his chubby arms from her neck.

'Quit it, baby!' she says. 'Your nails are like bleedin' daggers.' She turns the boy's face toward Annie. 'Teets, say hello to Annie. Annie, say hello to my gorgeous little sprog.'

Annie tries to smile, to catch the child's eye, but he's arching his back and struggling.

'Sasha!' Jude yells into the trees. '*Oi*! Sasha!'

A young woman wearing loose cotton pants with a towel wrapped around her shoulders walks from the dark of the woodland. She stares at Annie.

'Is there a bottle for him or what, Sash?' Jude says. Annie sees Titch rolling her eyes.

'He's not hungry,' Sasha says. 'Just over-tired. Give him to me. I'll take him back to bed.'

She puts her hands out and Teets lifts his arms toward her. Jude kisses him on the head and passes him to Sasha. Sasha nestles him under her towel.

'Where you sleeping?' Jude asks her.

'Where do you think I'm sleeping?'

'For sure. Yeah. Cool. Stay there, Sash. Annie and me'll kip in the bendy-bender.' She takes the mug of tea that Annie's been drinking, slurps from it, winking at Annie over the rim. 'Don't want my boy disturbed by any of your lovely sounds.'

'Maybe there's somewhere else I can sleep?' Annie says.

'Don't be a dip.' Jude says into her ear. 'It's a switch-bitch is all. That's what you're up against here.'

The last few mornings were frosty, but today it's raining again. Josie is cooking brown rice over the main fire. Titch, Scary-Mary, Bess, Hungarian Zsuzsi and a few women from Yellow Gate are sitting around it, dressed in a collection of hats, boots, coats and raingear, chatting and drinking instant coffee. Teets is playing beside Bess with the wooden toys someone brought from Yellow Gate. Over at the kitchen area, Annie and Sasha are chopping vegetables on the rickety metal table under the tarpaulin. The trees are shedding autumn leaves into everything, the rainwater in the basin is a dull, clotted brown and the vegetables keep getting muddy. Sasha reaches for a container of potatoes and winces.

'Shit,' she says. 'That fucker yanked my shoulder yesterday.'

'Roly-Poly?' Annie says.

'Yeah. Fucking sadist.'

'My arse is still sore,' Annie says. 'I think there was a rock right where they dumped me.'

'Are you going to Orange Gate later?'

'Yeah.'

'Me too,' Sasha says. 'Going to bring Big Bob to do some snipping on the way. If I can bend my arm.' She drops a washed potato into a pot of water. 'You still got the shits?'

'Yeah. I've been to the shit-pit at least six times already this morning. Probably that left-over dahl Welsh Sally gave us.'

'You really think you'll stay the winter?' Sasha says.

'If my arse-hole doesn't drop out first.'

Scary-Mary leaves the fire and goes into the kitchen bender. She asks if all the cheese is gone. Annie says it is, and also that they're running short of rice and onions.

'Okay,' Scary-Mary says. 'I'll do a food run with Zsuzsi. We need anything else?'

'Maybe more tins of tomatoes?'

Sasha starts singing 'Sarah's Song'. She has a beautiful voice, better than anyone else, and the little gang sitting around the fire gradually stop chatting and join in, harmonising. Annie drops her head to hide how emotional it makes her. It doesn't matter how cold or wet it is, how frightened she feels, when the singing starts, her heart swells. She doesn't know if it's because she's too happy or too sad.

Annie helps Sasha carry the pot of spuds to the main fire, and then goes to the shit-pit again. She's washing her hands in the shit-pit basin when Toni comes from the path near the fence and waves at her.

'Oi! Annie! Someone at Orange Gate looking for you.' She gestures behind her. 'She's on her way here now.'

Annie gives her a thumbs-up and goes back to the table. As she slides the chopped vegetables into the pot, she spots Lorna on the track near the fence, hands in her pockets. She drops the knife and chopping board and runs across the clearing, slipping and sliding in the mud. When Lorna sees her, she stops walking, grins. Annie grabs her and hugs her tight.

'You came!' Her voice is giddy and high.

'Jaysus! Glad to see me or what?'

Annie laughs, wiping her hands on her jumper and trying to catch her breath.

'I can't believe you're here,' she says. 'You got my letters then?'

'Yeah. The steady supply.' Lorna looks down at her boots, wiping one foot against the other. 'That's some fucking mud,' she says. 'And bleedin' cold too.'

Annie takes her hand and leads her toward the fire where Titch and the others are, but Lorna hangs back. She points to the kitchen area.

'Make us a cup of tay, wudja? Me throat's dry as a whore's knickers.'

'C'mon so,' Annie says, and they go to the little cooking fire near the kitchen. She pours just enough water in the kettle for two mugs and swings it onto the wire grid, poking at the embers to get the fire lighting again. Lorna plonks into a deck chair, takes a pack of Golden Virginia from her pocket and rolls a cigarette. She offers the pack, but Annie shakes her head, says she has the squirts and smoking makes it worse. Lorna lights her fag with the stick Annie used to poke the fire, tilts her head and narrows her eyes.

'So,' she says. 'This is where you're holed up.'

'Yeah.' Annie turns a log onto its cut end, puts a bit of polythene on it and sits while they wait for the kettle to boil. 'I can't believe you made it,' she says. 'I thought you weren't getting my letters.'

'Yeah. Well, like I said.' Lorna waves her fag toward the trees. 'So. How are you finding the shit pits, Lady Muck? And the general squalor?'

'It's grand,' Annie says. 'I mean. I feel filthy all the time, and everything's always damp, me poor kidneys, but so what?'

The kettle starts to boil and she stands, makes the tea, taking small sideways glances at Lorna, at how clean she looks. Her face and teeth, her hands.

'There's fresh milk,' Annie says. 'And *piles* of sugar.'

'Jaysus! Big Day at the camp or what?' Lorna takes the mug. She puts in three heaped teaspoons of sugar and a lot of milk. She sips the tea and nods in the direction of the women.

'They look a right dose.'

Annie glances across to the main fire. Lettie is bending over putting pieces of toast onto the wire rack. She's over sixty, with thin, straggly hair, but she's been inside the fence loads of times. She knows the location of every base in the UK and the numbers and types of missiles deployed. Beside her, Dublin Rosa is eating from a bowl. Probably muesli. She's the one who goes right up to the police horses, strokes them, puts her face close to theirs, says they're telling her they don't want to be there, lies down in front of them to stop the others being trampled during blockades. Bess is on the sofa, knitting and talking to Sasha. She's been arrested twice and already spent a week in

Holloway where they screwed up her insulin and she nearly died.

'They're *so* fucking great,' Annie says. 'You'd have to know them.'

Lorna scoffs. 'Yeah. Bet they're a laugh-a-minute.'

'Actually, they *are* really funny. Last week they poured super-glue into the locks at all the gates. The soldiers had to—'

'Right,' Lorna says. 'Hilarious.' She points at Dublin Rosa. 'I know yer woman's face from JJ's.'

Annie nods. She grabs a pack of biscuits from the tin box. 'Want one?'

'Cheers.' Lorna takes two digestives. She eats them like they're a sandwich and crumbs fall everywhere. 'So,' she says. 'You stayed.'

'Yeah.'

'What about the Big Degree?'

Annie tips the toe of her boot into the ash at the edge of the fire, then runs a finger through it, makes a women's symbol.

'I know. But, like, what's the point of a dickhead degree if there's no world? Might as well be here instead, doing something useful, at least try to stop them nuking the fuck out of everything.'

Teets appears from behind the sofa where Bess is sitting. He's crying, carrying something close to his chest. Someone has put an adult-sized jumper on him and tied the middle with string, so it's like a knitted dress. The front of it is covered in mud. Teets makes his way unsteadily across the clearing, his miniature red wellies a blast of colour against the November browns and blacks of the forest. He stands in front of Annie, tugs at her hand, whimpering.

'Not now, Teets,' Annie says. 'I'm talking to my friend. Why don't you find Sasha?' She points to the group at the fire, but Teets keeps crying, so she lifts him onto her lap and puts her arms around him. He stops sobbing, pushes a wooden wheel into his mouth and chews at it, staring at Lorna.

Lorna makes an incredulous face.

'Fuck me,' she says. 'When did you give birth?'

'Jude's away for a few days.'

'Away where? I mean, what the *fuck*? Is this what you mean by doing something useful? Living in shite to be Jude's fucking babysitter?'

Annie shrugs.

'It's not just me looking after him,' she says. Though actually, it sort of is. Her and Sasha.

Teets starts crying again, looking up at her.

'Whingy little brat, isn't he?' Lorna says.

Annie pushes Teets hair from his eyes. Sometimes, his high-pitched wail makes her want to kill him. That and the way he clings to her legs when she tries to walk away. She and Sasha call him The Barnacle, joke about taking him to some dark part of the forest and dumping him there, maybe dropping him into a shit-pit, or shoving him through one of the cat flaps in the fence, let the soldiers take him. Serve Fuck-Face Jude right when she finally comes back and goes looking for her boy.

She digs a teaspoon into the bag of sugar, swoops it high into the air.

'Get ready!' she says. 'Here come the Cruise Missiles.' Teets stops crying, opens his mouth wide to let the spoon in, and sucks the sugar thoughtfully. He takes the spoon out and examines it.

'I thought Green Gate was women only,' Lorna says.

'Except boys under ten. Are you staying long?'

'Nah. We're only passing by, hahaha.'

'Oh. Right,' Annie says. 'Is Viv with you then?'

'Yeah. She's the one who wanted to come. I just tagged along. She's up at Orange Gate.'

Teets's head bashes against Annie's nose. His hair smells like poo and she picks up a dirty towel and wipes his head roughly. He giggles and tries to stop her.

'That's where the blockade will be,' she says. 'Up at Orange Gate.'

'I know,' Lorna says. 'They're already dragging out pallets for a bonfire on the road. Not sure we'll stick around for that.'

'Why not?'

Lorna laughs.

'Not my thing. Playing mud-pies and war-games with all the vicar's wives. Slumming it with the middle-class ladies.'

'What are you on about, Lorna?'

Josie calls out for Teets and he squirms down from Annie's laps and trots over to the other fire.

'Just,' Lorna says, 'this so-called *wimmins* peace camp? Knitting fucken woolly spiders and rainbows and hanging them on a barbed wire fence to stop a nuclear war? Plus, all the pretty white faces? I mean, Viv is a minority of, like, one.'

The tops of Annie's ears are burning, her heart has started to race. She pours the last of her tea onto the ground between her legs.

'That's not true,' she says. 'Not everyone is white.' She wants to look at Lorna, but instead, frowns and pokes at the fire. 'Besides, even if they were—'

She stops and frowns. 'Why are you being such a downer?' she says.

Lorna looks up into the trees and shrugs.

'I mean, seriously,' she says. 'Don't you find it all a bit... swanky?'

'*Swanky*?' Annie wants to laugh at the old-fashioned word. 'We're at, like, four minutes to midnight, they could bomb the fuck out of planet earth any minute, and you're being picky about who's trying to change things because they're a bit *swanky*?'

Lorna turns toward her. Her expression is unreadable.

'Watch out, Annie. The world is always about to end. It's always Armageddon somewhere. But weirdly, this lot always have proper lives to go back to. All you'll have is the dole queue.'

Annie gets up from her seat. Her foot skids in the mud. She tosses her head.

'Why are you always—' she says.

'Think about it.' Lorna's voice is odd. Soft and kind. 'You love your books, right? And your family's not exactly rich, are they? So, you know, don't fuck up your chance.'

'Jesus Christ!' Annie's mouth is dry. 'You sound like my father.'

Lorna stands, zips her anorak and pulls her hat down over her ears.

'Yeah. Well, maybe your da knows a thing or two about how this world works.' She puts her tobacco into her coat pocket. 'Okay, I'm heading back to Orange Gate. See how my woman is doing up there.'

She punches Annie lightly on the shoulder, but Annie can't bring herself to look at her or say goodbye. She bends down, listening to Lorna walk away, rinses the two mugs with as little water as possible, pours the small amount of dirty liquid from cup to cup, then slops it back into the hand-washing basin. She feels a sharp cramp in her stomach, dumps the mugs on the trestle table and walks quickly to the shit-pit near the big tree. She squats over the hole. There's nothing but water and smell coming from her bowels, the sourness rising from between her legs. She hears Teets wailing and sees him through the trees, his nappy slumping down inside his pants, one little fist up to his eye. She watches silently as he stops for a moment, clutching the wooden wheel close to his belly, his small chest heaving. His head swivels, searching. She ducks down lower. If she stays here long enough, someone else will pick him up.

Notes on a Breast Reduction

memory floats in and out like the creak of a rocking chair like an old radio in a deliberately sentimental scene / memory floats in like you're standing very still and you're sixteen and you're standing in a kind of discomfort / memory floats in like a kind of discomfort like a stranger's breath close and wet down the back of your neck / you feel him turn and you feel him look away / and you look as the bra has been shucked and you look as the scars are shown stretching down and across / down and across like an anchor or the upturned curves of a cat's mouth in a kid's drawing / memory floats in and out but something stark like relief hits her face like an open window / memory floats in and out but the fishbowl glow of the television colours her skin green / memory floats in and you remember later, when he bends over your body, you watch as his hair slips over his face like a curtain.

Ríbh Brownlee

There are emerging reports that we should be adults soon

across the river the girls in shorts & backless dresses with legs the brown
    of a colour-toned canvas
are breathing out the thick summer air
& we think of how our skin

should be turning pink by now.
you've already a pack of cards in your bag

ready for negotiating rounds in a darkened pub corner.
we are here & we are somewhere else
& the sun around us perseveres

Ríbh Brownlee

Maura's Back (a novel extract)

Edel Brosnan

May 1927

If it was me who made the arrangements, we would have caught the Orient Express from London to the new Turkish state and driven by car: nothing mad like a Daimler, but still a model that offered some kind of comfort and decent suspension. We would have broken our journey for a few days in Venice and wandered down footpaths by the canals like real honeymooners. We would have stayed in a grand hotel—though not the Grand Hotel—and practiced behaving like lovers. I would have worn kid gloves from Brown Thomas and shoes with a thin ankle strap and a patent leather gleam. We would have eaten macaroni and thought ourselves smart when we worked out that the St Peter's fish on the menu was good old John Dory.

It was not me who made the arrangements.

On the seventh of May, we boarded a merchant ship on the dockside in Aberdeen. Our cabin had a porthole and two mean single bunk beds, and an empty water basin nailed to a bare wooden stand. The open deck smelled of oil, rope, stale sweat, and dried fish. A solid wall of grey drizzle followed us from Scotland all the way to Norway. By the time we landed in Bergen, the British police had raided the Soviet consul's offices in London. Accusations of spying and shenanigans and bad faith soon followed, along with rumours of war and invasion. Sabres were rattled, and strongly worded cables went flying forward and back across the continent.

Donal showed me the papers, three days old and damp from the newsstand outside the hotel. He read the Berlin news, while I thawed myself out with a cup of something that the waiter swore was tea, and that he clearly expected me to drink black, with a skinny half-moon of lemon on the saucer, because whoever heard of sugar for a cuppa, let alone a splash of milk?

'And that,' said Donal, 'is why we could not travel to Moscow by luxury train, with the British Empire's insignia shining like a target on the front of the engine.'

'And this,' I said, pointing to the paper in my lap, the newsprint smudging my cold fingers, 'is why we should have commandeered a sea plane, to get us there before they close the borders.'

He smiled, and I cracked a half-smile back. Never mind the secrecy; we did not have the funds to speed up our journey to St Petersburg—no, Petrograd—no, Leningrad—then on to Moscow. 'If it's still called Moscow by the time that we arrive, I'll give you half a crown,' I said, like somebody who had money of her own and could afford to be throwing it away. We would get there by the end of the month with a fair wind behind us, and we could endure no more delay, or Donal's mission would not go well.

'For the love of God, don't call it a mission, or you'll get us all shot,' he said to me, in jest but not even faintly joking at the same time. I promised that I would keep my rosary beads hidden away for the duration of our stay in the Red Republic.

That night, in a blissfully overheated hotel room in a Nordic sea port, in a bed the size of the boat we arrived on, he checked me for concealed holy medals and scapulars. And if I had been wearing any when the inspection began, by the time we were finished, there were none.

In the morning, the cobbles on the street below were gleaming like polished steel, the drizzle finally melted away and we strolled through a park where the air carried at least the hint of summer.

From Bergen to Stockholm by train, then Stockholm to Helsinki, and Helsinki to Leningrad. First class for privacy, for Donal had a ton of work to do. I read a book of folk tales to revive my *cúpla focail* of Russian, checking the handful of words I could not remember in a dog-eared dictionary. And I gazed out the window, at dark green forests of evergreen trees, and fields of cattle grazing on meadow grass. Wildflowers along the railway embankments filled the air with a scent almost but not quite good enough to cancel out the tang of burning coal from the Empire-free steam engine that dragged us closer to the place where we were headed, the lives we would be faking and the chances that we would be taking with our own lives, and the lives of those so eager to do business with us, and those determined to derail us.

Europe braced itself for war between two weary giants, while we quietly plotted to give a tiny nation the resources to survive, and make it to the tenth anniversary of its shaky independence. A nation that did not—yet—have the right to set up embassies or send diplomats beyond its borders, and was obliged to send unacknowledged deal-makers like Donal instead.

I grew to tolerate lukewarm black tea with lemon. I grew to love the mad, wild landscape of the north with its nineteen, twenty hours of daylight in late May. By the time our train groaned to a halt in Finland Station in the crowded heart of Leningrad, I was no longer homesick, or apprehensive. I was impatient for our great gamble to begin.

I was ready, but our hosts were not.

We unpacked our bags in a hotel room where the chandelier made me nervous; I moved beneath it, expecting it to fall on me the minute I turned my back. Clumps of dust spied on us from beneath the bed. The sheets were starched and clean, but tinged with grey, and I quickly learned to hide my soap because the maids kept stealing it.

I bought an electric plate in the hotel lobby from a timber merchant leaving for Canada. And I had learned how to use it for heating up pastries by the time Donal received his first summons for a meeting. Later, when I got to know Nadya, the friend of a friend of a man at the Trade Ministry, she taught me how to brew tea in the Russian way, and to drink it with a tiny spoonful of jam.

It tasted nice enough in its own way, though it was not the same.

Donal went to meeting after meeting, bringing me with him so I could listen in on the Russian small talk while he tried to make himself understood in a mix of schoolboy German, execrable French, UCD English and what he called the international language of the balance sheet. This was, after all, our cover story for being here in the first place: looking for new business ideas we could take to investors back home: vodka distilleries that could also make single malt whiskey; new high-yielding strains of barley or rye, equally suited to the bog or the steppe; or new ways to make cement, or silver-plated cutlery. So we drank tea with machine engineers as they met after a long day shift, and argued about economic theory, and with architects on building sites describing the new cities in the sky that they were building. Palaces that would be home to nearly ten thousand people, with cinemas and sports clubs, and canteens on the ground floor… fairer and more sociable than keeping staff, did we not agree? Well yes, as a maid of all work from the age of thirteen till my seventeenth birthday, I can assure you I agreed; I could barely resist the temptation to wave a red flag and sing a few bars of the Internationale while they showed us samples of tile work and parquet flooring and the communal dining rooms in the new apartment complexes. 'And everyone lives like this now?' I asked, unhelpfully. 'Everyone will indeed live like this, in good time,' they replied. And Donal believed them.

I liked our meeting with the women at the textile plant the best. They rattled off statistics about productivity and targets, and the average thread count in their rolls of cotton. But the kerchiefs that kept their hair tied back were colourful—pine green, red gold, or the watery blue of a clear sky in November—and the patterns were alive with hope, and the geometric shapes of dancers, and giant turbines and bluebirds soaring over soldiers marching in formation, the talking animals and heroes from folk tales blending into a jazz tapestry of revolutionary energy and light. All in a piece of cloth. I felt drunk just looking at their bold creations. The women in the textile plants knew that the work they were producing was utterly new. They complained about the factory bosses who wanted bolts of grey and blue unpatterned serge, and they took pride in the bold patterns they created instead. Soviets with style. The People's *Vogue*.

Donal worked his way through the contacts on the list he had made me memorise before we left Ireland: corn merchants from the American Midwest, geologists from the coal belt of England, and newspapermen whose nose for a story could not get past their host's determination to talk only about year-on-year improvements in steel production in the cities.

'Even in bed,' grumbled Nadya, shocking me by speaking so bluntly in front of the man she referred to as her fiancé, though Donal was sure that 'keeper' was a more accurate description. I rather liked Nadya, even when she flirted shamelessly with the commissars from the Party, ignoring their unbending, unspoken response that screamed, 'I am too serious to lie down with a woman who has a Marcel perm and red lipstick.' She did better with the waiters, who were less scandalised by her style and kept her glass topped up with sparkling wine from Georgia. If Nadya joined us at our table with her fiancé / keeper Petrov, I found myself unwinding, and her tipsy, gossipy chat improved my Russian far more than any of my attempts to make sense of Isvestia or Pravda had done.

Mostly, however, we dined with men who knew other men in positions of influence, men who promised to engineer introductions in a few days, a few weeks, when the time was right, but not now, before the ground had been prepared and conditions were optimal. Donal nodded and smiled and concealed his impatience and the men drank vodka, and I nursed a glass of Vichy water, and practised listening in on conversations at nearby tables to improve my vocabulary.

It took us a while to work out that Petrov, the fixer-in-chief, was the man most likely to do what everyone promised to do: he would get Donal into the offices of the people who mattered. We were supposed to disapprove of Petrov; our official hosts, who always seemed to have a more important meeting to go to, or a better party to attend, made that very clear. But Petrov never talked about steel quotas or dams or turbines. 'You don't have so many steelworks in rural Ireland, I imagine. It's all small farms and food exporters, yes?'

'Well yes,' we replied. And he complimented me outrageously on our lack of knowledge, which he called open-mindedness. 'Wipe the slate clean!' he would shout happily, as we clinked glasses in the hotel dining room under electric lights that flickered or faded, depending on how strong the current was on that particular day. He saluted Donal's ability to speak in both English and French and seemed completely unaware that I could just about follow a conversation in Russian as well. (Why did he think my university educated husband had bothered to bring me here, I wondered? It wasn't for my innate love of American jazz.) Oh, but when he claimed that my green eyes were a complete novelty in this city, that he had never seen anything like them, I felt like a goddess in a world without gods. The chambermaid who stole my bars of lily-of-the-valley soap had the same eye colour as me, and I doubted that her people came from a smallholding west of the Shannon. Petrov smoked Turkish cigarettes that smelled of first-class dining cars, but his mistress Nadya smelled of strong tea with lemon, sugar, and bergamot. She smelled like my old friend Hannah.

So I looked forward to the nights when we had no plans to meet with anyone important, and we might as well have dinner with Petrov and Nadya instead.

Donal was growing more and more frustrated in Leningrad. I was falling into a midsummer trance. Because it was daylight all the time now. The sun, the ever-present sun, shone on the Neva River and the watermelon sellers in the street markets. By now, Donal and I were playing the role of newlyweds with some enthusiasm. And though our marriage was as fake as the string of jet beads I wore around my neck, we strolled through squares and residential streets where the sky was still bright at midnight, shadowed only by our minder from the Party, and we kissed in shaded doorways.

Or we coupled lazily in our oversized hotel bed, in our immense and grubby hotel room, our bodies glued to one another by desire, and the summer heat, and our cover stories—shrewd businessman and his respectable bride who speaks in tongues—becoming tangled up with the grubbier details of who we really were and what had really brought us here. This convenient desire for one another became the honeymoon we needed and deserved. It was, I knew, more fitting than moonlit walks in Venice would have been.

And then, three days after midsummer, as Petrov and Nadya invited us to join them in the country for a break from the oppressive heat, the summons came. Our hosts were ready to meet us. And to talk about blood money, untraceable deals. And the Romanov crown jewels.

Skin Type: Dark

ma calls it 'wheatish with a glow'
this difference in shades is important
meaning: i'm not the dark of

bonded labourers working golden fields
in the afternoon sun to grow wheat
on hungry stomachs

not as dark as the untouchables
(*of course, not!*) because then I'll be
what ma hates—

> a *Santhali* maid secretly drinking water
> from the same steel glass as her lords
> tainting it with low-caste saliva

> thrill coursing through her ebony frame
> from a dangerous game,
> the cost of which: her life

—whitewash wheatishness
into desirable skin tone
for better matrimonial deals

top currency for highest bidder
I'm expected to surrender
uterine autonomy

for my family name,
face creams & breath mints
woman shamed, woman tamed

Sree Sen

What I Write Towards

The Stinging Fly is proud to partner with Skein Press on the Play It Forward Fellowships programme, which aims to nurture and amplify the talents of writers whose voices and stories have traditionally been underrepresented in Irish literature and publishing. Here, we asked the five inaugural fellows to reflect upon an emotion that lives at the core of what they want to convey through their work.

Home | Gonchigkhand Byambaa

Pre-dawn's beautiful light shines through a thick curtain. Birds singing, blended with cows' *muureh*, brings her nomad life to Dundrum.

A modern luxury apartment complex sits between farmland and busy shopping centre. It really is unique. Her apartment's bedroom windows face on to a big field with farm animals and beautiful, soul-nurturing native trees and their birds. Her living room's window faces the train track and the biggest shopping centre in Ireland.

This is the beauty she had always wanted. When she was growing up in the countryside, her dream was to move to the modern city, and yet she knows that her soul can't be separated from Mother Nature. She feels like the eternal blue sky has granted her wish. She is one of the lucky immigrants that has found a hardworking and loving Irish family here. At the same time, she is the unluckiest person in the world because she can't enjoy this life.

Grief, regret, and anger keep her awake most nights and she cries until her tears soak her pillow. And yet the wet and cold pillow gives her company and comfort, and becomes a safe space for her.

When she was a little girl, she used to get up before dawn to bring their cows to the mountain. Her mom always kissed her forehead and whispered to her, 'Remember to take your dog with you. Don't try to help if Banhar fights with predators. Make a loud sound frequently when you are walking to the mountain. Okay?' Her mom said this every morning in summertime.

This morning, she wakes with a slightly lighter feeling.

Life is funny, she says to herself.

She knows it is time to stop battling predators. Time to offer some food and ask for forgiveness from them. *Our dad's hunting journey is over, we must accept that. Mother Nature has blessed us with so many good fortunes.*

Thinking gives her no pain now. Today is the day she will call off her dad's cancer treatment.

She dials.

'I think we need to end his suffering. He is thin like paper. There is no cure. Just suffering. Our dad doesn't deserve this. He is a kind and intelligent man. He will understand why we want to stop the treatment. What if our dad's body will not be cleaned by predators and will not decay because of the chemicals involved? Those chemicals are very bad for the soil. This land is where he used to hunt. His hunting sustained our lives. It is just so wrong that my dad's body is going to harm many creatures,' she says in a hurry down the phone.

Total silence. She listens with great anxiety. For a second, she thinks her phone is off. This thought relieves her. *Thanks to the eternal blue sky my phone was off*, she says to herself.

She can tell it is around 4 a.m. by the light through her window, brightening the pane, inch by inch

Suddenly, a very frail voice answers down the phone.

'I agree with you. My son doesn't deserve this pain,' says her granny.

She puts family first in everything. Even so far away, she feels responsible to them, inspired by them, devoted to them.

Obsession | Sara Chudzik

I don't always feel like writing, but I always need to. A lot of the time I make it to the page. When I leave it, I feel relief, a particular type of stillness. There are also days when it's a source of frustration, when nothing seems to fit. But if I don't write, things feel wrong, almost tense.

I read because of a love for literature, but I write because of an obsession; for my characters, the fictional lives they lead, for their problems, for the words, for making it all work and making it the best it can be. I'm obsessed with the act of writing and what I'm writing about. The more I write, the more I'm sure of this.

I get obsessed with certain topics, the process of learning a language being the current one, and a way for me to live out this obsession is through writing about it. I create fictional characters living in the same world that we do so they can face the same struggles. When I obsess over a character, I try to inhabit their mind and to do that I have to take them along with me everywhere I go.

When you do that, you begin to share your selfhood with these people. I try to experience reality the way they would. I hear a song and think that it could be their favourite. If I'm buying clothes for myself I start to notice colours and styles they would wear. It can get busy in my head, so I really do have to get to the page to have some breathing space.

And getting it right; that's the hardest part of my obsession. The writing and rewriting when it doesn't feel right. You do a lot to make it better. Read your favourite texts over and over again to figure out what it is that makes them work. Not to mention the research: sometimes I go down a rabbit hole to find out what was the most desirable toy of 2001.

This obsession makes me forget my anxieties because perfecting the craft is more important than my comfort. It makes exposing my vulnerabilities easier. I know myself enough to admit it—I write because I'm obsessed with what I want to say and how I want to say it. I know I'll never get it right, but hopefully I'll get close.

Love | Majed Mujed, *translated by* Anam Zafar

In the annals of cultural history, poetry is never mentioned without a connection to love. In turn, a love story is never told without some poetic effect. They say that love was born with the spoon of poetry in its mouth; that the flame of poetry would not burn without love's spark. In other words, the fruits of poetry would not continue to adorn the table of life if it weren't for the great tree of love.

When the light of love first shone between two people, so did the concept of expression. The stone tip that transformed living objects into drawings and metaphors on cave walls was held by the first poet in love. After that, it was by the hand of another lover that the first engravings of language into clay became writing. Human civilisations began with love.

Love makes people feel powerful and connected, but it also makes them feel weak and fragile. This was human intellect's first test: how to reason between these two states—power and fragility—that have moulded human personality. From there, a form of expression was needed to give shape to this reasoning. Imagination was also needed, to bring order to the relationship between different words, and then between words and objects, to create work. This is how poetry was born, and from it would radiate literature, art, thought and philosophy.

It was when love lit up everything inside and around me, an overwhelming moment, that I suddenly felt I was a different person to who I used to be. The young woman I fell in love with became the only purpose for any of my concrete plans. Because of her I spent sleepless nights imagining angels and demons, my thoughts circling between hopes, dreams and defeat, insane happiness and crushing sorrow, and competing moments of clarity and conflict, testing the extent of my power and connectedness, my devastation and fragility.

I am just an extension of all those noble experiences in this human project. The only way I am capable of viewing myself and other things is through my window of love. It has become through this window only that I can beckon towards poetry's wide horizons and discover the secrets of the words that shape my works.

I have written every one of my poems—even those that were interrupted by the devastating eruption of violence in my country—while preoccupied with one of the facets of my love: either a moment of weakness and defeat when I used the poetic imagination to conjure images of victims and what had become of their lives, or a moment of power when I screamed in the face of every maker of evil and the ill fate that was bound to befall them, working through my poetry to draw a thriving future in a safe, free country fit for human life.

Every poet is a lover. Or maybe every lover is a poet's project in some form: lovers see the world through their love, as if love is their lens for an alternative vision of the world and themselves. And if there is no written expression for that vision, their different way of life will reveal it. For at its core, poetry is nothing more than an expression of the imagination for a different way of life.

Standing Out | Sarah Fitzgerald

The start of my journey as a Play It Forward fellow was fraught with imposter syndrome. *I'm not worthy. I'm robbing someone else of this wonderful opportunity.* Being the philosophical person I am, I felt that writing through it was the only way I could embrace the experience and overcome the niggling guilt that came with it.

Part of my reaction was normal for any writer, but feeling unworthy as a writer has another dimension for me. If you had asked me twenty-five years ago, when I was thirteen years old, what my view of disability was, I would've replied in a sunshiny voice that I accepted my impairment as part of my identity. This acceptance didn't stretch as far as admitting that I found the mainstream educational experience rewarding but draining; I thought that my refusal to use a wheelchair made me equal. Blend in with the crowd.

It wasn't until I started reading English in Trinity at nineteen that I realised that there was nothing wrong with me. That all my life, I had been led to believe that if I tried my best to conform, or if I downplayed the 'unsavoury' aspects of my impairments, I could have everything I wanted: a family, my independence, a satisfying career. Then in 2005, at the tender age of twenty-one, I met a man who shattered this warped belief system of mine. He was a wheelchair user. He couldn't dress himself, feed himself or even scratch his own behind, but he and others spearheaded a human rights movement that empowered thousands of disabled people in Ireland to take control over their own lives. His name was Martin Naughton, a true visionary and disability activist, and, above all, my friend. After his successful 'Operation Get Out' campaign which saw many disabled people being moved from institutional settings into the community, he and others set up the first Centre for Independent Living in 1992. He was also involved in the establishment of the European Network of Independent Living (ENIL).

Martin's fearless quest for equality has influenced my writing immeasurably. I feel an irrepressible duty to educate whoever will listen that impairment is personal but disability—and the exclusion we experience as a result—is political. I set up a blog so that I could write about the struggles facing disabled people, and now I am writing a novel about Rachel, a disabled woman caught between two worlds – the mainstream and the 'specialised'. Her story is provisionally called *Fixing Rachel*. Intelligent, artistic and feisty, it seems that Rachel is the textbook 'triumph over adversity' story. However, Rachel has internalised negative beliefs about her impairment, and comes to realise that it is only when she challenges these beliefs that she will be able to accept the flawed and wonderful person she is.

Once disabled people accept that we are not to blame for the way we are treated, then we can use our voices with confidence and strength. Finally, I can be truly proud of my place in the world, as a disabled writer.

Challenge | Neo Florence Gilson

I write stories to keep me grounded, connected and breathing. I see writing as escapism, a way for me to travel between the past, present and future.

My values, environment, faith, community and a host of other factors all influence my voice. The themes I explore in my writing often allow me to question the belief systems, anxieties and unspoken laws that continually shape our behaviours. I write to find the currency of love that runs between the blurred lines of injustice. I believe that class has nothing to do with social standing, influence or money; rather, it's about how people treat one another: with respect, and tolerance for differences.

The tales I write are inspired by the forces behind a whirlwind of meaningful experiences and life in urban cities and townships. These forces are culture, family, nature, religion, music, oral traditions, food and politics. The themes for my stories are identity, courage and perseverance. For instance, in my short story 'The Riverdance,' I gently explore the life lessons learned from living in an area where there is danger lurking everywhere. Its characters are believable and realistic, and have a touch of humour. The story is set in Kimberley, South Africa.

from 'The Riverdance'

> Susan rolls over. She feels as though her heart might burst from her chest due to its frenzied beating. She perceives a hand touching her shoulder, sees his face, and it all feels so real. Sweat is trickling down her forehead as she sits upright in bed. It is completely dark inside. The darkness is absorbing her tears. She sits in a dark room after suffering a severe blow from fate. She wants to spit out the seeds

sown by death and crush them beneath her feet. She puts her feet in her slippers and musters the energy to stand.

Some stories I write come from my experiences of life in Ireland.

from 'My Home is Nowhere'

Sarah clenched her teeth as she considered the little nuances. Then it was her turn to receive assistance from the woman at the counter. She was aware of how hurriedly the woman addressed her, and how agitated her raised tone of voice was.

'"Mosney Centre"? Is it a residential area?' the woman asked.

Sarah responded, 'No ma'am, it is a centre for refugees.'

'A centre for refugees, you say.'

The woman at the counter repeated everything Sarah said aloud, and Sarah could feel the eyes of the people in the room surveying her, their stares piercing right through her back.

In my work, I use everyday items as the defining characteristics of our environment and lived experiences. This can be anything that stands out to me, resonates with me, or feels significant in my life: food, an object, or even emotions, images, ideas and memories. Often, these items express a character's desire or trigger an idea or the voice of ancestors in the story. Everything plays a useful part.

The dream serves as the object in the story of 'The Riverdance'. Susan, the story's protagonist, dreams of her late husband and wakes feeling the desire to see him, but is faced instead with reality. The dream serves as my prop, allowing me to explore how Susan's loss and pain, which come from an external factor—the death of her husband—cause internal conflict.

What I have realised is that reading allows me to gain a worldview, whether it is through fiction or true stories, while writing forges a safe space to embrace one's vulnerability, doubts and contradictions; a space to create and explore life. The lesson I have learnt is that writers have a privilege to express things that are often left unsaid.

Often I am amazed at how quickly the blank white page can overflow with floods of words, and that is only achieved through insistence, creativity and diligence. My goal as a writer is to read, listen, learn, grow and to keep on writing.

Target Demographic

I am not the target demographic for a Friday night
presentation on osteo- or rheumatoid arthritis.

I am confronted by complex spelling patterns,
by muscle memory and inflammation.

I take notes on atmospheric pressure and painkillers,
on the double movement of a magic cure.

A tilt of the head tells me the difference
between being high and being high up.

It is nearly time for the squash and biscuits.
In a still moment I alphabetise my vocabulary.

Bebe Ashley

Walking Backwards

This time I remember it all—
the yellow lights
of a city strangening over our heads,
its honeysuckle smell & the dawn
that never rolls down the hill to catch us
as we walk backwards, down
to the edge of the sea
of Marmara. We take off
our clothes & get inside
the water, which isn't like
a mirror at all. It's hard
to tell the jellyfish
from the plastic, as they
both just float to the surface,
becoming light. I watch
you in the weird blue
glow, the calligraphy of your chest,
where there's more ink than skin,
I follow it like cartographer's lines, no
longer looking for a way home.
On the sea bed, we breathe, as
it's a dream and life has no lid—
it's more like an open window, where
outside, olive leaves dance silver
under the airless light & there's nothing
that cannot be altered—I know this
because you return.

Maija Sofia Mäkelä

Temporary Residence

And what if it doesn't end the way
you always thought it would? The first
lines around your eyes appear
like tiny rivers on a map—these eyes which
point to another continent, where
you've come again, knowing it never did you
any good to go calling back the dead
for an answer.

Anyway, the dead can barely recognise you
but when your eyes met
their own kind for the first time, sunlight struck
like a shock. Like light, the dead disperse
and you know assimilating wholeness
is not the same thing
as being whole, but you still stood there
right in the centre of the river
parting the current with your weird
white legs, expecting to be altered.

Your skin
the last man who touched you
said, *is so unusual*, striped with light
against starched white sheets
because you could only ever love him
in hotel rooms, making every space
temporary before you were, leaving
only a voice in the air

singing, because sound is a space
you can carry like a shell, taking a home with you
where you never overstay, where you always leave
before being left, and far away, in another
colonial hotel room, two alien breaths
fog up the window. Outside, the minarets release
a disembodied prayer, descending
like a gilded ceiling over the sky

and the dead are being difficult again,
with your finger pressed to the glass, nothing moves.

It was a rare rainstorm the night you arrived, so hot
you half-expected steam to rise off the streets
and you moved between unfamiliar rooms, like a ghost
yourself, or a widow, or a wind, afraid of what histories
could catch you if you stayed in one place for too long.

But what can the dead teach you, that you don't already know?
Even as you kept saying, *it's too late, it's too late*
you looked for signs in everything, lighting candles, bargaining ·
with pavement cracks, reading *11:11* in the jacaranda branches
its petals the neon purple of a mystic, unreal against the sky,
and when you meet a man who shares your birthday, another sign,
hold his hand at dawn, marking the ley line where bodies meet
on a rented mattress, in borrowed space, a borrowed hand,
and there is no terrain wide enough to contain all of your desire,
but you hold it still for a moment, in that basement under the city,
that catches only an hour of impatient sunlight, blotched
by the wide-leaved fig tree heaving against the glass

and even the dead are still
when you wake at last in that one sunlight hour
and watch his body, without a shadow,
as it passes through the door.

Maija Sofia Mäkelä

Something I Love

Tríona Bromwell

Let me tell you about something I love.

Something I loved.

A gut feeling always made me go. No matter the state of the house or how tired or frazzled I felt, on Wednesday evenings and Saturday mornings, I handed our sticky-fingered children to my husband and walked out the door. Often it felt like a massive derogation of my duties as a mother to drop everything and walk away, away from my chaotic house, two chubby-cheeked toddlers, precariously piled dishes draining by the sink and a mountain of washing waiting to be ironed, which only ever seemed to increase in size. I was bone-tired. The days back then were manic: dropping the girls to crèche, driving to work, working a full day at my job, leaving work, collecting the girls, getting home, cooking dinner, cleaning the house, doing bath-time and bed-time. The ticked boxes on my list, the stepping stones of my day.

The second I sat into my battered Opel Corsa I felt the weight of the week starting to lift from my shoulders. My destination was a room above a local restaurant with a laminate floor and grubby walls, the drab surroundings transformed by the slow smoking scent of incense, the ringing of a bell and a row of rectangular rubber mats. Our teacher, tall with dark eyes and long dark hair, moved with the grace of a ballet-dancer, exuding strength and calm in equal measure.

In the previous decade, the popularity of yoga had exploded. Studios had sprung up all over Dublin, offering classes in many different forms: hatha, ashtanga, vinyasa, hot, parent and baby, outdoor. I found this particular class, in its unassuming venue, through the recommendation of a friend.

What attracted me to it, out of the multitude of yoga classes being taught around Dublin at that time, was its spiritual nature, its emphasis on self-awareness. This was not just an exercise class, not a pair of fancy lululemon leggings between us. We were a diverse group of six or seven women, an assortment of shapes and sizes, whose faces became as familiar as the yoga poses themselves.

For years, I travelled the same road to the same room. At the sound of the bell, we began by following the teacher's lead, pressing our hands together and touching our hearts. Her lilting voice guided us, my body somehow responding to the ancient Sanskrit terms long before my brain learned what they meant. I loved being barefoot, my feet planted on the mat like the roots of a tree, my body standing strong and tall. Raising my arms overhead, I opened my chest and my heart to the universe, moving through the sun salutations and beyond. The warrior poses were my favourite. There was something so positive, so optimistic about lunging forward, feet wide apart, one hand stretched in front to the future, one behind to the past, my core strong and stable in the centre, directing my gaze beyond my extended fingers at what was to come. I am a warrior. I am strong. There was joy in breaking out of the mundane movement patterns of daily life: stretching to the sky, widening my stance, shaping my arms into beautiful arcs, my stressed, tightly-wound body extending into rainbow-shaped backbends. Breathing fully into every tiny alveolus in my lungs, my rib cage floating. Revelling in the feeling of being fully present in my wondrous body, in that particular moment. Developing enough confidence in my strength and stability to dip my head backwards into the unknown, when the unknown was not something to fear.

My mat became a sacred space for exploration and self-awareness. I discovered that leaning into discomfort and resistance was something that I was adept at. 'Pigeon' was my least favourite of all the poses. A tortuous hip-opener, one leg was stretched straight out behind with the top of the foot pressing into the floor and the other leg bent in front, the calf pressing into the floor. The muscles and joints were pulled to their limits, the feeling of stretch almost merging into pain. Breath by breath I learned to quiet my mind, to be present and allow my body to surrender.

While I appeared to have a reasonable capacity for dealing with resistance, I discovered that I was rather averse to risk-taking. Hand, head and shoulder-stands felt way beyond my capabilities. These were the positions that we usually tried at the end of class, when we were feeling light-footed and limber.

Over the many years I had been practising yoga, I had attempted headstands and handstands on hundreds of occasions, all to no avail. My teacher assured me that I had the control and the strength to do these poses, but I just could not seem to master them. To this day I am awestruck when I see elastic little girls flinging themselves up into handstands and spinning cartwheel after cartwheel on the local green. I was never one of those children. I was firmly indoctrinated with the belief that I would hurt myself if I attempted these unnecessary manoeuvres.

It was only when I began to practise yoga at home on my own that the voices in my head softened and change became possible. On a March morning, the rain which had been loudly drumming on the kitchen rooflight quietened to a gentle putter. Thousands of droplets were strung on the washing line like rows of glass beads. I rolled out my mat against the wall to attempt the elusive headstand. Kneeling down, I lowered my head to the floor, breathing in the sharp aroma of the rubber mat. My hands were clasped behind my head, my two elbows resting on the mat, forming a tripod of support. I pushed my back up towards the wall in a form of 'downward dog'. This was the point at which I would inevitably fail, unable to take the necessary leap of faith and raise my legs. Until that dreary morning, when suddenly my body seemed to know what to do and I exhaled, extending my legs and pointing my toes towards the ceiling. The wonder of letting go and succeeding; I was upside-down, my body a pillar of strength, viewing the droplet-strung washing line from a new perspective.

I don't know the exact dimensions of a yoga mat, but within that rectangle was a whole world.

Until my body betrayed me and my world crumbled.

It was a slow, insidious betrayal in the end. Degree by degree, I struggled to raise my arms to the sky, my chest and heart less open to the universe. My movements became tentative, hesitant. Poses which had been automatic, the motor plans well established in the sulci of my brain, became stilted and onerous. My warrior was weak and trembling. My core was shaky and unreliable, unable to support the lifting of my arms and legs into the air, or the playful placement of my head in space. My limbs were withdrawing from the world, no longer able to seek out joy and adventure.

It all came to a head one Wednesday evening when it became clear that a pose I had been doing with ease for years was no longer within my capabilities.

I caught the pitying glances of my fellow yogis. A couple of degrees more movement had been lost; the scales had finally tipped in favour of my disease. The class ended and I rolled up my mat, my eyes brimming. The sum of all the losses was too much to bear. I bypassed the usual chat after class and headed home from the drab room for the last time, devastated.

My yoga teacher contacted me the following day, having noticed my water-heavy eyes and quick exit. We arranged to meet in a local coffee shop where she presented me with a brightly-coloured bolster cushion. We talked at length and agreed that the group class scenario was no longer appropriate for me, not because I felt that I was in competition with everybody else, but because it was too painful a reminder of what I had been capable of doing. She convinced me to continue my practice at home and, at a later date, taught me how to adapt the yoga poses using props such as the bolster cushion and a kitchen chair. When I could, I continued with active poses, and when I felt weak, the emphasis was on restorative practice, supported by props and focusing on beneficial body positions and deep breathing. In this way I was able to reap the benefits of yoga for a lot longer, but I missed travelling the same road to the same room and enjoying the time set aside for me alone.

In the coming years, I watched as the black magnetic resonance imagery scans that signposted the progress of my disease lit up with constellations of white scars. These bright, innocuous looking spots were responsible for blocking the messages from my brain to my body. As my ability to function plummeted, my history of yoga enabled me to avoid serious injury as I did backbends over toilets, jack-knifed my legs in the shower, tumbled downstairs, arched over open dishwashers, and fell face-first hanging out the washing. My flexibility was my superpower. It also meant that I started from a reasonably good baseline in terms of my muscle strength and range of motion.

As well as the physical benefits of practising yoga, I learned that my body was capable of more than I ever realised. The thousands of micro-experiences on the mat, using the power of my breath to remain present and overcome resistance within my body, were like drops of water, slowly, gradually filling up a well of self-knowledge. Successfully attaining poses that I thought were too difficult showed me in a very tangible way that sometimes risk-taking can pay off. I decided to throw the kitchen sink at treating my disease. In addition to a whole raft of lifestyle modifications, I embraced the search for new treatment options. I was confident that I could overcome the unpleasant side-effects and pain associated with serious medical interventions.

Entering this niche world, I became familiar with a strange new lexicon, terms such as sphingosine-1-phosphate receptor modulators, humanised monoclonal antibodies, autologous haematopoietic stem cell transplantation. Terms which, many years later, would still not roll off my tongue. I participated in a clinical trial, with countless tedious hours spent at the hospital to confirm the safety of a new oral medication, one I was more than happy to try in the hope it might stem the tide of deterioration. When that failed, I tried intravenous monthly drug infusions, spending hours hooked up to drips alongside my fellow patients, hoping that the 'rare' side-effect of an illness worse than the one I already had would not be visited upon me. When that failed, I gambled big, pumping my body full of chemicals, destroying my bone marrow in an attempt to birth a new immune system that would not attack itself, hoping against hope that I could halt the deterioration. But my hopes—my dreams—would not be realised. With all the potential avenues of treatment exhausted, I was left with the wreckage of my body.

I know the exact dimensions of my iPad, and this glass rectangle is my portal to the world.

It sits propped up on the tray of my wheelchair, all day every day. I rely on it to plan, organise, shop, read, watch, research, and, most recently, to write. These days my left arm is a dead weight and rests on my lap, like an alien appendage. I have some residual function in my right arm and hand, enough to open and close tabs on the iPad, but I cannot type, my fingers unable to complete the careful choreography required. Writing in the conventional sense is no longer possible; I will never have a favourite pen again, chosen for its snug fit, the ink running just right. Scratching words onto a page, feeling the nib working its way across an expanse of paper, is a distant memory.

When I could put pen to paper, it was always perfunctory in nature: scribbling shopping lists or spontaneous notes for my children's lunch boxes, jotting appointments on the family calendar, signing the weekly spelling tests. It amazes me now that when I could have expressed my thoughts in beautiful curlicued script or careless pencil scrawlings, I didn't. And now that I can't physically write, I am compelled to express myself using the written word. I always had to be awkward.

Sometimes I wonder if even one hand worked, would I be a better writer? But then perhaps I would not feel compelled to write at all. Maybe I write because there is not much else I can do. So my voice is my quill, vibrations of invisible ink travelling in the warm air from my lungs, moulded by my hard and soft palate, my tongue, my teeth, my lips. I speak the words and phrases, hear the vowels expanding, the consonants popping, the sibilants hissing, and the sentences magically appear on the screen.

During the precious time I carved out of my busy life to practise yoga, I always gained great satisfaction from the physical endeavour of trying to attain a pose and then maintaining it. Encouraging my obtusely-angled knee joints towards straight lines. Squeezing my shoulder blades towards each other. Extending my arms and stretching my fingers towards something unknowable. Now, in my spare time, and I have lots of it, I write, which is made easier by the use of some readily available technology. Writing for most people would probably be described as a sedentary activity, but for me it involves a significant physical component: the brute force I have to expend to extend my wrist; the concentration with which I have to uncurl my index finger from its family of four, furled tightly in the palm of my hand; the balancing of my hand on my forearm, the weight searing through my bone-bruised elbow; the determination required to direct the tip of my index finger towards the cursor, microphone or delete buttons. Completing these movements does not bring any satisfaction. It is the painstaking price I must pay to make a mark, my mark, and I am willing to pay it.

From my first tentative attempts, it became clear that writing with my voice is not the same as simply speaking; the words seem to come from a different place. I am never sure where they are going to take me, or what I am going to find out. I have learned that I think unexpected thoughts that only arrive on the written page. Thoughts that surprise me, thoughts that I don't always like, thoughts that I am not always proud of. It has been a revelation to realise that I do not know myself very well. Joan Didion famously wrote 'I write entirely to find out what I'm thinking, what I'm looking at, what I see and what it means. What I want and what I fear.' At the beginning of my foray into writing, I was petrified by the possibility that what I may write about my life could weigh on the side of the intolerable, the undoable, even the unliveable, because in writing, I, too, find out what I really think.

A visceral pain intensified in the pit of my stomach as I wrote about my increasingly restricted body, my restricted life. I composed sentences I never wanted to write, about the corruption of my body by its own cells and systems, how this corporeal self-sabotage has made my life smaller than it perhaps otherwise would have been. The feeling of imprisonment due to my extremely limited hand function, surely our most innately human way of interacting with the world. The intrusive daily timetable of kind-hearted carers assisting me with essential daily tasks. My life as a wheelchair user, in a society where wheelchair users are rarely considered, or worse, rarely welcomed. My chair-shaped body's experience of varieties of pain I never knew existed. The loss of my professional career. The censorship of my feelings, how I stop myself from expressing any annoyance or anger with people, as I rely on these same people to live. The claustrophobic realisation that I will never spend a day on my own again. My daily struggles, as a disabled mother, a disabled wife. The constant wondering—am I enough?

Still I did not expect to find, within the confines of a small glass rectangle, an endless scroll of white space, an infinite sky. As I began to write, my inky breath took the shape of a bird, soaring, swooping, skimming through the air, allowing me to see my life from different perspectives on its way towards the page. When I write, I see a landscape gouged by chronic illness, scorched by pain, and yet it is no less beautiful. Reflecting on moments of joy allows them to be elevated, appreciated again in hindsight. The giggles skittering from my eldest daughter's heart-shaped mouth, the limpet-like hugs from my youngest, the burgeoning roses planted in our garden, the smell of morning coffee, the freedom of my wheelchair, the craic with old friends around the well-worn teapot, the scaffolding of my family, the warmth of sun on my bare skin, the escapism of reading, the endless love of my husband. This smaller, not lesser life.

Somehow in the space between the thought and the page, the painful realities of my life are often transposed into a narrative that I can accept, even embrace. But not always; toxic positivity does not have a place here. Chronic illness permeates every single aspect of my life. I'm not 'differently abled'. I'm not 'special' or 'inspirational' either. I am a disabled person. There are many things that I would like to do that I can't do. I'm still restricted. I'm still in pain and most likely always will be. Part of me will probably always wish things were different. Sometimes, no matter the perspective, there is simply heartbreak. Writing does not change this, but I delight in being able to say what I want and decide how I want to say it, how I want it to feel, how I want it to sound. I find joy in the weaving of words, beauty in the construction of sentences and the shaping of paragraphs. I rearrange twenty-six letters to express the innermost workings of my heart. In this way, I am free.

My favourite part of a yoga class was at the end, when all the strenuous work had been done. I would lie on the mat with my arms and legs loosely rolled out to the side, close my eyes, and my body would descend into a delicious stupor. I have not experienced that feeling since, nor do I expect to again. It is lost to me now. But the more that is lost to me, the more valuable what is left behind. Writing, while messy, emotional, arduous and demanding, gives me a sense of freedom that I cannot experience in any other aspect of my life, and leaves a feeling of great peace in its wake. I love the feeling I have after I have written, the words smoothing the sharp edges, sweetening the bitter pill. Emily Dickinson wrote, '"Hope" is the thing with feathers'. My feather, this quill, is my hope.

fruit

Passed back and forth
between departments
and tests

I hear opinions

An opinion
formed and shared—
an opinion I will live by

I adore the doctors
rich knowledge
in their veins

I am passive
they are hard
I flail they know

I don't joke
I'm not joking

I want them to tell me
I want the certainty
don't tease
fuck me that truth

The chemicals, each pill
an anchor at sea—
the waves rise
the gales blast
and I stay still
—medicated

Maybe you don't know
you don't know pain

and you eat fruit
and you think
we should all
eat fruit

David McGovern

Throwing an Orange Up in the Air

Tom Roseingrave

1

On a clear, bright evening in Dublin, Finola Devlin, known to friends as Nola, takes a right from Marrowbone Lane onto the smaller Forbes Lane. It is late spring; Nola is in the seventy-third year of her life.

In her hand is a brown paper bag, which in her hurry, she forgets is there. When she remembers, she panics that it is empty, and despite knowing it is not, sticks a hand inside to check. There they are. Her oranges. Round and bright as the sun in the sky.

For no particular reason, Nola decides to introduce an orange to the evening. She holds it in her hand and tosses it up, and it moves past her chest, her eyes, her forehead. It rises, rises, until it reaches its turning point, where the forces of will and gravity are in balance.

Nola is thinking.

It had been a shock. No, not a shock: a disturbance. Yes, that's what it was, a disturbance, but only a short disturbance that would pass. Disturbing, though. Yes. An intruder. No, not an intruder, that's not... Come on, Nola. Just her own bad luck. Could've happened to anyone. No point in telling Barney.

It had been morning, a time she kept for herself. When she heard the knock, she had been eating breakfast in her garden. She had been allowing clouds to pass overhead.

He was, at first, a figure behind a door. Then she opened the door and he became the man. The man stepped back with exaggerated politeness. The man was smiling with intent.

—There is still time, he said.

Bony and tall.

—There is still time, he said, to upgrade your alarm system.

Nola laughed. But the man was deadly serious. He had a long, pale head and clothes too heavy for the day. He wore a satchel, like all those with trampled dreams.

—You'll forgive my directness, Ms Devlin, I hope. I am here today on behalf of Securi-System, your home protection provider. Your alarm system has not been upgraded in seventeen years. This means, Ms Devlin, for a woman of your demographic, you have put yourself in a precarious position.

Pre-car-i-ous. He spoke each syllable precisely. In his round eyes Nola saw a man who had not had much luck.

—Call me Nola, she said. Please.

—I'm Graham, he said. Apologies, I neglected to be delighted to make your acquaintance.

Graham explained that the system was out of date. There were burglars who could disable the whole thing over the internet. They might be working from Costa down the road, and they would know when she was out and then... Well, the lock might as well be made of fresh Irish butter.

Nola wished she could return to her breakfast. These were the things Ronnie had looked after. His smaller side of the bargain. The things that could easily get out of hand.

—I've lived here for thirty years, Graham, and not once have I had the slightest bit of trouble.

—Well, said Graham. Aren't you lucky.

The man's shirt, under a gilet that was too tight, ballooned around his waist. He had the look of a chancer, Nola thought. These were the jobs chancers did. She would know: Ronnie had been a chancer.

This poor man must've been out since morning.

—I'm admiring your boots, she said. You're getting good use out of them today.

—Oh yes, he said. Yes, good quality boots. Sturdy. Leather. Walk a mile in my shoes and you'll be... just fine! He stopped, sensing diversion. But look, the plan, it's very reasonable. There's a small installation fee, you'll understand, and then a monthly subscription of twenty-one euro ninety-nine. Euro. Per month.

—That's grand, Graham. And thank you very much for the information. Do you have a leaflet I can take?

—A leaflet? Why?

—So I can take a look and get back to you.

—Oh no, said the man. No, no, Ms Devlin. The offer is ending very soon, you see. Today is the very last day you can sign up. And given the sensitive nature of the details, well, it's not exactly a matter we can discuss—he indicated the street with a slim finger—in the public arena.

Oh. The man was insistent. Nola was stuck. Nola rubbed her forehead with the back of her hand, then kneaded the skin. Maybe this is how things work? These bills, she thought, they could get out of hand. Ronnie had been on top of it. And what had he left her with?

—I'll have a think about it, Graham, okay? And you can come back another day.

The man sighed. He straightened up. The man looked away down the road.

—Another day, he muttered, shaking his head. Another day. Do you think I can just skip merrily down here on another day?

—Pardon me?

He looked back at Nola. Then he craned his neck and leaned quite close.

—Do you think, Ms Finola Devlin, that I can just skip merrily down here on another day?

The loose floorboard creaked under her backward step.

—I don't know, Graham. I don't know the first thing about you.

The man lifted his head suddenly, and did a little laugh, like it had been a joke all along. But then he was over her, and he had curved his neck like a giant swan, and he had pressed his face into a desperate smile.

—I'm sorry, that was... I don't know, I'm sorry. Look, I'll level with you, you seem like a good person and... I'm up against it, I don't mind telling you. I've two boys at home, okay, and I... I've a few debts, that's the truth, to people you don't want to owe money to... Do you understand? And my two little boys, y'know, they're starting to ask questions. They're going, Daddy, Daddy, why are you sad? Daddy, why are you so stressed? And it's tearing me apart, okay? So look, I'm asking you, and I would never normally do this, I wouldn't dream of it, but you seem like a good person, and it's simple, I guarantee you. I'm asking you to take an upgrade today. All right? I get the commission, and if you want, you can cancel the whole thing next week. Easy. You get your money back and you do someone a very good deed.

He brought his face closer. Nola could smell his breath, spicy and ripe.

—Do you think you could help me, Finola?

—Oh, Graham, I don't think so, I don't —

Beside them, the next-door neighbour's door opened. The man froze. Nola went silent. A bicycle wheel appeared. Then the next-door neighbour appeared. The woman with the barbershop haircut. Wearing a yellow coat.

—Finola, she said. How are you?

—Oh, hello… yes! Good, good!

The woman was clever. She looked between the pair and caught a whiff of something she didn't like. Nola couldn't remember the woman's name for the life of her.

—Is everything okay?

—Yes, yes, Nola said, Graham here is just telling me about an upgrade opportunity for my alarm system. On the wall there, do you see?

Graham did a short smile, or perhaps he twitched. She was quiet enough, the woman. A quiff with those shaved sides, the way a lot of those women had. Nice though.

The woman looked again at the scene.

—Well, I'm free now if you fancy a cup of tea. Right now. I've plenty of time.

What was her name? She had been living there six months now. Worked all hours. Bit of an air about her, a professional, that confidence.

—No, Nola said. No really, I'm fine. But thank you. Graham here—she repeated his name—is coming inside to do some paperwork.

The man's eyes flickered.

— Are you sure?

— Yes. Yes, of course!

—Well, okay, said the woman. As long as you're happy.

—I am happy. Come on inside, Graham.

Those meaningful glances.

—Another time, said the woman.

—Another time.

Nola let the man in but lingered at the door. She watched the neighbour cycle away, her back straight and strong. Nola had never asked her for help.

Nola turned, and she shut the door. She was inside with the man. He had gone all the way to the kitchen and was rattling the back door in its frame.

—Entry and exit points, he said. Just checking.

He turned to the window and yanked it hard.

—Oh, no, no, Graham, said Nola, You'll have to push down the keyhole with those. Do you see? The button. On the handle?

The window burst open and he swung it on its hinges. Then he slammed it shut. BANG!

—Hunky dory, he said, moving towards the table. Hunk-yyy dory. He chose a chair and sat facing the garden. Tell me this: have you coffee in the house?

—I do, said Nola.

The man tossed his satchel on the floor and unwound his scarf. There was a smell of clothes dried slowly in a damp room.

Nola did not take out the French press, but made them cups of instant instead, spooning in grains as soon as the kettle boiled. When she served it, the man poured milk from the jug, then stirred his coffee with a finger and sucked it clean.

—Just you in the house then?

—Just me.

—Lonely, I suppose.

—Not much.

—I didn't tell you earlier actually, but… my wife's gone four years now.

—Why would you have told me that?

—I don't know, he said.

She looked at the clock behind where he was sitting. Ronnie would've had him away at the front door. The man sloshed his coffee like mouthwash, and swallowed. Ronnie had a nose for trouble.

—Monica, he began. That was her name. Monica, my wife. Separated now. I take it you're not married? No. Well, for the first year of our marriage I woke up every single day, and I actually said thank you. Out loud, like. And you're probably thinking this bloke's a weirdo, he's a nutcase. Fair enough, I am a bit of a nutcase! But I was just happy, just happy out. Of course we started talking about kids, and why wouldn't we? The whole kit and caboodle. The house with the dog and the nippers running around. I always wanted to be a daddy. But Monica, well, some people, they're not made for it. That's just the way. Anyway, the two boys come along, twins, I was delighted, and healthy, thank God, and I keep telling Monica the hard part was over. How wrong was I? But I wasn't thinking straight. I was in love! Pure ecstasy. Purpose. But Monica, she just… she just couldn't see past the sleepless nights, the nappies and all that… I tried to be there for her, I really did. She left two days after the twins' first birthday. *Whoosh*. She was a selfish bitch, Finola. What can you do?

Nola drew back at the word. She looked down at her cup.

—Lives in Meath now. With an acupuncturist, I kid you not! Found her on Facebook. The man sighed. What about you? Any kids?

—No, I never—

—I sensed that, said Graham. I could sense that.

Nola gripped her mug and allowed it to burn her palm. She took her hand away and felt the sting.

—I'd like to have a look at the documents now.

—My two boys, he said, they got me through the whole lot, the whole mess she put me in. Do you think I want to go knocking on people's doors, selling alarms? I've got a university degree for fuck's sake… I bet you didn't think that, did you? Be honest! Well, look, I'll tell you a story, right? I was in a shopping centre the other day, with the two boys. Coming out of Tesco's. They're five now. And Conor, he's a handful, Max is quieter, but you don't want to let Conor out of your sight, otherwise… Well, look, we were coming out of the Tesco's, and suddenly Conor's gone. Vanished. I can't see him anywhere. Max is beside me, but Conor's disappeared. And I look around and I'm starting to panic now. Missing person. Child abduction. Head going like the clappers, of course it would be. And, d'you know what, this is mad now— this is weird—but I started to think, and this isn't a nice thought at all, of all the fucking paedos out there. Cos every day I hear about some fucking paedo or other… some fucking nonce… and I start thinking, if Conor's been taken… if someone's taken him away… I would hunt that person down. I would tear that person limb from limb. Not a fucking bother to me.

The neighbour had seen him come in.

—And look, sure Conor appeared then, he'd only gone and hid in one of those photobooths, with the curtains, y'know? Haha! The messer. Big sigh of relief from Daddy of course. He's bawling and I don't mind telling you so was I. But I'll tell you what, and this is the point now, right, long story short. That night, I went home, and I put the boys to bed.

Barney would know something was wrong. He'd drive over, or he'd get one of the kids to come, he was good like that, Barney was, vigilant.

—I went downstairs, and I just sat with myself for a moment. And I thought, I actually feel amazing. Like, incredible. And this, right, this is the whole thing. We're wired for it, y'know? That animal urge. Protect the young. Be good. Be responsible! It's what we're built to do. And d'you know what, Ms Devlin, I have no problem in saying this, none at all; there's no law in this country, no fucking authority, no police that would stop me protecting my kids. I'd rob for my kids… I'd kill for my kids.

He'd only banged his fist lightly. A rap. Against the table. He'd actually stopped his fist just before so he didn't hit it with full force, so it didn't make that loud a sound. You would've had to be in the room to hear it, it was that quiet, it could've been an accident, nothing really… But Nola… Nola was crying out. For Ronnie… for someone! For God's sake! For someone to be here for Jesus' sake to know what was happening to her right now in this moment!

The man looked at her as if he'd woken from a dream.

—I'm sorry, he said, I get like this. It's… I don't know why I'm telling you. You seem like a good person. A good listener.

Nola felt her body shaking.

—I, she started, I have listened to you, Graham. And you have done nothing but intimidate me since you entered my home.

Graham did not react at first; his eyes stayed on Nola. Then he brought his head into his neck, and sucked air into his mouth. Raised his eyebrows. Looked at Nola as if she were not in the full of her health.

—You invited me in, he said. But fine, fine. I understand. I'm sure you have things to do. As do I.

He reached into his satchel and removed an electronic tablet.

—Now. Are you going to sign this for me?

It is a warm evening, and Nola decides she will walk to her brother Barney's. She wants to forget the man, forget the morning. Barney has invited her to a barbecue because he worries that she's alone. Barney, the bloody patriarch, hahaha.

Nola walks along the river, and then up to Christchurch. When she is close to Barney's, she stops to buy a box of Milk Tray, because Barney is an insufferable traditionalist, but the shop is one of those places that looked like a granary, and sells nothing usual, so she buys him six oranges instead.

Near Barney's house, Nola takes a right from Marrowbone Lane onto the smaller Forbes Lane.

She smells the hops that scent the air around here. There's still time, she thinks. But you can't still time. Distil time, maybe, make it richer. That is how time could be still.

In her hurry, she momentarily forgets she is holding a brown paper bag. When she remembers, she panics it is empty and sticks a hand inside to check. Her oranges. Round and bright as the evening sun.

For no particular reason, Nola decides to introduce an orange to the evening.

She holds it in her hand, and tosses it up, and just before it falls, she sees out of the corner of her eye—Him! The man? That fucker!

The orange falls into her hand and she goes to throw it.

She will throw it at his head. She will throw it right at his head and it will lodge in his mouth and he will choke and splutter like a dog. She will kill him. She will choke him because he made her feel old and alone and she never feels old and alone, not ever, and she lifts her arm and in that moment she is powerful and huge and she is going to get him she is going to fucking get him!

Her foot catches. It sticks. It lodges in a crack in the pavement. And in an instant, her ankle twists and she falls, and when an orange rolls from her hand it is a lonely resignation.

2

On a clear, bright evening in Dublin, Finola Devlin, known to friends as Nola, takes a right from Marrowbone Lane onto the smaller Forbes Lane. It is late spring; Nola is in the seventy-third year of her life.

In her hand is a brown paper bag, which in her hurry, she forgets is there. When she remembers, she panics that it is empty, and despite knowing it is not, sticks a hand inside to check. There they are. Her oranges. Round and bright as the sun in the sky.

For no particular reason, Nola decides to introduce an orange to the evening. She holds it in her hand and tosses it up, and it moves past her chest, her eyes, her forehead. It rises, rises, until it reaches its turning point, where the forces of will and gravity are in balance.

Nola is thinking.

She had woken with a freshness on her face. The window had been left open, and it was cold, and she heard the sound of children playing secret games outside. She willed herself out from under the duvet and sat up.

Nola went downstairs along Ronnie's grip-rail, which was an awful thing, white and plastic, so different from the rest of the house. She opened the blinds: nothing had happened while she was asleep.

She made breakfast and ate it in the garden. The garden was hers, more of a yard really, twelve foot by six. Fuchsia in baskets, and daisies and begonias in the low beds at her feet.

Nola's only place, in a house where Ronnie's things were everywhere still. His big glass bowl in the sitting-room, with the hotel matchboxes. The Adelphi, The Crystal, Palm Court: the places they'd toured. Ronnie Hand, the showband man, the electric guitar man. The genius with the good-time gut.

There came a knock at the door, and Nola went to open it. Behind the smoked glass she could see a shape holding a clipboard. She opened the door and the shape took on the form of the man.

—There is still time, he said.

Bony and tall.

—There is still time, he said, to upgrade your alarm system.

The man told her that her alarm system was out of date. There were burglars who could use the internet to disable it, and they could enter her house without resistance.

Nola didn't care. She wanted to go back to her garden. She felt only pity for the man, who was forced out on a Saturday morning to do his work. She thought of Ronnie's call-outs for the phone company, the milk-subs, the dreary jobs he did after he did his back in.

—I didn't catch your name, she said.

—Graham, the man replied.

—I'm Finola.

He never went back touring after that. Those damn jobs. She'd sat Ronnie down and told him she had enough money for the both of them, and he was getting too old anyway. He'd taken some convincing. Some warped principle... Then he told her, like it was his idea all along, that it was all a swindle, a cod, and he wouldn't be doing another fucking day.

—Look Graham, I've a few things to do today, but why don't you give me a leaflet and I'll get back to you.

The man wouldn't hear of it. He was insistent, twitchy. He said the information was too sensitive to be discussed on the doorstep.

—I'm going to close the door now, Graham. It's nothing personal, really, but if you could just step back—

—Ah no, Finola, ah no, now...

He was frowning at her.

And he went for the closing door.

The man put his hand through the opening, grabbed the side of the door and pushed in. Nola was knocked back into the hall, and she was not expecting it, and the door crashed into the house like a snapping jaw. She didn't fall, but was stunned, and thought for a terrible moment that she might give in to the man. But then she recovered, and in a blind rage, she went for the bastard. She grabbed him by his shirt collar and she pushed with all her weight and she sent him stumbling backwards onto the path.

—You fucking maniac!

Next door's door opened and her neighbour came reeling out, with the TV remote in her hand. The woman with the shaved sides. She looked between Nola and the man.

—What the fuck is going on?

The man tried to muster a few words, but they wouldn't come. He looked to Nola with round, shocked eyes, and then he turned on his heels and took off down the road at pace.

—Finola, Jesus Christ, what just happened?

—I, well, I, he—

Nola saw herself standing at her front door as if from above, and she thought she looked like a plucked chicken: grey and prone.

—Oh God, said Nola. He was trying to come inside to, to get me to sign this thing…

As she spoke she came back to herself.

—Wait there, said the woman. Let's go inside.

The woman threw the remote into her hall, and closed her front door. She stepped quickly over the garden fence. She seemed to be following a set of procedures.

—Thank you, said Nola.

The woman followed her into the kitchen, where Nola sat down. She began to rage.

—I don't want to think about him for a moment longer! That bastard, she said, That bloody bastard! How could he do that, how could he take advantage…?

Her breath became shallow and she stopped. She could never stay angry for long. She was exhausted. The woman placed her hand on Nola's shoulder, and Nola squeezed it.

—You're so good to come in, Nola said. You're not in a rush, are you? Will you have tea?

—I'll make it, said the woman. You stay there.

She turned away to the kitchen counter, and Nola settled and watched her. She must be fifty-five, Nola thought, sixty at a push. A body well cared-for.

—You know something, said Nola. I don't even know your name. Isn't that terrible?

—We're as bad as each other, said the woman. I only know yours because the postman mixes us up. I'm Helen.

The woman put two cups of tea on the table and sat opposite. Her hair was styled in a black quiff, with a white streak at two o'clock.

—How are you feeling?

—I'm fine, said Nola. I'm just annoyed I let it happen. You must think I'm a bloody fool.

—Ah, no, come off it now. You shouldn't go blaming yourself, said Helen. That was an awful thing to happen.

Nola wasn't used to being comforted. She straightened her back, like she had been taught in school.

—You know I don't know the first thing about you.

—Well this is the first time we've talked.

—What do you do with yourself?

—For work?

—Well, we can start there.

—I'm an anaesthetic nurse, said Helen. Which might explain why we've never been introduced. I work odd hours.

—Oh, that's a big job.

—The last face you see before you go under.

—You could do a lot worse.

Helen laughed.

—I like it. Busy enough. A lot of responsibility. You speak with the patient, and you settle them. Tell them to think of a beach, or their kids, or something, as the drugs kick in. Monitor their bloods. They go to sleep. Amnesia, analgesia, muscle relaxation, they don't feel a thing.

—Sounds like heaven.

What would it be like if Helen put her under? Nola might think of her garden, or the evening sun in the kitchen. She might think of Helen's hands.

—I like to care for one person at a time, Helen was saying. You don't get that in other departments.

—And you've been next door six months now?

—Longer than that, said Helen. Moved in this time last year.

That explained it. Why they hadn't met: Ronnie went in May. In the hospice since March, where he had died every day.

—Worked out nicely, Helen said. I'd actually moved down from Belfast and I didn't know a soul in the city—she scratched briefly at her eyebrow—I'd just, ah, I'd just separated from my partner, my wife, actually, and everything was all over the place. As it would be.

—That's a tough old road, said Nola.

—Best decision I ever made! We were kind to each other, mind you. But I couldn't stay. We've the same friends, I was bumping into her mammy in Tesco's, that sort of thing. I can't spit for someone I know in Belfast.

—I'm the same for here.

Partner, wife. There was a moment then, she knew, where she could've introduced Ronnie. Should've. She could've told Helen the whole lot of it, who she was, what had happened, the whole thing, the way she'd do to anyone. But she didn't, because she didn't want to be pitied any more that day.

—Do you work yourself?

—Me? No, no. I'm retired now. I was a teacher at Saint Raphael's, do you know it? The special school, it was called. Not anymore, thank God. I loved it, oh, I loved it. Loved the students. I'm retired a while now, but it's funny, I don't look back. Thought I'd miss the place, but no… I suppose I'm easily pleased.

—Life's a bit of pleasure, isn't it? said Helen, and raised her cup to her lips. Nola noticed her shoulders and thought she might be a swimmer.

An easy silence came.

A rush of wind over the yard.

Nola watched as Helen's eyes moved across the room. They settled on her basil plant, sitting on a bright blue saucer in the middle of the table. They considered it. Then her hands moved away from her cup, and travelled to the plant, and made for the dead, brown stalks at the bottom. Nola realised Helen was talking. She was telling Nola about her new life. As she did so, she pinched a stalk and removed it. She placed it in the palm of her other hand, and deposited it by her cup.

—I thought that stage of my life was over, she said, That I was slowing down. But I found more things, other things…

Her hand was back at the plant. She pinched another stalk. She brought it to join her little pile.

Nola watched her hands and her fingers. What would happen, she thought, if they were to go upstairs? Right at this moment? Or, if they kissed each other here, across the table, touched each other… and then went up to Nola's bed?

—I walk from here to the sea, and I think, I'm almost sixty, and I'm starting again.

To be in Nola's bed together, with their legs wrapped around, rubbing each other… Is that what Helen and her wife did? Nola wanted to do it too.

Helen burst out laughing.

—I've made a right mess here!

Nola! Nola.

Helen was pointing behind her.

—Is that your husband, then?

Nola knew the photo. The only holiday they ever went on.

—Oh, no, said Nola, I'm not, eh, I'm not that way inclined.

Helen's eyebrows raised, and she smiled very briefly. Nola did too because it felt so nice. But then she began thinking, hold on, she didn't mean… no, and she suddenly realised what she said, it could be taken up wrong, when she had only meant that… she could upset Helen, and Helen could be confused! And Nola thought it might actually be fraudulent, what she had done, illegal, it could be a case of false identity, she didn't know what about these things, she could be arrested, she could be charged with—

Helen was talking.

—Here, Finola, she was saying. We should go out one night. We should go out and get to know each other. Would you like that?

—I would, said Nola, Very much.

But Nola saw Ronnie, his moustache and leathery skin, laughing away— he'd be enjoying this—and she knew she had to tell her.

—Oh, Helen, she began, I should have said earlier, I didn't, I don't know, I just—but in the photo there, that's my husband, Ronnie. He was my husband. That's what I meant. We're not married now, because… he died, you see, very soon after you moved in… My idea of a joke! Not funny, I know! Silly… I'm very, I'm very sorry if there was any—

—Christ Nola, there's nothing to apologise for! Helen said, and she smiled kindly. I'm so sorry to hear. But a glimmer went from her eyes and she looked at Nola the way she had looked at her on the doorstep.

—I miss Ronnie, said Nola. I miss him, she said again, in case he was listening.

Nola takes her time dressing for Barney's barbecue. She chooses a loose tunic, olive-green, with grey leggings and a denim jacket, and in her excitement, she knocks over a tube of lipstick and has to get on all fours to fetch it from under the bed.

It is a warm, bright evening, and Nola decides to walk. The streets are busy with activity, people getting in and out of taxis, wearing new clothes and painting their faces in the hope that something might happen to them.

She is seventy-two, for god's sake! She's lived her life; she is happy. An oncoming car beeps and brakes. Sorry! Ronnie had been her partner, they'd stayed true to each other and she had cared for him. That was her life!

A woman cheers from the window of a passing taxi. She married Ronnie and wants to go to bed with Helen. Why can't both be true?

Helen looks out to sea and is happy. Nola looks across Thomas Street: two men disappearing into a doorway with a mirror, flower-sellers packing up for the day. Ronnie used to say about the showband singers, *It's not their wives they're singing about.*

Nola remembers she has no present for Barney, and stops into the nearest shop to buy a box of Milk Tray, because Barney is an insufferable traditionalist, but the shop is one of those places that looks like a granary, and sells nothing usual, so she buys him six oranges instead.

Nola walks the curve of Marrowbone Lane. From the walls of yards, purple flowers grow. Buddleia, they are called; a friend had told her. She remembers when Ronnie first went into hospital, in James's, up the road; it took a collapse for him to finally go, and when they arrived he was so frightened, and the nurses took him away down a corridor, he was effing and blinding everyone in the place, he had been such an awful patient, and Nola could do nothing but sit in the waiting-room, so she did that, with a change of clothes for Ronnie. And then in came Barney, blustering, and raging, and demanding that he speak to the doctor RIGHT NOW!, no the *FUCKING CONSULTANT!*, as if Barney could fix it all, and Nola thought that the receptionist must be trained to deal with people like Barney, and she was so *tired*, knowing that she would have to deal with Barney next, and then with Ronnie. She would have to rely on the training she had learned all her life, caring for Ronnie, living under Ronnie, and she felt the wasted years like a hunger. She went up to Barney and told him to sit down, to call his kids, just to give him something to do.

Ronnie had never cared for her.

She is delighted he is dead.

Nola takes a right, from Marrowbone Lane onto Forbes Lane, and panics her bag is empty. She sticks a hand inside and relaxes: there they are. Six oranges. She takes an orange out, and for no reason at all, she decides to introduce it to the evening. It is round and bright like the sun in the sky.

Nola holds out an upturned palm and throws the orange upwards. It rises, rises, and at its turning point, she makes up her mind.

The orange falls.

She is thinking of Helen.

It is wonderful to be asked a question.

The Knee

after Jane Hirshfield

The knee is not a city
Of hollow cathedrals and patella gates
Of stitched ligament and
Stretched tendon and
The empty agora, where the blood once
Gathered, then evacuated.

It is not the velcro crunch of itself
As it bends and carries,
The ache and the strain, the
Burden of movement.

It is not even the nudge into
the crook of your bent leg,
The puzzle piece of it,
Where it whispers to your tendons
In the night.

It is not a rock face,
Pock-marked, water-carved
Allowing itself to be hollowed and
lived in and
River-rushed.

Only in rest is it a mountain range,
Both busy and silent under a dark sky,
Allowing safe passage
Through a burdenless night.

Chandrika Narayanan-Mohan

The Trellis

This house is like no other I have lived in
with its porch come study (which, I'm told, is very
Wisconsin), its twelve-foot windows and its ochre tiles
filigreed with patterns of emerald and violet leaves.
Aside from the damp in our windowless bathroom—
no home is perfect—these rooms would not be out of place
in Chiswick or Notting Hill, except the walls made of
Belfast brick have no cavities and let the cold in.

Through the window I see you weeding in the shade
of the cherry blossom tree, wresting ivy
from its bough tattooed with white rivulets.
You hold the shoots above your head and form a trellis;
beyond the hedge, the Malone Road surges along
thick with four lanes of traffic. The Black Superba
plant on the kitchen table hoovers up a spray
of formaldehyde and invisible iron filings.

At dusk, the thrush sings in the din, an octave
higher than it used to, and it hasn't seen its mate for weeks.
On the sofa, two rugs coloured onyx and chartreuse
fold back on themselves in a double weave.

Eoghan Totten

Patch Notes – 14.8.2006

Brenda Romero

Introducing *The Divorce Update*

Our 14.8.2006 update resolves a number of substantial issues that players have identified, addresses the game's economy, and presents an expensive expansion DLC[1]. In addition, *The Divorce Update* permanently resolves the long-standing conflict in the successful running of *Brenda*.

|------------Player Avatar-----------|

» Created new player Avatar class: Divorced.
» Changed player Avatar class from Married to Divorced.
» Added Change Name functionality. Note: the player is required to Change Name in each instance that the Avatar's name appears. At present, the system does not support a universal name change. We recognise this will be irritating to players, particularly as old names may appear for years, even decades.

|----------------NPCs----------------|

» Created new NPC[2] Class: The Ex.
» Created new NPC AI[3] Faction[4]: The Ex In-Laws.
» Set The Ex and The Ex In-Laws' state to 'Hostile'.

|----Environment: *New DLC*---|

» Instantiated[5] new one-bedroom apartment.
» Relocated player Avatar to one-bedroom apartment.
» Established 'minimalist' texture and item set.
» Purchased Ikea couch, Ikea chair, and Ikea table for apartment.
» Purchased Walmart kitchen utensils, pots, pans, and plates.
» Initiated ownership transfer of espresso machine from NPC on Craigslist.
» Purchased double mattress. Note: In this update, the double mattress is on the floor, but a bed frame is on the roadmap for a future update.

|-------------Economy-------------|

» Transferred all $40,000 from *Brenda*'s large retirement account to Hostile AI Faction.
» Transferred all $20,000 from *Brenda*'s medium retirement account to Hostile AI Faction.
» Emptied $3,500 from *Brenda*'s checking account. You already know where it went. Note: we recognise that the low amount will irritate some players, but it's been difficult to accumulate anything with only *Brenda* working.
» Closed *Brenda*'s savings account. There was no money.
» Transferred full control of core systems and all game inventory (furniture, appliances, car) to Hostile AI Faction.
» Flagged as 'shared' a single asset (House) that may be sold on the Market at the request of the Hostile AI Faction.
» Note: Data was unavailable and unretrievable for assets owned by Hostile AI faction. These assets were deemed unnecessary and undesirable for the successful running of *Brenda*.

|--------Statistics & States---------|

» Buffed[6] the improves-over-time rate of the player Avatar's Morale.

» Deprecated[7] 'Cheated on' state as it will no longer be required in the *Divorce Update*.

» Deprecated 'outsidewomen [100]'[8] array as it was also no longer necessary and frequently caused memory leaks and disrupted functionality of core systems.

Note: 'outsidewomen' was an unapproved mod[9] to the existing base *Brenda*. Once the popularity and unauthorised integration of the mod was discovered, we worked to remove it from the codebase.

» Raised base Vitality[10] statistic for player Avatar. The statistic appeared to have been artificially nerfed[11] due to the unauthorised introduction and integration of the 'outsidewomen' array.

» Fixed an issue in which *Brenda* mistakenly used items from the class 'Food' to raise both the Morale and Vitality statistic.

» Fixed an issue that caused the player Avatar to doubt the validity of game data. The issue was due to multiple NPCs refusing to acknowledge in-game events. This in turn caused the player Avatar to question the validity of said events, even though the player Avatar had direct knowledge of said events.

|-----------New Content-----------|

» Introduced three new player Avatar mission chains: 'Accumulate Savings', 'Separate Truth from Fiction', and 'Sex and Other Things You Gave Up On'.

» Instantiated two new items: 'STD Test Kit' and 'AIDS Test Kit'. Note: Our roadmap includes 'AIDS Results' and 'STD Results' in our next update.

» Note: New content is limited in this update as the economic changes make purchasing any new content unlikely.

|--------------Combat--------------|

» Deprecated Combat.

|--------------Inventory--------------|

» Fixed a memory issue in which old panties, nighties and lingerie—however worn and no longer used—caused players to experience loss of Morale. This required deletion of all old panties, nighties and lingerie.
» Addressed a similar issue by removing letters, cards, mementos and photos from the player Avatar's inventory.
» Fixed an issue causing existing wearable inventory to fit too tightly, if at all, caused by the 'low morale eat food' bug.

|----------Gameplay Fixes----------|

» Temporarily disabled Co-op mode.
» Fixed several noticeable visual issues caused by lack of self-care.
» Fixed an issue causing periodic spells of hopelessness.

|----------------Magic--------------|

» Introduced an alpha version of Magic 1.0 for the player Avatar. Note: this does not yet introduce actual Magic, but it establishes the possibility for it to happen.

---

[1] DLC = Downloadable content. An expansion on the base game.
[2] NPC = Non-player character. A character within the game that is not controlled by the player.
[3] AI = Artificial Intelligence.
[4] Faction = Like a clique, but for AI. They share properties and make decisions as a group.
[5] Instantiated = To bring into being.
[6] Buffed = When something is purposefully increased by the developers of a game.
[7] Deprecated = To remove from use.
[8] outsidewomen = The term the Hostile AI Faction uses to describe women outside the marriage.
[9] Mod = Modification to an existing base game, often created by people external to the game.
[10] Vitality = Vitality is a stat that is often used to determine the lifeforce of a character, their will to live.
[11] Nerfed = When something is purposefully lowered by the developers of a game.

Irish Sonnet Sonnet

Forgive me the fuss of breaking in with MUJI pens,
throwing some canvas on the smithy's anvil, and making
myself at home (and home, it must be made). I'll explain.
The tatty fabric of this too short song that compensates
by being awfully broad is a box ill-omened
yet capacious for the aches and anxieties of an
Irish minority, now overseas, shocked to be seen
as emblematic as the embassy. This story
is best told piecemeal through uneasy sequence
of ephemera from all islands of Europe's dark
archipelago. I may pin it all in this form
or let it unfurl, the jumble of history and I,
to be loosely tied like ribbon by an English rhyme.

Viv Kemp

Balance Sonnet

on George Best

Balance was vital, you said. Like the sixpence perched
on your little toe to be flicked into a breast pocket
stuffed with a book of Wilde quips as a party trick.
Like the ferry roiled between Belfast and the Mersey Docks.
Like an apprentice carrying lunch to the Ship Canal
Offices. Like a painter's ladder positioned
at a bedroom window in the dark. Like ten thousand
letters stacked and leant against the closet. Be glue. Connect
the back page clippings meant for Cregagh, *Britannicas*
memorised by a prospective printer, and the silent,
sober, un-dancing teen in the Twisted Wheel all night
to the wizard dribbler, fifth Beatle in a sombrero,
who died before his da in a hospital named 'Cromwell'.

Viv Kemp

The Untameable Donkey

David McGrath

The Crack was near becoming the worst sheep farmer in Ballybalt. His sheep approached the tractor doing their best to trust again after the Christmas shortage. 'I'd stand well back, sheep,' The Crack told them. 'This might be ugly.'

The Crack beeped the horn on the tractor to get them scrammed, but it was broken. Everything was always broken.

'Go on now, sheep. Get.'

The withered auld sheep backed off but encroached again when The Crack wasn't looking.

'I don't know what's going to happen when I open the tailgate.'

The sheep didn't understand and told him as much.

'Suit yourselves, so.'

The Crack backed the horsebox into the paddock. When he jumped down into the muck, he kicked out of his way bits of pallet and split bucket. He looked inside the horsebox to see how The Untameable Donkey had travelled. She was in there calm as bottled water.

'You just look like you need a good wash.'

She stomped.

'You don't like authority.' The Crack said as he unlocked the tailgate. 'That's all. Like myself. Willy! Come out here, Willy!'

Full of welcome, Little Willy trotted over towards the horsebox. He was such a grand and lovely little donkey. The Crack hoped The Untameable Donkey would see the manners on Little Willy and take emulation.

'I need this donkey tamed, Willy,' The Crack said as he unhooked the latches on the horsebox. 'Or we're in trouble. So show her the ropes. Promote grace and good manners.'

But no sooner had The Crack dropped the tailgate did The Untameable Donkey shoot from the horsebox like a natural disaster. The Crack realised she'd been biding her time in there, not calm at all, now unleashing, charging hard for Little Willy who didn't know what was about to hit him.

She chomped down on his ear.

'The poor little crater!' The Crack shouted and made to find something to hit her with, but Little Willy hadn't the time to wait for rescue. Before he lost it, he pulled his ear out from between her broken teeth and brayed away back from whence he came for cover.

The Untameable Donkey turned around and eyeballed The Crack's sheep, who were no dipsticks and knew trouble when they saw it. They hightailed it for the hills. The Untameable Donkey tore after them, neverminding gates and their usage, ripping through the paddock fence instead. She galloped across the hillside in assault of the sheep, kicking and tripping them, snapping the backs of those that fell and when they were down, she mercilessly stamped their heads into the muck.

'My poor auld sheep,' The Crack cried, and when enough sheep were dead, The Untameable Donkey turned her sights to mankind. She fired back for The Crack with brain-soaked fenceposts flapping from her hinds.

The Crack ran up into the horsebox for cover. 'A donkey that will kill us all,' he said and off beyond, a poor auld sheep baa'ed its last baa to confirm it.

The Untameable Donkey stamped up the tailgate into the horsebox.

The Crack backed into a far corner and hunkered down in it. She approached slow. He saw that the dirt in her coat was dried blood. They'd been whipping her something terrible. Ulcers clawed under her teeth and she drooled slime and filth onto the toe of his boots. She was rain-scalded—malanders on her forelegs, maggots in her ears, mange in her mane and a bloodsodden hatred in every fibre of her being for mankind and its bloodsports. She reared up on him, showing him the hooves he was to be trampled with, to melt him before death in fear and sheep-slaughtered stink.

But The Crack was not going out death by donkey.

Because The Crack was last of the old-school alcoholics. The Crack may have been near becoming the worst sheep farmer in Ballybalt, but he was Phelan's best customer with a weekly consumption of alcohol that read more like an inquest. Graveyards of men had their photographs nailed to the wall in Phelan's after reckoning their whole lives that if The Crack was alive—despite the drink he packed away, and the calamity he endured—they would be grand, realising only in their dying moments, with nothing but stories of cirrhosis and misadventure to conclude them, that The Crack was a miracle of human biology and impossible to kill by circumstance.

And so, without knowing that the stars above them shone in The Crack's favour, The Untameable Donkey stomped down for the kill only to miss The Crack's head by a dripple. A slat of the horsebox had come loose from all of her kicking. It was enough to squeeze through. The Crack landed badly in the muck outside but he was alive to go on outliving all men and donkeys.

The Crack ran back around to lock her back in, then leaned on the horsebox for support. He took from his coat a flask of whiskey and drank back a slug. And another. Then another.

'There are six traits a species requires for domestication,' The Crack said when the world had settled. 'And I'm not talking about *taming*. One can tame any animal out there. But to take a *species* out of the wild and into the field, it must have several characteristics. The species must reach maturity fairly lively. Man can't be dawdling for decades, paying for copybooks and gap years so some sheep can find inner meaning on a beach then go exploring its sexuality, all to get only a few chops and a woolly jumper out of it. The species must breed in captivity. I know one particular ram and I'm not codding you, donkey, he'd find a tup if you strapped a straitjacket on him and fired him forty miles out to sea. And the species can't be a picky eater. One can't be scaling Icelandic cliff faces for a specific type of lotus every time a sheep wants breakfast.'

The Crack slugged back more whiskey. 'The species has to be part of a social hierarchy that man can place himself at the head of. Sheep are a flock animal, gregarious, with a dominance hierarchy. It means they have a natural inclination to follow a leader to greener pastures and I, their shepherd, shall be their trailblazer all day long, donkey.'

The Crack knocked on the horsebox. 'You listening in there? This applies to you. We need to get you tamed or we're all fucked.'

The Untameable Donkey roared and screamed.

'The species can't be nervy,' The Crack told her. 'I know sheep jolt. But not like when I tried to raise deer that time. Little Willy moseying on over to take a look at the deer, and the deer take off, and Little Willy gives chase because he thinks it a game. Next minute Little Willy is droving the whole herd into oncoming cars on the Carrickbeg road at thirty miles an hour. A fuckin disaster.'

The Crack emptied the flask into himself. 'And finally, the species must have a pleasant disposition. I know some sheep can be cantankerous but they're not skulking around in the dead of night ripping the throats out of sleeping children, or stamping other sheep's heads into the muck and cracking their skulls.'

The Untameable Donkey turned in the horsebox to kick out, an effort to take The Crack's head clean off.

'I need solitary confinement for you,' The Crack said and returned to town with The Untameable Donkey smashing his horsebox to pieces in his rear view mirror.

'No,' Tom Phelan said in Phelan's.

'Little Willy's allowed in.'

'Little Willy has manners on him. He sits and does harm to nobody.'

'I'm not asking that she come in here. I'll keep her out in the barrel yard.'

'No.'

'The barrel yard was once the livestock yard.'

'On mart days. When was the last mart day in Ballybalt?'

'I'll pay you rent on it.'

Tom Phelan had a famously big turnip head on him with which he pretended to think about it. 'What if she does any damage?'

'I'll financially amend damage if there's damage.'

And that was that.

The Crack reversed around the back of Phelan's. He opened the tailgate to release The Untameable Donkey into the pub's barrel yard. She kicked around in rage, cracking the yard brush and making shite of the old barstools. And when everything was good and broken she upended the empty beer barrels. Their dregs gushed out of their valves and drenched her in stale stout, and onwards she smashed, thrashing at the steel gate that had her imprisoned.

The whole of Phelan's came out to marvel at the hatred in her blackball stare, hatred that began as far back as her African wild ass ancestors who were hunted by the Egyptians, speared and roped and roasted whole, hatred that spiralled when the Sumerians made the wheel and stole her from the scrublands to pull it, to haul their stone to the fertile crescent of Mesopotamia for the first cities. And she hauled their ore to the smelters in Damascus, their rock out of Nubian gold mines. And on the Trabiz and Trabon trade route she was 45,000 strong, a caravan of work, thrashed and whipped onwards to expand empires, powering the water pumps and the grain mills, ploughing earth for the vine, then carrying the wine to market. And when the dying civilizations needed scapedonkeys she was there, thrown over cliffs as retribution for the death of Osiris. And when the dying towns needed a symbol to bear the weight of their sins and failure of their crop, she was there to burn alive. She carried their prophets and their Christs, and she was whipped into war, pulling in supply carts only to pull out the wounded, dying *en masse* in French mud, blown to pieces on the beaches of Gallipoli, freezing to death while carrying screw guns and cannons across Alpine mountain passes. And they saw her parachuted into the Burmese jungle and strapped with bombs in Kandahar, watching her children castrated and starved as she was thrashed to the grave, or called vermin and shot from helicopters in Australia, or massacred by the tens of thousands in South Africa where she was shot in pens through her back and head and legs to die screaming or hacked alive for pet meat. Jilted and ghosted. The odd-toed ungulate. The idiot. She became the joke, the indolent and stubborn fool, reborn again and again to cruel wagon-masters who beat her with rods, and she forgave, and forgave, but ne'er forgot, carrying man on her shoulders, being whatever was needed for their stories, resurrected time and time again, the sign of good or the sign of evil, the God or the fool, the king or the peasant, the right or the wrong. Until she had the blood-mad dogs set on her, a Rottweiler hanging from her throat at the bottom of a pit, fifty beery men cheering on her death, and enough was enough.

The Crack and Tom Phelan and the rest of Phelan's watched The Untameable Donkey exhaust herself and fester, reeled and rattled. Her black eyeball stare dared any one of them to step a foot inside the barrel yard, to put one more finger on her and see what fuckin happened.

'She's the worst donkey I've ever seen,' Tom Phelan said. 'A fuckin tiger wouldn't be in it with her.'

And as long as anybody in Ballybalt could remember, The Crack had never dropped a drink. But after The Untameable Donkey took a drink from a puddle of stale stout and picked herself up to try and climb the wall of the barrel yard, The Crack's pint slipped from his hand and shattered at his feet.

Tom Phelan's penny finally dropped. 'When the bould clan were in the other night, Crack... '

'Large one, Tom. Please.'

'... and you were talking to them about domestication. When I told you never to be talking about domestication ever again.'

'Large one, Tom.'

'Did you bet, Crack?'

'Large one, Tom.'

'Don't tell me you bet. Did you bet? Did you bet with the bould clan?'

'I said, and I've always said, one can tame any animal out there.'

'Did you fuckin bet, you gobshite?'

'I bet the farm,' The Crack said. 'The farm. Now can I have that large one?'

'Jesus Christ, Crack,' Tom Phelan said, the heart put crossways in his chest. Best customers were not best customers when the farm was gone. They were liabilities with sob stories.

The pub crowd returned inside like The Crack had smallpox. A sinking ship. Stick a fork in him: he was done.

A goner.

Tom Phelan turned back for one last question. 'And this bet—what's in it for you?'

The Untameable Donkey screamed at the wall and kicked empty beer barrels, some clearing the barrel yard to bound down Bridge Street, crunching wing mirrors and denting bonnets.

'When I die I want to be shot into the sky from a cannon, Tom. Then if I don't fall back to Earth you'll all know I made it.'

'What's in it for you?'

The Crack crunched glass beneath his boot. The road had soaked up his stout and he cursed the road. He needed a large one.

'Well?' Tom Phelan pressed.

'They'll tell me where he's buried, Tom. Is that enough for you? Now a large one. And another after.'

In the days thereafter, The Crack sat up on the barrel yard wall with his pint and thought on how to tame The Untameable Donkey. The Untameable Donkey stood in the barrel yard where the shade was deepest and thought on how to climb walls.

The Crack poured shampoo on her back to treat her rain-scald. He poured some antiseptic down for the cuts and claws. She reared and screamed in pain.

'You don't go through pain, donkey. You grow through it.'

The Crack thought maybe cruelty was the way forward. Deprive and starve and persecute, Stockholm Syndrome the fuck out of her.

The Untameable Donkey looked at him and said go right ahead.

The Crack thought maybe to hook her around her forefeet with a catch rope: crash her to her side. He'd half-hitch her hinds with a slip-noose and hobble her… but then what? The Crack would be sat on the neck of a nightmare hoping the nightmare would be happy about it. The Crack was too old and too drunk. There was too much hate inhabiting The Untameable Donkey. Too much godlessness.

'I lost God,' The Crack told her. 'A donkey found Him for me again. Would you believe that? I wanted to be a monk as a young lad. I carried everywhere with me an auld bible. Don't know where I came on it. I took to learning it anyway. To this day I could recite it for you back to front. *Then Samson said, with a donkey's jawbone I have made donkeys of them. With a donkey's jawbone I have killed a thousand men.*

'And anyway, after a disagreement with God I took this tattered auld bible up the mountain and flung it off. It went so far down into the valley that I didn't even see it land. Take that, God, I said. Then I set off back down the mountain. It was then I first met Little Willy, the donkey whose ear you bit up at the farm. To this day nobody in Ballybalt knows where Little Willy came from. But there he stood looking sent from God Himself. And you know what was between his teeth? My tattered auld bible. Little Willy walks up to me full of purpose and presents it to me. A miracle, I says. And Little Willy looks me square in the eye, and I'll never forget it, he looks me square in the eye and he says, it's not really a miracle, Crack. Your name is written on the inside cover.'

The Untameable Donkey was not won over.

'It's a joke,' The Crack said. 'Only an auld joke. Because donkeys can't talk let alone read.'

The Untameable Donkey kept looking like it was all just words.

'You're smarter than you're letting on.'

The Crack thought maybe if he rang a bell every time he dropped down cabbage to her he could condition her, but when he looked into The Untameable Donkey's black eyeball stare, he decided no bell in existence was big enough to neutralise the hatred of a thousand generations.

The Crack thought maybe if he lived as a donkey for a time, and ate cabbage with her, and walked around on all fours, some solidarity could form. There was a lad up in Dunlavin living as a badger for the last seven years. His sett was out on the Carrickbeg road. The Crack had often seen him in Dungarven hospital being sewn back up after being shred apart by unaccepting badgers, highly sociable and familial creatures who for the longest time couldn't get their heads around this lad being one of them. Still and all, this lad mustered onwards, eating earthworms and snuffling in the mulch and loam, and now, having *not* been shred apart by a badger in a year or two, swore never was he happier. The Crack however, did not have years to realign his consciousness so that he could forget words and their abstractions, or to thoroughly investigate the interconnectedness of things by abandoning the human condition.

From atop the barrel yard wall, The Crack saw the bould clan giggling in their vans out on Bridge Street, scouts sent to see how he was faring, and The Crack was very much reminded that he had only three months until Easter Sunday to tame her, or the farm, and life, was lost forever.

The Crack watched The Untameable Donkey push down a valve on the newest of Tom Phelan's empties, scraping for spray and dregs, never once taking her eyes off The Crack as she did it. A burst shot into her mouth and The Untameable Donkey clopped and chawed on the tops of more empty barrels. The Crack realised she'd acquired a taste for stout. She swayed when she had her fill and paced the barrel yard feeling good, her ailments soothed and her rage for mankind suppressed. The Crack threw his pint into the bucket and lowered it down to her.

'Here,' he said. 'Have some more.'

A month later The Untameable Donkey woke with a cruelty of shite in her head. She was on the tail end of a ferocious bender, mostly blacked-out, and now she was bright-sore. She had to move to stop the spinning. She got to her hooves but retched and slouched and puked. She staggered around the barrel yard, dribbling sick and stumbling at the barrels to find one with enough barrel-dreg to silence the buzz in her teeth and the fuck in her brain. She found every barrel well and truly exhausted. Tom Phelan had stopped storing the spent barrels in the barrel yard since the brewery complained about the state of his returns.

'Drink some water,' The Crack said from atop the barrel yard wall. He lowered down the cabbage bucket by rope. The Untameable Donkey raced for the offering and checked it for stout. When none was found she pulled on the rope with her broken teeth: an effort to drag The Crack into the barrel yard. The Crack kept balance.

'Suit your surly self, so.'

The Crack looked at The Untameable Donkey and knew she was mad for a drink. Or a hammer, one just as good as the other. She lay down until she could not any longer. She wanted a drink. She needed something to take the edge off. To not drink terrified her. She wondered how she'd ever have an emotion without it. She wondered how she'd feel confident. How she'd cry. She worried about Christmases and weddings. She popped puke and the retch was too much for The Crack, too close to the bone. He went into the pub and returned with a breakfast pint in hand, first of the day. The cream on the inside of his glass marked the volume and speed of the two swallows so far taken. The Untameable Donkey berserked about the barrel yard, kicking the empty barrels in protest of not having what she wanted when she wanted it.

'I'm often doing the same in the pub bog in the mornings. I sleep in there some nights. Too drunk to walk home. And when I wake, it's with nerve endings soaked and fingertips fried and a head like a microwaved banana. My stomach heaving up the whole gloopy meal—memory and regret—the body purging up the toxic soup. But there's a rush of euphoria in the exodus, isn't there? A breathless piece of calm. A rush to the head when the confession to yourself happens, heart not beating, lungs not breathing, and in the morning mini-death over the toilet bowl you become a cleansed thing, absolved and ready to go again.'

The Untameable Donkey looked at the pint in The Crack's hand and stomped a hoof.

'When you're not drunk you're fuckin sober,' The Crack said. 'That's the problem. Both states claiming to be the solution to the other.' The Crack took a third swallow and The Untameable Donkey watched its mightiness in the morning sun.

'Breakfast pints are not for donkeys,' The Crack said, regarding his pint.

The Untameable Donkey was having none of it. She stomped again.

'Give until the Angelus. You start going straight through and there's no peace in it. I'm telling you that now.'

The Untameable Donkey was getting annoyed and The Crack knew it. 'You want some of this delicious stout?'

The Crack took a fourth swallow and the pint was near slain. 'Donkeys cannot appreciate the devotion and dedication it takes to drink this first thing in the morning, this sweet-smelling stout with a malt nose, frost-silk taste and a velvety coffee-note to finish.'

The Crack finished the pint.

'How to become an alcoholic in five easy steps. Step one: begin drinking in the 1970s. Step two: continue drinking for the whole of the 1980s. Step three: continue drinking for the whole of the 1990s.'

The Untameable Donkey asked just what in the name of fuck The Crack was talking about. She didn't have a problem with alcohol. She just needed a drink to fuck off the hangover.

'I don' know if its nature or nurture, donkey. It takes a certain mix of genius and stupidity, that's all I can say, both in equal measures. I've been bundled into the backseat of cars a few times, the father holding on to me all the way to St John of God's for alcohol rehabilitation and a month of reciting the Serenity Prayer. An auld alcoholic queer, he called me once. So I married to spite him, to look respectable and inherit the farm.'

The Crack went into the snug and returned two minutes later holding two ruby red pints of stout. 'God, grant me the serenity to accept the things I cannot change. Courage to change the things I can, and wisdom to know the difference.'

The Crack poured a pint into her cabbage bucket and lowered it down. 'Fine. Have some. But don't say I didn't warn you.'

The Untameable Donkey horsed into the stout. She finished it violently. The bucket near didn't make it. She stomped a hoof for more.

'You're an insatiable bastard of a donkey,' The Crack said. 'We're at nothing with these pints.'

The Crack went back inside the snug and returned rolling a full barrel, carrying a bottle of whiskey he'd persuaded Tom Phelan to sell him. It was the last of his cash. He'd need to start selling off vehicles and machinery.

The Crack opened the barrel yard gate and kicked the barrel inside to The Untameable Donkey.

'Now, eleven gallons of the bastard. Eighty-eight pints. Get that into you.'

The Untameable Donkey rushed on the barrel, all clop and bite. She straddled its side with a hoof, ripped the cap seal off and pressed her cheek-teeth into the valve. The foamy stout shot into her mouth.

'Send out The Crack!' The Crack shouted, to peacock, so the bould clan out on Bridge Street would hear him. 'Bouldest clan in the country, donkey. That's what they call themselves. Sitting out there in their vans beneath a barbarous load of murderous intent and bad haircut. The same clan that does give the rest of the clans a bad name, disowned by the peripatetic culture, the same clan plastered all over the newspapers for pipe-bombing homes of gardaí and doing hit-and-runs on grannies! A disgraceful clan of cunts!'

The Crack squared up to the clan watching on. 'A clan comprised of bareknuckle boxers and mad-in-the-head muck-savages with not a birth certificate nor a passport between them, not on any grid unless it was your cattle grid they were driving over to pilfer your house a week before Christmas, with or without you in it. Isn't that right? And then again in March when you have everything replaced with the insurance. And then sell drugs to your daughter suffering PTSD from all the robberies, maybe pimp her out to the forestry workers when she's addicted and can't afford more.'

The Untameable Donkey drank back her stout something ferocious.

'Their names, donkey? All of them are either a John or a Joe. These are the only two names given to men of the bould clan. Joes have Joes as brothers and Johns the same, all regardless of what you think the rules are for naming men, donkey. To differentiate between themselves there are Big Johns, Other Joes, JJs, Johnnies, Joeys and John Boys.'

The bould clan out on Bridge Street, who were now out of the vans and listening, told The Crack to keep talking and see what would happen.

'Except once when a baby boy of the bould clan was christened Ulick after a thirty-hour labour. The bould clan deemed it a bad omen for a baby to drag on the womb for so long. The name was to toughen him up and make him bould. But Ulick did not turn bould. Ulick turned out a soft and beautiful soul. Ulick liked dancing and wearing his sister's dresses. And when he was older he loved to talk. And he sat up at the bar beside me sipping glasses of white wine, and we loved one another, not a bit of shame on either of us regards it, me with a wife at home and Ulick undermining the bould clan's reputation to the country.

'And one night a van stops beside us on the Dunlavin road. The bould men inside offered us a lift. Ulick tells them we're fine, to go on, that the walk would do us good. But the men spilt out and I was knocked unconscious.'

The Crack took a swig on the bottle.

'The Lord is my shepherd, there is nothing I shall want. Except help with bottle-feeding the lambs at four intervals daily. Maybe a bit of a dig-out with castrating them, ear-tagging them, tail-docking them, mucking out the pens, making sure the racks are topped up for the ewes. Some help with plumbing in water. Then there's the worming, the blue-tongue and the blow-fly vaccinations, the footbaths to prevent the foot-rot. The shearing in August. The mart in Autumn and the flushing to make sure the ewes gain weight. Tupping in October then a five month gestation takes us back to March. The circle of life over and fuckin over. Time is circular, Untameable. No beginning, no end. Don't let anybody tell you different.'

The Untameable Donkey drank herself into delicious nothingness.

'No end ever,' The Crack said, and took a drink. 'So don't be expecting one like some arsehole of a donkey. You're no arsehole of a donkey, donkey.

'And only marry for love,' The Crack said, as an afterthought. 'I married to look respectable and inherit the farm. But I possessed not one single trait a species requires for domestication. Any little thing set me off and into a blind rage, throwing tantrums and storming out, like a baby, not to be seen again for days, a horrible cantankerous bastard at the best of times and worse at the worst. Unable to be told by anyone. Heeding no warnings nor paying no respect to nothing but myself. Only happy when drinking pints. *The Crack*.

'Cheers,' The Crack said, and swigged hard.

'I wouldn't give the woman I married any children, this dull and frumpy person with hips and tits and a sour face.

'That's not fair.

'No, that's not fair of me. The nicest, kindest… *nicest* person you could ever meet and I made her absolutely miserable. On purpose. Just to feed off of her pain. To see her wither before me. I drank with Ulick for days on end and she'd leave and I'd keep winning her back just to be cruel to her. I was so nice to that woman when winning her back that it was cruel.

'Just let me go, she said.

'I cannot, I told her. I love you.

'Stop she'd say. Please stop.

'You're the best thing that's ever happened to me, I'd say.

'Stop.

'Without you I'm nothing, I'd say.

'Please stop, she'd say. Please stop.'

The Crack swigged on the bottle like he was drinking fire. 'Everything I ever held has claw marks on it.'

The Crack saw The Untameable Donkey looked like she wanted to slap him.

'And so you should,' The Crack said. 'I deserve a comeuppance. I widowed that poor girl when I married her.'

The Untameable Donkey hit a slump from the morning drink.

'Didn't I tell you?' The Crack asked. 'You go straight through and there's no peace in it. The sun is too bright. There's too much left in the day. Too long to go.'

The Untameable Donkey stomped a hoof.

The Crack howled and tried to eat the sun out of the sky but came nowhere near.

The Untameable Donkey stomped harder.

'I got you drink,' said The Crack. 'More drink than you can drink.'

But drink was not what The Untameable Donkey was looking for. It was comeuppance.

'You want comeuppance? *Here!*' The Crack balled a fist and gave himself a shot in the nose with the knuckle.

The shot smarted. The Crack's nose bled.

'There—there's comeuppance.'

But The Untameable Donkey shrugged it off by drinking more stout. The shot in the nose was nothing. Nowhere close to comeuppance.

The Crack took a swig from the bottle.

Fine.

The Crack balled another fist. He punched hard on his cheekbone. He'd kept his elbow high and followed through. The Crack fell from the barrel yard wall from the force and landed in front of The Untameable Donkey. She inspected the cut that had opened on The Crack's cheek.

She approved of it. She kissed it.

'That's enough now,' The Crack said, winded and dazed, but The Untameable Donkey wanted more. The Crack got to his feet, took a deep breath to ready himself then inflicted an almighty slap to his own bollocks.

It dropped him to his knees.

'You dirty rotten bastard,' The Crack wailed.

The Untameable Donkey kicked a bit of rubber hose towards him.

More.

The Crack took the hose and beat himself with it. The Untameable Donkey watched and drank.

Come nightfall, The Crack was black-eyed, scraped, whipped, swollen and bloodied. He couldn't take it anymore. He had whipped himself with the rubber hose, clonked himself with bits of barstool and washed disinfectant into his eyes.

He'd kicked the complete and utter shite out of himself.

The Crack stumbled over to the barrel yard gate and opened it. 'Go on, then, Untameable,' he said. 'I'm not able. Go on! They can have it. They can have the farm. Fuck it all in anyways. Nothing but a landlocked lagoon of conformity. To fuck with it.'

The Untameable Donkey did not move.

'The surge and settle,' The Crack said, as he swayed. 'It's inclement. It's an inclement sale of indulgences. Fuck off I says. But then comes the madness that makes what it wants of its stories, twisting and wrangling the ends. God grant me the serenity with your sawn-off endings. I'll weld new ones. It's the faggot here, God. Won't be happy till you have us all swinging from the rafters. Dragging everyone down with you. Johnny look-up-and-spot-the-rocket I called him. The lad calls an ambulance on himself, donkey. All the time singing, then you're sneaking mini-bottles into the hospital. A drink? I'd be just as happy with a hammer. One as crude an anaesthetic as the other. To dieth by musket or by pot. Men and donkeys: all but detritus. Courage to change the things I can and wisdom to know the circular circumference.

'You want The Crack, donkey? You got him. Here's The Crack.'

The Crack held himself out like Christ on the cross. 'I'm plunging into darkness here, donkey. Have a cross on your back for all time for your service here today. Last man out, turn off the lights.'

The Crack fell face-first to the barrel yard cobble, unconscious.

The Untameable Donkey looked at the opened gate. She could go live on the mountain, never again to be seen by man. She could live off the land and roam in peace. She looked at the gate and realised that the thing she wanted wasn't after all what she wanted. She looked down at The Crack beaten unconscious by his own hand.

The state of it.

Fuckin men and the notions they have of themselves.

She approached the barrel and sucked back a good luck gallon. She then approached The Crack and bit down on his collar. He stank. He needed a wash. She dragged him to the pub's back door and used her hind leg to open it. She dragged him through to the pub bog and put him to bed on the floor in there, Tom Phelan watching it all unfold from the old kitchen as he slurped on a cup of hot tea, saying to himself that now, there and then, he'd surely seen it all.

Entomopathogenic Fungus

In January 2022, a new species of fungus
was identified at WWT Castle Espie.

At first it was no more than a descent of fine
mist, a shiver that settled, like dew
on the battement tendu of the cellar spider
that porcelain arachnid; Art Deco—

climbed, in time, into slippery joints;
unctuous cavelets under exo-
skeleton shield. A complex: vulnerable
to persuasion of the psychedelic kind,

or perhaps amphetamine, it anoints
its mycelial threads in the blood's rich juice.
And maybe the brittle spider never knew
before such a rush of unutterable joy, such

lust, such clarity: as the spores tingled
through the abdomen, reaching to the tips
of the legs & coursing through the brain
in its life up to this point, in the warm

dark of the gunpowder shed, as it climbs
to the highest corner. And when the toxins
numb it, perhaps it is a relief to give over
all your liquid, and be a dry husk

and finally, to spore into a ghost tree
so unlike the body you knew.

Kate Caoimhe Arthur

The Brotfressor

Shane O'Neill

Wolfgang's garden, filled with its spectacular assortment of inane items, is an abomination. The hood of his antiquated car remains permanently erect and rusting. The engine within is in no better shape. This defunct vehicle is parked next to a wheel-less golf buggy, itself casting shade on a children's play castle which lies in front of the entrance to Wolfgang's house. Stubby, unkempt bushes protrude from between the rusting machinery. Nearby rusts an old-fashioned hydrotherapy bath which has done little to assuage Wolfgang's nerves, if the display is anything to go by. The house is a discoloured brown, sun-faded and desperately in need of a fresh coating of paint. Despite it being a sweltering July, an inflatable Santa Claus peeks from behind the curtain of the second-floor window. Meanwhile a porcelain, human-sized lady-of-liberty stands aloof on a rooftop balcony, a length of rope tied around her neck and shoulders, perhaps an overt symbolic gesture, perhaps simply a convenient place to keep one's rope.

This garden stands in stark contrast to those of other suburban households in the Saarland, a state in western Germany from which my partner Sandra hails. When I first walk through these neighbourhoods, I am unable to pinpoint what it is that gives them such a profound sense of homogeneity. The houses, mostly built in the seventies, are quite dissimilar to one another, often remarkably so, but there seems to be a societal expectation to keep one's front garden perfectly manicured. For most, gardening is a pastime, yet in the Saarland gardens are maintained as though it were enforced by law. Perhaps this emphasis on impression stems from the country's not-so-distant, ignominious past; if nothing else, this kind of external order suggests a capability to maintain the status quo, whether that be on a local, national or global stage. Any divergence from this measurable normality is disdained and derided; all miscreants are viewed as pariahs in their locality.

I ask Sandra if, by describing them so, I have in any way unjustly stereotyped the people of her country.

'In what way can orderliness and conscientiousness be conceived of as a bad thing?'

It is a reasonable point and one for which I have no counter-argument.

Having spent the first three months of a global pandemic locked-down in a small cottage in Connemara, Sandra and I are still struggling to readjust. Our flight to Germany was stressful; we took every precaution possible, wearing not only masks on the plane, but goggles too. Only after two weeks of self-isolation are we sure we haven't picked up the virus on the plane, and are not at risk of infecting Sandra's parents, who are in their seventies. Now installed in the apartment, I spend my days writing at the kitchen table, sometimes moving to the living room where I can stretch out and read on an enormous L-shaped couch. From here I have a vantage point overlooking the neighbourhood's pristine gardens, the one exception, of course, being Wolfgang's. Repelled by the displays of carefully-pruned homogeneity, I obsess over this aberration, seeking solace in the chaos.

From the outside, Wolfgang—not his actual name—is an impressive specimen. He has a luxuriant mane of long, scraggly hair and his face is deeply woven with wrinkles, as if he has been too exposed to the sun or sunbeds. His resulting tan is almost Trumpian. His small eyes sit in his boxy face, peering from beneath his large, lined forehead. When their attention is caught by an unfamiliar sight, such as a stray Irishman, they dart feverishly before receding behind his nose. Although short in stature, he resembles a professional bodybuilder; was indeed one, asserts Sandra, back in the eighties. Germany, of course, is the country that gave birth to what would be later classified as German Volume Training: a weightlifting regimen characterised by intense work and rest periods. Wolfgang now works as a personal trainer; this explains why a considerable portion of his home has been converted into a gym. Despite his aversion to clothes that are not loose-fitting, tent-like shirts, up close it is still possible to perceive Wolfgang's unnaturally defined abs.

As the summer wears on, I find myself spending more and more time analysing Wolfgang's garden. What is the likelihood that he is a student of the Frankfurt School of thought, and that his garden is a staged production—his response to a continent besieged by consumerism, neoliberalism and capitalism? Indeed, should Theodor Adorno or Walter Benjamin have laid eyes on Wolfgang's display, would they have written some profound thesis? More likely, themselves being German, they would have been stunned to silence by this ugly vision of neighbourly neglect.

Take for example Wolfgang's Mercedes rusting in the driveway. For as long as cars have existed, masculinity and motoring have been inextricably connected. A man's car might reflect the state of his virility, the size of his sexual appendage and the wealth that he has acquired. Nowhere is this more true than in Germany. The care with which German people maintain their vehicles borders on neurosis: their interiors will always be recently vacuumed, their windows will sparkle and the tyre pressure will have been correctly adjusted. By making his wrecked car the centrepiece of his display, Wolfgang, whose physique stands as a testament to manliness and machismo, inverts the gendered cultural expectations associated with vehicular upkeep. It might not be such a stretch then to suggest that his garden is in drag; indeed, it represents a queering of societal norms. Such a reading helps me better understand his neighbours' distaste for the spectacle he has created.

Some symbols are more overt than others. A sign in the yard reads 'Brotfressor', with a lying-face Pinocchio emoji beneath. I puzzle over the word. 'Brotfresser', with an 'e', might mean 'bread-eater'. But the strange spelling suggests that more is at play. Googling the word, I find it to be a neologism from Joyce's *Finnegans Wake*: a combination of 'Brot' (Bread) and 'Professor'. Wolfgang is thus the self-professed Bread Professor. This title that he has given himself hints at a layer of genius behind the façade. However, how can we take his word for granted when the cartoon beneath suggests an inclination towards mendacity?

In an attempt to further my inquiry, I ask Sandra's friends about Wolfgang.

'Do you really think he's a lunatic?'

'Yes, isn't it obvious,' they reply in unison. 'Look at the state of his front garden.'

Unsatisfied with their response, I persist.

'But why does uniformity signify sanity?'

To this they have no answer; they simply consider me with sympathy.

As if I, the outsider, could, with so little effort, understand the machinations of German society.

Feeling like James Stewart in a Hitchcock film, I return to the window, day and night, to study Wolfgang's behaviour as the summer progresses.

In much the same way that Wolfgang is an oddity within his neighbourhood, the Saarland is an anomaly within Germany. Geographically, it borders France and Luxembourg. It is the smallest county in Germany and has found itself pieced apart and divided between different powers over the last couple of centuries. The region was once the French *Département de Sarre* (1798–1815) and, at other times it belonged to the Prussian Rhine Province and the Kingdom of Bavaria. Then, having been established as a French state in 1920 after the Great War, residents of the Saarland voted to become part of Nazi-governed Germany in 1935. After World War I, the French were eager to hold on to the Saarland because of its wealth of coal deposits. The region 'feels' much more German than French—indeed, I encountered few French speakers during my two visits—and many residents of the Saarland seem to dislike the French on principle. It is no surprise that residents of the Saarland speak a dialect foreign to the rest of the country. From a linguistic perspective this dialect—a hybrid of German and French—is fascinating. The syntax often closely resembles that of the French language, while the words are phonetically linked to German.

I also observe many similarities between Ireland and the Saarland. One third of the county is forestland, which Sandra regularly compares to the landscape of my home county of Wicklow. It is notable too that the Saarland is—historically at least—one of the most religious states in Germany, with around 57 per cent of its population identifying as Roman Catholics. The conservative nature of the Saarlandish people, at least in relation to the appearance of their gardens, may well be the result of a conservative Catholic culture; Catholicism, we might note (taking the opportunity to invoke once more the spirit of Joyce), ensured that Ireland remained a 'priestridden Godforsaken race' late into the last century, until those Godforsaken priests found themselves being chased away by the roars of a feral Celtic Tiger. Capitalism is the modern opiate of the masses and perhaps this is the message of Wolfgang's display, where vehicles turn to rust and Santa is not so much the dimpled mascot of consumerism as he is a home-invading Krampus.

Considering my growing obsession with Wolfgang and his activities, it might not be unfair to call into question the state of my own mental health. Since the beginning of the pandemic, I have been unable to train Brazilian Jiu Jitsu, a grappling sport that necessitates close proximity. Having trained in combat sports since the age of ten, it is only now I realise the extent to which they form my sense of selfhood. The shape of my body has become unfamiliar to me, reflecting months of a mostly sedentary life, and for the first time in years I am self-conscious about my appearance.

Might this new awareness be linked to my obsession with Wolfgang? His chiselled body stands as a testament to male fitness and strength. And yet even his body has a strange contradictory quality, being somewhat unnatural, *unheimlich*, almost unwholesome at his late age. In this manner, even his physical appearance pushes him further out of the periphery of what his neighbours might consider 'normal'. Wolfgang's self-identification as the neighbourhood Brotfressor might suggest his own difficulties with these perceptions of normality and the words being spoken to him. Indeed, anyone familiar with *Finnegans Wake* will be aware of the linguistic challenges it poses and its seeming impenetrability. On this level, I too can relate, being an outsider this summer, trapped within my own linguistic purgatory, and skirting the borders of cultural comprehension. I struggle to communicate with Sandra's parents, despite no lack of effort on their part. Her father, Manni, is sympathetic to my cause, constructing short sentences using lyrics from English songs that he loves. Sandra's father has the profound distinction of being the founding member of the Saarland's first fan club of The Rolling Stones in the sixties; from all evidence, the group did little more than smoke weed and listen to The Rolling Stones, a noble enterprise if ever there was one.

'Sugar in the morning,' he calls to us each morning as we breakfast outside on the balcony. Then later in the afternoons, he drapes an arm around his daughter and quotes Stevie Ray Vaughan: 'She's my pride and joy,' words I might consider more threatening (*Don't upset my daughter*) were his general disposition not so jovial. When we dine together in the evening, he insists on quoting lines from Jewel Akens's 'The Birds and the Bees', blissfully unaware of their sexual overtones. Sandra's mother has better English than her spouse, but is nervous speaking it in front of her fluent daughter. Each time she addresses me, she speaks to me not in the dialect of the region, but slowly and with emphasis in 'proper' German, believing that I'll have a better chance of understanding her. She used the same technique when raising Sandra, leading to some confusion during early developmental stages when Sandra noticed that her father (who preferred to speak the dialect) and her mother were speaking to her in different languages. Sandra's mother's tactic is unsuccessful, however, and I spend much of the summer in a state of profound bewilderment, not helped, of course, by an increasing awareness that two years of a scheduled three-year doctorate have elapsed, and I need to redouble my efforts if I am to submit to schedule. My PhD research, somewhat ironically, is also a study of translation, specifically of Samuel Beckett's self-translated dramatic works. Balancing English, French and what little German I know exhausts me and I find myself at a linguistic impasse from which there seems no easy escape.

The pressure of my research has slowed my efforts to learn German, which have been consistent, if not a little perfunctory, over the past few months. I spend on average ten minutes each morning on my phone using a language-learning app, to mixed results. The app performs a double function, however: as well as improving my German, it allows me to satisfy my own obsessive-compulsive inclinations as I watch my streak climb daily. For the same reason, I subscribe to a meditation app that I employ every morning. While in use, my mind tends to drift off (the opposite of what it tells me I should be doing), but is ultimately appeased when I watch the 'days meditated' number increase. Perhaps Wolfgang too suffers from some kind of compulsive disorder, one that manifests itself in the exterior disorder on display outside his home.

One day, on our way back from a walk in the forest, I see Wolfgang in the distance, his back to the road, leaning over the open bonnet of his silver Mercedes. The car is switched on and the rusty engine hums. As I approach, I realise that he is eating a large portion of lasagne in an aluminium tray off the warm engine. Fascinated, I want to stay and observe, but Sandra tugs at my arm.

'Don't let him see you watching, he'll get suspicious. He's really paranoid.'

Paranoia does not explain this spectacle, but I don't stop to argue the point. However, as the evening wears on, I find it hard to unsee the image of Wolfgang hunched over his aged vehicle like an animal, gorging from a metallic tray.

As night falls, I suggest a brief stroll around the neighbourhood. It is dark and the streetlights illuminate little. All is still but for the intermittent whining of mosquitos. Picking our steps carefully in the darkness, we stop when we spot a large figure moving catlike across the road in front of us. The figure is clearly Wolfgang; his broad silhouette gives him away. Before I have time to marvel at his stealth, Wolfgang illuminates himself with his phone's torch. The resulting effect is that Wolfgang's head bobs in obscurity, like a bodiless phantom from a Beckett play. He has positioned himself before a car, which he is now peering into. The light inside the car comes on suddenly and two petrified girls are shrieking at Wolfgang. The girls rev the engine, and, tyres squealing, depart, pausing only at a safe distance to roll down the window and hurl insults at Wolfgang. We hurry back to the apartment, where Sandra informs me that Wolfgang sometimes feels it is his duty to patrol the neighbourhood and ensure that there are no obvious strangers lurking, up to no good. I ponder such acts of vigilantism; they suggest something about Wolfgang's character, a quality I have yet to clearly identify.

The systematic doping of athletes in East Germany during the seventies and eighties is well documented; however, in 2013 it was revealed by the Humboldt University in Berlin that doping was carried out to a similar extent in West Germany, an area encompassing the Saarland. Neither is it a secret that steroid abuse often has long-term mental health implications: side-effects include mania, hypomania, paranoia, depression and anxiety. Perched as I am by the window, a literal armchair psychologist, it is easy to attribute such characteristics to Wolfgang. His behaviour—which Sandra assures me has worsened in recent years—borders on mania at the best of times and his furtive vigilantism may well stem from a fevered paranoia. And yet I cannot help relating with him on a personal level. Since the beginning of the pandemic I am admittedly more withdrawn, more introverted. State-sponsored encouragements to keep one's distance from others have been effective: I too am paranoid of the outsider, despite being one myself. This prompts me to consider to what extent Wolfgang has been affected by the pandemic. Has he also become more inward-focused, more insular? Or it may be that he is blissfully unaware of the extent of the global crisis, having shut himself out of the loop many years ago. It dawns on me that I have never seen him wearing a mask, although I have only ever seen him engaged in outdoor activities. Maybe he believes that his fitness and impressive physique will act as a shield against the invisible enemy. For all he knows, the pandemic is all part of a global conspiracy to shut down local businesses such as his gym, a concern, it seems, that both he and his wife share.

The woman Wolfgang is married to is either a psychologist or a psychotherapist, which raises immediate questions as to the nature of their relationship. She is blonde, was perhaps once glamorous, and wears glasses in what seems to be an attempt to obscure the rapid movements of her receding eyes. Her skin is leathery and weather-beaten; I assume that she and Wolfgang tan together on sunbeds.

Before Wolfgang married, Sandra's father Manni used to greet Wolfgang with a military-style salute each time he passed him in his car. Wolfgang would reciprocate with a salute of his own. One day, however, Wolfgang blanked him. Not unused to Wolfgang's eccentricities, Manni thought little of the snub. Some days later, Manni found himself being accosted by Wolfgang's wife who accused him of mocking Wolfgang through their ritual. It was not long after that Wolfgang erected his 'Brotfressor' sign.

Another sign in Wolfgang's yard alludes to the annual meeting of the global elite at Bilderberg. The sentence is garbled and makes little sense, but similarly to the 'Brotfressor' sign, there is a Pinocchio emoji printed above the word 'Bilderberger'. This sign too, affirms Sandra, was erected soon after the incident with her father. Perhaps Wolfgang perceives his neighbours to be members of this elite class of Illuminati overlords, or perhaps he considers them to be blind to conspiracies to which only he, the Bread Professor, is fully attuned. Indeed, Manni affirms, Wolfgang believes that he is under a relentless assault from his meddling neighbours who are united in their efforts to shut down his indoor gym. This effort, according to Wolfgang, is all part of a larger government plot to drain resources from honourable working people. This was as much detail as Sandra and I could glean from Manni, who did all he could to piece together years of Wolfgang's garbled diatribes.

It was after he married that Wolfgang's paranoia of his neighbours truly manifested itself. He had always been reclusive and untrusting, yet willing to allow his neighbours to pay him visits to use his gym. Manni is convinced that his wife is only interested in Wolfgang as a case study for her profession—or brotfression—as a psychotherapist. Such an hypothesis might lead us to believe that she is exacerbating his mental instability for her own gains: monetary, sexual or otherwise. Perhaps Wolfgang has become her test subject. I imagine them locked away in his gym, her applying electrodes to his skull, zapping what remains of his mind into oblivion, or standing watch as he steeps himself in the hydrotherapy bath, which now sits discarded in the garden, a failed experiment. One conclusion is that she too suffers poor mental health, and clings to Wolfgang for stability. This scenario strikes me as unfortunate, like watching a non-swimmer attempt to save a drowning child—in few such scenarios will there be a happy ending. If I were to reach a less cynical conclusion, however, I would posit that what others see as madness, she sees as charisma; that his idiosyncrasies are exactly what she finds attractive about him.

The summer is drawing to an end and our return flights to Ireland are booked. We start to mentally prepare ourselves for the ordeal of masks, goggles, disposable plastic gloves and disinfectant spray. The sweltering weather has been unrelenting and I am inside trying to finish a chapter of my thesis. The electric fan whirs loudly, and at first I do not differentiate the shouting noises outside from the low-volume heavy metal emanating from my laptop speakers. Pausing the music, I go to the window, where outside, Wolfgang is aggressing a student of the driving school owned and run by Sandra's parents. From what little I can glean, it appears that the man parked his bike in front of Wolfgang's house. Perhaps the juxtaposition of the man's gleaming bike with Wolfgang's prized collection of junk upset the overall effect that he is trying to achieve with his collage. The cyclist is the taller of the two, but has a hanging gut, in stark contrast to the mass of muscle standing before him. He is a paltry sparring partner for Wolfgang, who must outweigh him by thirty kilograms. The cyclist probably thinks that he is safe, protected by the many laws that are supposed to deter humans from violent acts.

But Wolfgang is a law unto himself.

My poor grasp of German making me quite impotent in such situations, I call Sandra to the window. The cyclist's voice has risen and, to our dismay, he prods Wolfgang's enormous chest with a finger. There is no time left to de-escalate the situation. Wolfgang swings back his fist and lands a heavy blow on his adversary's skull. The thud echoes horribly through the neighbourhood; the crack as his helmeted head meets the concrete is somehow even more unpleasant. Wolfgang stands over his dazed victim, muttering to himself in a low, unrepentant monologue.

This act of violence unsettles me. The summer has been a unique period of monotonous circularity during which I found myself endlessly re-treading the same walking routes, actively searching for something to divert my attention away from the sheer sameness of the quotidian. I was acutely aware of what it meant to be an outsider and so my obsession with Wolfgang was inevitable. I spent the summer trying to empathise with him, only to bear witness to this act of brutality.

At different points throughout my stay, I considered Wolfgang to be either a genius, a lunatic or an anarchist. The act of proclaiming oneself the Bread Professor of the neighbourhood suggests an underlying intelligence, while the punch he delivered and the state of his garden—along with his long, impressive, rockstar hair—suggest an inclination towards anarchism. By creating his garden display, is Wolfgang actively seeking the derision of his neighbours, perhaps hoping to use their scorn as a catalyst for confrontation or contact?

A lunatic would be, I think, the saddest category to place him under. It may be true that years of steroid abuse have affected his brain function. In this case, rapid mood-swings would not be uncommon should his brain not receive the requisite supplies of serotonin and dopamine. Furthermore, his early career as a bodybuilder suggests that he wants to be noticed and admired. Should he have failed throughout his career to get such approval, he likely turned to drugs in order to enhance his performance. Still not receiving the praise he so desires, he effectively leaves society while remaining within it, to the scorn and degradation of the outside world, which now perceives him as a failure and a madman. He finds solace in modernist works that seem to reflect his own thought patterns, such as *Finnegans Wake,* of which I am sure there is a fine translation (though with my limited German, it's not something I will be seeking out any time soon). This teaches him to dismantle the symbols of normalcy in favour of those of chaos, allowing him to effectively raise a middle finger to the society that has neglected him in his time of need. He is therefore not a figure to be ridiculed, but one that deserves our compassion and empathy.

I wonder how Wolfgang would feel if he read this essay. Would he be enraged to learn that he had become the object of such close examination, or would it satisfy some longing within him: that is, a longing to be noticed by those within your vicinity. Would he sense compassion in the words of another outsider, or would it cause him to withdraw more forcefully than before?

It comforts me, somewhat, to see how quickly Wolfgang's victim stirs. Already, Manni has emerged from the school and is dragging the bewildered cyclist away from his meaty aggressor. Sandra's mother has called the police and a siren can be heard in the distance. Nobody attempts to stop Wolfgang as he makes a hasty retreat back to his house—it would be futile to try and derail such a behemoth. Minutes later, when the police arrive at his door, he accepts his fate with composure, allowing himself to be cuffed and led to the car where he is squashed into the backseat. We watch from the window with some relief as he is carted away. The siren fades and the neighbourhood is still. People slowly return to their front gardens to water their plants, mow their lawns, trim the hedges and unearth the weeds.

I'm not angry just disappointed

after The Walking Dead

Turning 28 and thought I'd know how to drive by now. Everyone on TV knows how to drive, I only know how to watch. In the zombie apocalypse they're always driving away from the newest lesson in *fear the people, not the dead*. I eat my reheated leftovers and think, I'd be that one straggler on the road with a bag full of family photos and the bell from my cat's collar. Right? Look, there I am, screaming for mercy after an ex-cop in a shitty Prius. His lawless kid, his well-weathered gun in the backseat. They don't even stop to look at this sorry son of a bitch and I don't blame them. I'm running after life in too big shoes. I forgot my good winter coat. My useless hands carry nothing but the past, nothing but *I wish I had / if only I had / I might have by now.*

Eva Griffin

Say Yes

after GLOW

In the women's dressing room
something like friendship
comes close again. The ridiculous
swing of your breasts towards me.
The beauty of dancing so badly
in an abandoned showgirl headdress.
You knew you would hate Las Vegas;
for the love of what do you stay?
Backstage flowers die eventually,
the lights go down each night,
and I have learned so carefully
how to stick my fingers down
my throat. How to stand up,
wipe myself clean, and look at you
approaching me from behind;
your silly tits bouncing in the mirror.
The only person who doesn't tell
me I look good these days.
So, I say yes to dinner. Yes
to keeping the lights on. You
laughing back into my life
through this basement, knowing
that the bouquets would wilt
the same way anywhere else.

Eva Griffin

The Roof Has Fallen In (a novel extract)
Aoife Esmonde

'He as good as killed her,' some woman hissed as I approached the counter with Brendan, wrist braceleted to wrist, the metal of the handcuffs already as warm as skin. Brendan jostled into me so close that there was no drag between us, just the polite half-intimate slide of his body behind mine. I knew Brendan must have heard the woman, but when I looked at him, he was staring up grimly at the menu board, already compromising over his choices. As soon as I'd ordered, I unlocked the cuff on my wrist, letting them all see me do it.

The Coke was a dismal, greyish colour, and half the cup was ice, but Brendan sucked on the straw with a sort of fierce enthusiasm, cheeks hollowed, nostrils flared.

'Can I have curry chips?' he asked, mouth full of anaemic-looking burger.

I wondered if he'd ever had fast food before. There was a chipper in the village but it was only open during the summer, and Greta had never been one for eating out. I thought of her little vegetable patch, the sideways lean of her rickety greenhouse, the glass milky and warped with age. Walking into it had been like a descent, that slow underwater pull of greenness and moist heat. And anyway, I doubted there had been much money for luxuries.

'It'll be nothing but muck once I get to Finian's,' Brendan said. 'A lad I was talking to at the courthouse said you wouldn't believe the shite they expect us to eat. This is the last time I'll get anything nice, I'd say.' His eyes rolled with pleasure as he licked ketchup off his fingers, like he used to with the cream off the top of the pail when Greta had him milking. For a second I was back there in the animal fug of the barn, the tentative wet nudge of Clodagh's nose against the thin skin of my inner wrist, and Greta in the doorway, a darker shape against the opening arc of light as the door swung in. 'Fingers out!' she'd always say to Brendan laughingly, warningly, and he always would do it, whip them out quick as could be, obedient. It didn't make sense that I was bringing him to St Finian's, him who had always been such a good boy.

'Why did you do it?'

I wouldn't have been sure that I'd said it out loud but for the fact that he went still, a quivering, tense sort of stillness, like the moment before the unfolding of wings. He looked skyward, as though he could see through the polystyrene ceiling tiles to the opening blue above. I wished again the weather wasn't so fucking nice. It should have been a day for rain.

Then, after a long pause, with the crinkle of ice into a distant cup, the ding of the cash register, he relaxed again, shoulders dipping into insolence, the curl of his mouth the same sly smile he'd given his lawyer and the judge and me when I'd sat him into the back of the Garda car.

'I didn't,' he told me, 'but you know that, don't you?' He shook his wrist at me, the loose end of the cuffs trailing. His smile slipped. 'But it doesn't matter anyway. I might as well be inside as anywhere else, now that she's—'

He looked away from me as he stuffed the end of the burger into his mouth, before saying indistinctly, 'I would have preferred it to be me, you know?'

The worst part was that I could see it so easily: the arc of his blood, not hers, fanning out across the wall; his beautiful eyes swollen shut; the slack hang of his sulky mouth; maybe even—if they did a good enough number on him— the halo of the camera flash around his cleaned-up face on the metal slab for the autopsy photos. He knew what I was thinking, I could see it, because he laughed, meanly, and sucked on his straw again.

'I'll get the chips,' I told him. 'Stay here.'

Nancy was behind the counter, her hair sliding out from under her hairnet like dandelion fuzz. Her face was still smooth and joyful and fresh, like a teenager's. She told me once that her hair had turned grey overnight, when they'd found her husband. She'd been only twenty-four then, with a small baby and a new business to run, and he'd gone and cracked his skull falling into the overflow ditch on the way home along the canal one night. He had drowned in six inches of water, she told me bitterly, like he had done it on purpose. I liked Nancy. I had been stopping in at least twice a year since I made full Garda because it was always me who ended up bringing the boys to Finian's, and I wouldn't want to send them off to that place without something warm and filling in their stomachs.

'I'll be with you in a second, Guard,' she called, wiping a damp forearm over her forehead, dunking the metal cage of chips into oil to a hushed sizzle. She nudged her sloping chin toward Brendan. 'Another one for the Home?' When I nodded, she tutted a bit, then shovelled an extra large portion of chips onto the plate. Her curry sauce was lurid, sludgy. Brendan would love it.

'Where's your young fella today?' I asked.

She looked frazzled, alone behind the counter. Her quiet, tall son was normally at the fryer, hands always moving, back turned to the world. Nancy looked delighted I had asked.

'He's got himself an apprenticeship over at Fogarty's, the accountant, you know?'

I didn't, of course, had never set foot in any place in Killyboyne other than the café, but I nodded anyway. I could see that would be a step up for him, out of the smell of cooking fat and the tang of artificial lemon cleaning fluid.

'Anyway.' She pushed the plate across the counter to me. 'That's on the house. Poor little lad.'

Brendan was sitting where I'd left him, not that I thought he'd try anything. He was pushing the sticky ketchup bottle around the table with one finger, though he looked up and smiled when I came back with the food. He could have been ten years old again, hands all mucky from helping me with the garda bike, listening to my instructions with that curious, cool, appraising manner of his, like he had all his feelings tucked behind his teeth and was keeping them there.

Grief lapped at me. It felt muscular, like my sadness was a living thing. I didn't need the handcuffs for Brendan, I knew that, and I took his wrist, still boy-thin, and silently unclicked the bracelet.

He'd nearly finished the curry chips before we spoke again. I wanted to tell him that I knew he didn't do it, but he was gasping and smacking his mouth at the heat of the spices, and I couldn't be too loud, not with Nancy leaning against the counter with the radio down low. Whatever song was playing reminded me of Greta moving around the pub with a swing to her walk. These days, everything reminded me of her.

'I wish it could have been me too,' I told him, and for the first time since it happened he looked at me gratefully, like he used to. 'I miss her,' I said, just like that. 'I miss her so much.'

It wasn't as though I was going to cry or be foolish about it all, but the journey yawned ahead of me, the long, dismal road ending in nothing but that awful grey building, and then the lonely drive home, maybe the radio fuzzing in and out, maybe just a silent stretch of country, the miles clicking by like a metronome. And the drive wouldn't even be the end of it all, because once I was home it would be hollow days and evenings in and out to the hospital, which was already almost unbearable, and the unknowable shape of her under the sheets, smaller than she had ever looked. And after that? Maybe the rehabilitation centre, if she made it that far.

Brendan was still so quiet. Maybe he was thinking about her too.

'You'd better use the jacks before we go,' I said, and he flushed, angry, or embarrassed maybe. I could understand that. At least I wouldn't have to be cuffed to the hand that wasn't holding his prick, like I had with some of the tougher lads before.

We stood, and he wiped his mouth with one of the plasticky napkins, leaving a saffron smear. I moved with him around the table, careful to apply that little bit of force, something at once jovial and threatening. Nancy was watching. I nodded to her, elbowed Brendan to do the same, and after he smiled at her I caught his arm and steered him, hard, towards the door. Nancy's gaze was flat and unimpressed. We had to walk past the counter to get to the jacks, and I pushed Brendan in front of me as we followed the TOILET sign that blinked on and off in a lacklustre rhythm.

The door shut behind us, and we were in a clean, quiet corridor. I could hear the maddening low hum of the strip light above us. It made me want to shake my head, dislodge the noise somehow. My hand was damp and too tight around Brendan's bicep. I let him go, abruptly, and he stumbled as he went ahead of me down the corridor, all the way to the end where the Men's were. It was cooler out here than in the chipper, and the walls had that sheen of damp that looked like sweat on skin. There were no windows. It could have been any time of the day or night.

'Get in there, quick.' I shoved him between the tensing wings of his shoulder blades with the heel of my hand. Then we were in the bathroom, lit only by a dim haze through the frosted window over the toilet. The empty socket of a broken light swung gently overhead.

He had a slash and washed his hands carefully, meeting his own eyes in the small mirror above the sink as though it was the last time he would see himself. Then he squared his shoulders, his poor boyish chest shifting to angles of tension as he steadied himself, and I realised what I was going to do.

'Listen to me,' I whispered, and he actually jumped, the poor stupid child;

he jumped and shivered when I went closer so I could speak low and quiet, mouth to his ear. I felt so angry with him, all of a sudden, like it was his fault I was failing in my duty and breaking my oath in the dingy bathroom of a greasy café thirty-five miles and a lifetime away from home.

'You're going to take this'—my hands were unsteady as I opened my wallet and took out the stack of notes—'and then we're going to get that window open and you're going to climb out. And you're going to run, do you hear me?' I pressed the money into his hand, wrapped my own fingers around his so he held on tight.

'James.' He closed his eyes, opened them, blinked as if against some brilliant light. For a moment, he looked like her. I could see the thread of her running through him in a way I had never appreciated before, him with his dark eyes and dark curls, and her so pale and clear-eyed and her fair hair like the floss of a baby chick's feathers. It was pity I saw on his face, I thought, and I hated him all over again. 'James, I can't—'

But he was already disentangling our hands, shoving the cash into the deep pockets of his grey tracksuit bottoms. He backed up against the wall of the toilet cubicle. The partition rattled. He was shaking.

'James,' he said again, my name tight in his mouth. 'I can't leave until you promise me you'll get him. Do you see? I appreciate'—he waved his hand, encompassing the cubicle and the window and the wad of cash in his pocket—'all this, but I can't just go knowing she's back there, like that, and him walking around free as a bird.'

'What do you think my fucking job is, Brendan? Do you think she'd want you stuck in Finian's getting clattered or worse by the bigger boys and the padres? Just give me a break and get out.' The two of us were like half-drowned kittens there in the gloom, shivering together. 'You know I'll do everything— anything—to make him pay. And go north, will you. Get yourself to England if you can. You know where I am. You can write later with your address. Keep the head down for a while and we'll sort you out, okay?'

We had never touched much—he wasn't that kind of young fellow and to be honest neither was I—but he wrapped me up in himself for a minute, and the feel of his arms around me made my eyes prickle. He still smelled of the house: turf smoke and the thin lemon of her homemade soap and the brackish undertow of well-water. I had to push him off in the end, feeling too rough and too tender all at once as my hands skimmed over the bird-bones of his shoulders, the strung-bow tension of his muscles.

'Go on,' I told him. 'I'll sort it out, don't worry. Just…'

There wasn't much point in saying any more to him. We both knew there would be no guarantees.

Together we climbed onto the ledge behind the toilet seat, kneeling in the slanting light, penitents. We had to peel back the wire covering the window, but then one good tug had it off the wall, and after that it was just an open window and a short drop and he was gone, loping slow and easy and inconspicuous past the big rubbish bins. He made for the stretch of scrub grass that lay between the chipper and the back road.

I didn't even bother to try to put the wire back over the window, just let it fall with a clang. I felt clammy inside the wool of my jacket, tight right up to my throat behind the starched collar of my shirt. I kicked up the toilet lid, because I suddenly needed to piss, and badly, so much so that my hands were clumsy and fumbling over the button of my uniform trousers, and I barely got it out in time before the stream started, hot and noisy in the quiet of the cubicle.

After, I spent a lot of time washing my hands, ticking down the seconds in my head. He'd have the good sense to keep off the side of the road anyway, though he might have already been lucky and found a lift, but I still wanted to take my time before I went out and put everything in motion. Every minute that passed gave him another minute to get further away. The mirror was warped and foggy, and in it I looked half-drowned, melting.

It was in the corridor, when the door to the Men's crashed shut behind me, that I saw the man. He was half-crouched in the near doorway, which was shut and unmarked, probably a cleaning cupboard. He was wearing a suit, or maybe the suit was wearing him; it was a yellow-olive, lightweight thing, boxy at the shoulders, squared off and flappy at the legs. He should have looked ridiculous, but his stern, fine-boned face had a sort of dignity to it that stole the attention from his clothes. His hair was overlong, curling past his ears, a rich brown that lightened to russet at the tips. When he saw me, he straightened. His hands fluttered expansively below the too-short jacket sleeves. His fingertips were shadowed with ink. He looked me in my face when he spoke.

'Where's the boy, Guard?'

For the Border Sheep

You graze the mist in basin country
where reception fuzzes out and in again,
arrange your slow deck-stacking shuffles. Then
your bony rumple rolls, the gravity
of the flock begins to tilt. You flee
to what the EU and the Revenue
would view as your annihilation,
your detonation into specks and strands of fleece—

and reassembly. So, counted and recounted,
drift off to your dreamy counter life,
your masquerade soirée among the outcrops.
Dance a quickstep with your mirror-tinted
counterparts, but don't go touching: leave
just wisps on wire connected up.

Chris Kitson

The Afterlife

Leopold O'Shea

It is the day of my execution. From where I have been positioned on the stage, I cannot help admiring all the work that has gone into decorating the assembly hall. My classmates have spent the week folding sheets of coloured paper and cutting snowflakes out of them, writing messages of encouragement and sprinkling them with glitter before sellotaping these Good Luck snowflakes to the windows. One of them reads AU REVOIR ET BONNE CHANCE, for we have been learning French and our teacher Mrs Hanrahan always makes sure to reinforce what we have been learning in all our activities. Whether it is asking to open a window or making farewell cards, always we are improving our French.

Mrs Robinson is going over the dance routine with First Class, reminding them to perform for the back of the room, while Sister Amanda opens a small black deposit box on a desk set up next to the doors.

The hall is always hung with tinsel and garlands for these sorts of occasions, and it is true that the snowflakes are not a new idea. But maybe because this time it is my execution I feel that there is something special about this one in particular.

My mother has arrived early so she can say a word to Mrs Hanrahan and save seats for my friend Rudy and his parents, who will also be here this evening. My brother has not been able to make it because of a long-running Dungeons & Dragons campaign at a friend's house, but says hi. She sits alone on an empty bench, my mother, wearing earrings, eyeliner and a light billowy dress. My mother is in a good mood. She is waving up at me. Now she is mouthing something. I do not know what. I smile, but also I am trying to stay still for fear of the cone falling off my head.

There is only so much eye contact I can make with my mother before it gets awkward and we must look elsewhere. She adjusts her dress, finds a strand of hair or a fleck of glitter which she rubs out onto the floor. When the doors to the hall open, she turns to see if it is anyone she knows, a smile slowly fading each time as she turns back to consult her ticket, making sure that she is in the right seat, checking her watch.

The assembly hall is filling up nicely. There is much waving among the children and there is a kind of excitement among the parents, who lean over benches to shake hands with someone they have not seen since that birthday party or the parent-teacher meeting, how is your cousin and what happened with the veranda. Together they admire the work of the children. They agree that they have never seen anything like it, the French snowflakes, the gold loop-garlands, the use of pipe cleaners and googly eyes on the cone this year, and the other arts and crafts which the school has mobilised in a single collective effort.

My mother looks worried now. She does not know how much longer she can hold on to Rudy's parents' seats, and she is getting more and more embarrassed every time she must tell someone they are taken. She barely ever looks up at me. She turns the bracelet of her watch to read the time, turns to the back of the hall and sighs.

My best friend Rudy has arrived. He performs our secret hand signal as he and his parents pick their way through greetings, reunions, and impromptu catch-ups that will have to be continued at some later date. I think they have forgotten the arrangement with my mother for they have gotten into a conversation with Colin Sweeney's parents and now are taking their seats with them.

The dance of First Class in their donkey masks begins. Sister Amanda dims the lights and plays the music. Mrs Robinson is motioning to her students to stay in position and to be as expressive as possible, but their timing is embarrassing. Their masks are cut from cereal boxes and look nothing like donkeys. They are merely disquieting. But it does not matter to the audience who have forgotten what a donkey looks like and clap along regardless. To think that I too was once in First Class. At Christmas, Rudy and I had to cover our mouths as we giggled through their production of the nativity. But I am not laughing now.

The bolt is not firing and my teacher, Mrs Hanrahan, who smells good and has dressed very nicely for the occasion, is gesturing to the principal that there is something wrong.

Mrs Robinson is telling First Class to keep dancing so as to buy Mrs Hanrahan some time. But the more they dance, the more they are out of time, the more amateur the whole thing appears. Mrs Tracy, the principal, has had to step in for Mrs Hanrahan, whose face has gone red because of Mrs Tracy's impatience, which is starting to show like the brands of the cereal boxes from which the disquieting donkey masks were made. Everyone is taking a deep breath, I am doing my bit, the cone has not moved from my head, but it is a tense situation.

To keep my mind off the cone, I try to guess who has written the messages on the snowflakes. I do not think that I will ever know for certain.

Mrs Hanrahan, following the instructions of someone in the audience, turns everything off and on again. Mrs Robinson has finally told the donkeys to stop their dance and is trying to help, but she too is saying all the wrong things. I think that Mrs Tracy is under considerable stress due to the presence of the inspector. No one has thought to turn off the music. Mrs Timoney, who is substituting for Mrs Creevy, asks if Mr Curly could have a look since he is the one who deals with technical matters, repairs the radiators, scrapes the hardened chewing gum off the tables every summer. There is a man on the stage asking Mrs Tracy if he can help, maybe the firmware needs updating. Mrs Tracy is holding her head and dropping her arms in defeat. Soon we are joined by two other parents who must know each other from birthday parties. Mrs Timoney, acting as if the idea has just occurred to her, asks again why they do not call Mr Curly who set up the equipment. In the end everyone agrees with Sister Amanda's idea of asking Mr Curly for his help, as he is the one who deals with these things.

I am wondering who it is who could have written AU REVOIR ET BONNE CHANCE on the snowflake and I conclude that it can only have been Anne-Sophie, with whom I share a desk, for it is exactly the sort of thing Anne-Sophie would write to impress our teacher.

I was supposed to be executed on Monday but because of corrosion to the bolt it has had to be postponed.

My teacher is whispering to me at my desk that I do not have to complete her fill-in-the-blank exercises anymore. I am free to go outside and play in the schoolyard during class time, or to draw to my heart's content or occupy myself however I wish, for the school understands that my mother cannot take the time off work and an arrangement has been made that while I am awaiting the new date of my execution, the school will keep me on the premises. No more subjugation of the hand to the practice of writing, the mind released from the memorisation of tables, the reshaping of the spine by the schoolbag, straps cutting into the armpits.

I turn around to Rudy and fist pump triumphantly. As my first act in this new lighter state I raise my hand and ask for permission to go to the schoolyard. Mrs Hanrahan comes back to my desk and whispers that I do not have to ask for permission anymore. As long as I am quiet while the others are working, I can come and go as I please.

It is not clear from where I am standing in the middle of the schoolyard whether Rudy can see me fist-pumping, because of all these reflections in the windows, and so I pump my fists harder than before and bare my teeth again in case he is looking out at that moment.

Mr Curly's clothes are drying on the roof of the school. I find half a tennis ball. The shrill voices of First Class are droning in the distance and I am fist-pumping.

I am admiring the card I got from my class before the execution. It reads ADIEU NOTRE AMI on the front and each letter is personalised by a different classmate. Crêpe paper frames the card and it is dusted with gold and red glitter in the most spectacular fashion. Match sticks and strips of felt, it cannot be denied, add an extra dimension to my farewell card. Inside are all the names of my classmates wishing me all the best. It is a spectacular card. The only one of its kind.

My mother is examining the most recent permission slip which she has to sign if my execution is to go ahead. The tickets from the first execution, I reassure her, will remain valid. Money is a perennial concern of my mother's, the duration of showers and the turning off of lights a constant source of tension in our house. Whenever I ask my mother for anything these days she simply grumbles, and so usually I prefer to leave the permission slip next to her and slink out of the room.

I am standing in the doorway of my brother's bedroom looking at the poster of an elvish woman in thin leather underwear, asking him if today he will help me write my Dungeons & Dragons character. It is not a game for homosexuals, he tells me, and so I continue to my room.

It is obvious from my mother's silences, from the way she closes doors and turns off lights when I am still in the room, that she is not happy about something.

It is ruining my enjoyment of the Rice Krispies, whose crackling I like to hold my ear to in the morning. Unfortunately, my mother will not be able to make it to my execution, she says, as Friday is the opening of the French Film Festival. This may be the last time we will see Alain Delon on the big screen for some time. I am trying to listen to my Rice Krispies and instead I must listen to my mother, when I know, as my mother knows, that she will be there earlier than the last time, regardless of the French Film Festival, because of how she thinks it would reflect on her that she did not attend her own son's execution.

It is true that I am no longer obligated to wear the school's uniform but I do not feel right going to school without it even if it does cause me routine discomfort. It is the same with the schoolbag to which I have become attached despite the constriction of the armpits and the pressure at the base of the spine.

I am sitting next to Anne-Sophie and I am raising my hand to answer a question, for that is what I have always done when I have had the answer. There is only so much aimless wandering of the corridors I can do. The schoolyard in reality is a windy place without the other bodies to shield you and there is something I do not like about the sound of women's shoes echoing in empty corridors. Outside Mrs Hanrahan's class there is nowhere to hide from the strange rumours and chantings of First Class. Though in many ways long division and French nursery songs do not apply to me any longer, as a matter of habit I cannot help joining in. And so I follow the lessons of Mrs Hanrahan, complete the homework and sometimes, even now, wake up sweating in the night thinking today is the long division test, and what will I do with the remainder. I am extending my arm as far as humanly possible, rising from my seat slightly, which Anne-Sophie says is not allowed. If I extend my arm any further, I am thinking, I will surely dislocate it.

I do not think that Mrs Hanrahan can see me.

At lunchtime, while the other boys throw gravel at each other and the girls rehearse dance routines, my best friend Rudy and I add to our already elaborate handshake. Now Rudy has invited the homosexual Colin Sweeney, and I look on as he tries to teach him our handshake, shaking my head at Rudy's naivety, for I doubt if Colin will ever be able to grasp it.

Is it because of the uniform that my mother sees me as the embodiment of the school, I am thinking, and, according to her, the exorbitant demands made of the parents. Always you are springing something new on us, she says. We are always haranguing her. My mother is listing all the expenses on her fingers, of school trips, bake sales and no-uniform days, which though not mandatory come with a kind of social pressure and which, according to her, the school uses to extract money from the parents. Maybe the parents cannot afford to pay for a school trip, my mother says, and yet they must because of the rules of conformity. As soon as a bolt is corroded or the computer room needs new mousepads, the school invents a pretext to extract money, of which she is not made. You demand that we buy uniforms, and we buy uniforms, then you invent a day on which we send the children to school without their uniforms, the so-called no-uniform day. This is how my mother speaks, as if I am a representative upholding the logic of the school.

I cannot help feeling that something has changed in my relationship with Mrs Hanrahan who during the roll-call looks up and smiles at whoever is answering PRESENT but ever since my execution does not look up at me. I cannot be the only one who has noticed this awkwardness, where she stumbles over my name as if it is an obscene drawing someone has done in the roll-book. Is it because of the time I raised my hand in class and called out my mother's name and some people laughed, I am wondering. Now, I am raising my hand for questions I do not know the answer to, knowing that I will not be chosen. I am trying to talk about this with Rudy on our walk home from the school, but he has invited Colin Sweeney and the two of them are talking about Dungeons & Dragons. Why has Rudy invited a homosexual, I ask him loud enough that Colin will hear it, but there is only a kind of unnameable silence. As we cross the main road to our estate I am thinking that Mrs Hanrahan wishes to forget what happened in the assembly hall, for even though it was not her fault Mrs Tracy was depending on her, and though it was not my fault either it must be that I remind her of this perceived failure. I walk ahead and for the first time I do not say goodbye to Rudy.

At dinner, my mother is holding her head over her plate. She is mashing her food in a hostile manner. Now and then she mutters something under her breath. There is a sense that things are about to come to the surface and my brother is looking at me shaking his head with level-ten enchanted daggers in his eyes as if I am responsible for the darkening of the mood.

Do we understand what it means to work and study for a management exam and have to do the shopping a second time this week because of an extra person, she does not think so, no, we do not know what it is like to be harangued for money by the minions of the school. I want to explain to my mother that she does not have to pay for the tickets again, but I know to keep my eyes on the cauliflower.

There is no less disregard, says my mother, omitting the first part of her thought.

My brother and I are eating as fast as we can, but I think that I have never seen so much cauliflower in my life.

Why do I not ask my father to sign the permission slip, my mother says, as I rise with my plate.

When I leave the kitchen my mother is still holding her head and playing with her food.

As I am hurrying up the stairs I hear my mother's voice in the kitchen calling up to ask my father, ask your father to sign the permission slip.

We are watching television when my mother comes back from the kitchen. She tells me to choose a side. I choose the left wherein is revealed my second favourite flavour of yoghurt. She hands me a spoon and says that she will go to my execution but that she will not pay for new tickets, she is not made of money. She tells me to ask my brother if he wants to come and I fall asleep nestled in her side.

Sister Amanda has finished running through the procedure with me but I think that I would have liked to go over it again to make sure that I do not get anything wrong and that if I could I would ask her to please go over it all again one last time. I am concerned that it will be a repeat of the time the teacher asked me to bring her the blue crêpe paper and the yellow glitter for the Easter celebration display and instead I brought her the yellow crêpe paper and the blue glitter, which could not have been further from what she had asked for. What a humiliation this glitter-crêpe-paper mix-up turned out to be that to this day I cannot forget. I hope that the cone on my head will not fall off as it has done with other children in the past, that I will not make a funny face, for the eyes of the school will be on me, and some of the parents may want to record the execution for posterity.

Because of a long-running Dungeons & Dragons campaign at his friend Gerard's house, my brother was not able to come and watch me die last Monday. If it had been any other day, said my brother, he would definitely have been able to come. And so now that my death has been moved to Friday, I think that my brother will have no option but to come and watch me in my final moments. But as it turns out, thinking I would be dead, my brother has already planned on going to the birthday party of a girl on our estate. My brother makes an hourglass gesture with his hands and a thrusting motion with which it is impossible to argue.

I am looking at the permission slip on the sideboard in the hallway and I see that my mother has written her name down as attending but has not yet signed. Every day the school asks me if I have gotten the permission signed and every day I must make up an excuse why my mother has not signed the slip of paper. It will not be possible to enjoy the crackling of the Rice Krispies until my mother does this very simple thing. She is saying that she never agreed to sign the piece of paper despite the fact that I heard her say so last night in front of the television.

Though I am to be executed on Friday, I cannot help worrying about the long division test. It is possible, I tell myself on the way to school, that the teacher will simply forget about the long division test, but also there is very little evidence that our teacher would ever forget, since she has never forgotten a single test to this day, unlike Mrs Robinson who used to forget about tests all the time. There is no avoiding it. The long division test is inevitable.

I am telling Rudy about how my brother, his friend Gerard and I are at a crucial juncture in our Dungeons & Dragons campaign. Then Colin changes the subject to his own Dungeons & Dragons campaign. I tell him that Dungeons & Dragons is not a game for homosexuals. There is a silence and I apologise to Colin for my short temper but I am under a lot of stress due to the long division test that is coming up.

We are chanting our conjugations when Mr Curley shuffles into the classroom. He does not knock or say anything to our teacher who pretends that there is not this old man standing in one of the aisles. We must continue chanting this dreary song the same as before, as if there is no Mr Curly looking around like he has forgotten something. He is bending down at the linoleum floor and looking into the forest of chair legs and table legs and children's legs. We are doing the present continuous now and he is crawling around and I cannot help feeling that there is something I cannot name that is going on.

My best friend Rudy is explaining to me why he does not think he and his parents will be able to make it to the execution on Friday. I can only sympathise with my friend Rudy. This Friday, I tell him, is an especially inconvenient date as it is the opening of the French Film Festival. It is typical, Rudy, that of all the days the French Film Festival could have opened it had to be this Friday. Who knows when we will have a chance to see Alain Delon on a big screen again, I say, letting my arms fall to my sides with exasperation. But Rudy, it turns out, is not there. He is talking with Colin.

Examining the farewell card again, I find that the glitter has been applied to it willy-nilly. There is also crêpe paper on the card though it is barely worth mentioning because of how willy-nilly the application is. If it is worth saying anything about the crêpe paper on this farewell card it is how willy-nilly and uninspiring it is. It is hard not to see the imperfections of the card, the superfluous inclusion of the felt and the match sticks, glued or rather flung onto the card, weighing it down so that it is impossible to stand up and always flopping over like a pig's ear.

Behind the door to my mother's room, I hear crying. I open the door and find that my mother is sitting on the end of her bed, sobbing. I give my mother a hug, for I am not the only one under a lot of stress at the moment.

It is time to practise our French pronunciation, each of us repeating after Mrs Hanrahan who puts her head back and gurgles in the manner of the French. It is the most hilarious thing we have ever heard. Even Michelle, who is the shyest creature and is barely audible and buries her head in her arms, makes us laugh uncontrollably. There are tears rolling down our faces as it goes around the room, sounding more and more preposterous and less like the original every time. Now it is my turn to gurgle absurdly. Tears are rolling down my swollen face. I am ready to explode with laughter, but Mrs Hanrahan decides that we have had enough French for one day.

On the way to the school, I think that maybe I will step onto a bus and that instead of the school I will go to the beach, for it is the day of the dreaded long division test. There is a bus stop on the way to school where I am waiting with some other people who, like me, are looking for an escape. I have never skipped a day of school before. I do not know what I would do at the beach, where it will certainly be cold and windy, and what if I was seen by one of the parents and it was reported to Mrs Hanrahan and our principal Mrs Tracy. And so, in the end, I am unable to step onto this bus or the next.

The nib in my pencil has broken during the inevitable test and I must ask Anne-Sophie for her pencil sharpener, the embarrassing pink Clefairy pencil sharpener. Though it is sitting right next to me, it is not as simple as taking it, for Anne-Sophie has put her ruler down between us to divide our separate halves of the desk, there is no arguing with the three-sided non-slip aluminium ruler. And so I must whisper to Anne-Sophie in the hope of not being detected by our teacher. Anne-Sophie is pretending not to hear me. She will pretend not to hear me until I have called it by its full name, the pink Clefairy pencil sharpener. That is the rule. Every year I pray that I will be assigned to sit next to Rudy and every year our hopes are dashed.

I am trying to put the broken nib back into the wooden shaft of the pencil, like a tooth that has come loose in a dream. Anne-Sophie, I can see from the corner of my eye, is grimacing at my misfortune. Is it something about my essence that I cannot hold a pencil without the nib breaking again and again, I ask myself. I try to push the nib back in but it is like trying to smile with a wobbly tooth. What is wrong that my pencil keeps breaking and that I must sharpen it until all I have left is this, the tiniest nub of a pencil imaginable. Always, I think, I should stop sharpening this pencil. This time is the last time, I am thinking, the pencil is sharp enough. But then, as usual, because I feel somehow that a finer point is still possible, I perform what I tell myself is really the final twist this time. It is then, without fail, on this last turn of the pencil, just as I am about to stop, that the nib decides to break from the shaft of the pencil.

With the nib, I wish that my agonies would end, but instead they are compounded by the eraser which far from erasing merely smears what I have written. Have I been using an eraser all this time, I ask myself, or the rubber stopper of a chair leg; all over my work are these stains which cost me points on presentation. How is it that Anne-Sophie's eraser remains in such immaculate condition, I am thinking. She will never let me use her eraser for fear of soiling its white immaculacy, its clean edges and perfect corners. And because my hands, she says, are not clean enough to hold it. If it were not for the non-slip ruler separating my half of the desk from Anne-Sophie's, I think that I would take her eraser by force.

During our lunch break, I take a handful of the gravel and throw it at Colin Sweeney the homosexual's face, who of course begins to cry, and now Mrs Hanrahan, whom I barely recognise anymore, tells me I must stay in the schoolyard until it is time to go home.

I am throwing pebbles at the windows of the classroom. Mrs Hanrahan is trying to ignore me but eventually she is forced to come out and tells me to stop as if there was never anything between us, and I am starting to scrunch up into a crying face.

At the end of school, I am racing to put on my coat and bag to catch up with Rudy, but he and Colin Sweeney are running away from me and I do not think that I will catch up with them. I am calling for them to wait, for with the bag on my back and the school shoes it is almost impossible to run.

My mother is standing over me saying that she will do her best to be at my execution on Friday, though she cannot make any promises because of the French Film Festival and Alain Delon. I am lying on my back under the rug in the hall. It is important to my mother that I know the sacrifices she must make, but I have other things on my mind and I do not feel like arguing.

Because I am not answering my mother she asks my brother if he has seen me anywhere, where has your brother gone, even though it is obvious I am lying under the rug at her feet.

How about this, my mother is saying. Tonight I can stay up until 10 'clock.

My mother does not realise that I am done with speaking, that I have committed myself to silence and to lying still here under the rug in the hall, probably forever.

I can hear their whispering on the stairs and after a grumble my brother says reluctantly that he will help me with my D&D character.

I do not feel like speaking, I will lie still, covered by the rug.

My mother is sighing and lets her hands fall to her sides because of how difficult I am being. Because she has had enough, according to her, she turns and walks away, flip-flops slapping the soles of her feet.

Then, a few moments later, my mother returns. She says that though I have already had a last meal she has decided that exceptionally we will have my last meal a second time, but there will be no last meals after that.

It is difficult not to smile under the circumstances. Instead of the cauliflower to which I had resigned myself, we will have my beloved hoisin duck and egg-fried rice one more time. I am drying my face on my sleeve and trying to hide the smile from my mother, who is kissing me on the head.

Though I am to be executed on Friday, I cannot help feeling excited about the weekend. Probably I did better in the test than I first thought and I am looking forward to telling Rudy and Colin about my campaign. QUELLE PLAISIR DE VOUS AVOIR CONNU MON AMI it reads inside my farewell card in the immaculate handwriting for which Anne-Sophie is well known. Anne-Sophie is a friend of mine, I tell my mother. She is the smartest in our class.

Burrow

It's in the air and fog,
that quiet spongy sense
of trespassing where
I hadn't meant to go,
regardless of intent,
and landing foot-long
into a bog or creek or mire.
Earth sinking,
and the trees starting
to thin out.
I look for the lichen,
for the sickly ochre
mushroom rings
and wonder what
to think of these things.
Named by someone,
known by others—
careful footed
forest men who've
sunk here before me,
who pursue roots,
rabbits and other edible,
elusive figures.
They avoided
danger colours—
nothing bright or waxy,
sticking to the mud,
to earth shades,

eyes adept at singling out
the tawny wiry pelt from
the tawny wiry brush.
Breathing in the bracken scent,
swallowing primaeval rain,
they'd found a use for it all.
Now, not knowing poison
from pigment, not knowing
the truth of a berry—
still, I come to wallow,
to draw out juice,
and search for the hare.

Cait Phenix

Ghosts of Saint Francis

Alan McCormick

Saint Francis Psychiatric Hospital dominated the town where I grew up. The vast red-brick Victorian asylum stood in parkland, bordered by woods that massed towards the Downs, a long spine of hills separating us from Brighton and the sea beyond. It held the longest inner corridor in southern England, a third of a mile long, where shuffling patients picked up butts, and a blurred dread and melancholy tainted the walls nicotine yellow. A village retreat for the disturbed and fragile, with its own farm, laundry and chapel, where Gran and Mum would come to convalesce after discreet breakdowns and botched suicides.

In 1980 I applied to be a porter there in a year break between school and university. Dad tried to persuade me not to apply, as if Mum's depression were enough to cope with, and working with other mentally ill people would risk further contagion. In the patients' canteen I waited to be called for my interview. I took in the higgledy-piggledy arrangement of rickety chairs and tea-stained tables, ubiquitous pale blue plastic teacups, the rude clatter of metal trolleys, women in borrowed clothes, often too short and tight, men in gravy-stained suits with absurd high waistbands. An odd shriek amidst a slow melancholic drudge of repetition: confused conversations with no end and no beginning. I felt oddly calmed, listening, watching, distracted and sleepy in the familiar—I'd experienced it all before, already having visited Mum and Gran in asylums and discreet seaside convalescent homes—becoming so comfortable that I lost my grip, letting go my teacup and emptying its contents onto my lap. Trousers sodden and bottom sticking to the chair, I pulled myself up and attempted to dry myself in the patients' toilet, with its rank splatter over the bowl that I'd come to recognise as heavily medicated freeform shit.

Mrs Nettles came to collect me in her grey East German prison guard suit. In the interview she didn't mention the England-shaped damp patch on my crotch at first, but, after offering me the job, she advised me not to drink in the patients' canteen anymore.

'It's very loyal and patriotic, but you're one of us now,' she said.

I loved working there, trying my best to avoid being a voyeur, being witness at a freak show. I found myself instinctively empathising, taking it all in but also sometimes revelling in the otherness, the defiantly different.

I'd recently finished reading Ken Kesey's *One Flew over the Cuckoo's Nest*, and showed Mum a video of the film on her return from hospital after one of her nervous breakdowns, hoping she'd find some kind of kinship, familiarity, a home from home.

'Why did you show me that film?' she asked.

'Bloody well unbelievable!' Dad said.

Kesey's McMurphy was a wild, charismatic rebel, a con faking madness to stay out of prison. Harry was a patient who'd been imprisoned after fighting with a prostitute in Brighton and attacking the policeman who'd arrived to arrest him. In prison he'd babbled and hurled himself at the walls and was sectioned to Saint Francis. Like McMurphy, he arrived to the ward full of wild energy, joking and raving whilst handcuffed to a prison guard.

He was a sociopath who beguiled and wove spells. A tanned bear of a man with long blonde tousled hair, he burst through my flimsy defences back then. He ran barefoot, talked fast, harangued and freewheeled as if he were permanently drunk. Occasionally, he could be charming and funny, even thoughtful. I lent him books: *Cuckoo's Nest* (naturally), *On the Road* (trusting him with my prized original UK edition paperback), and *Keep the Aspidistra Flying*. Orwell's book was his favourite; he liked its subtle subversion of suburbia, the hidden humour appealing to his own disdain for the everyday and normal.

I witnessed his character change in an instant, starting with repetitive jibing of the nurses.

'A fucking mess, a wonderful fucking mess! Eh, Paddy, what do you think?'

'Less of the "fucking", Harry.'

'Never do much fucking, Paddy, you're right.'

'And less of the Paddy.'

'Right you are, Paddy.'

'Harry!'

'Paddywhack, Paddywhack, Paddy whacked a Paddy.'

'Last warning!'

Then suddenly he was running, roaring, and emptying a jug of water over the nurse. A shout for help from a crowd of cowering patients, and Harry was taken to the ground, four nurses on top of him.

'I'm the crazy guy here, and I'm supposed to be looked after, not oppressed. What a sorry state of affairs.' He caught me looking. 'Hey, Adam.' Harry never got my name right. 'What do you think? It's a fucking disgrace, is it not?'

A heavy knee to his chest and he went red in the face, struggling to breathe.

'My inhaler, get my inhaler!'

Before he left for prison again, he returned all the books I'd lent him, folded page marks neatly turned back.

'I'd like to have discussed them with you but my brain is frazzled. You know?'

I did know but I also knew not to tell him where I lived in case he came calling when he was released from prison.

Gordon was a retired bank manager on Kingston Ward. He sat on a big armchair, which he positioned to face out onto the grounds. He loved looking at the branches of a particular old oak tree and he'd sit staring at it for hours. I'd bring him a cup of tea—he preferred a cup with a saucer to a mug—and take the seat next to him. There was something relaxing in being by his quietness and stillness. Sometimes he'd ask about my life outside the hospital and offer advice.

'Keep living, son, and don't get depressed if you can help it.'

Often he'd read.

'The books in here aren't really my cup of tea though.'

I wasn't surprised. The library hadn't much beyond Steele, Archer, Cartland and Wilbur Smith. I gave him Graham Greene's *The Human Factor*, a perfect, sombre book. The next day he'd nearly finished it.

'I'll get it back to you as soon as it's done,' he said.

A couple of days later I was back on Kingston. Gordon's bed was bare. He'd slipped away from the nurses' attention and slit his wrists in the bathroom the night before. A nurse handed me back my book. There was a note inside.

'Thank you, it was very kind of you to lend me the book. I've always liked Graham Greene and I really enjoyed this one. All the best, Gordon.'

Suicide, a familiar chill, a curse running down Mum's family line; I shuddered when I saw the stripped mattress, I knew the form. 'As soon as it's done' he'd said, but I hadn't been listening carefully enough. Thankfully, the bathroom had already been cleaned, so I took a cup to his chair and sat for a while and looked out. The oak tree, quiet and unmoved against the shifting sky.

At thirteen, I'd watched out of my bedroom window as Gran's tiny body, hidden under a bright red blanket, was carried on a stretcher into a waiting ambulance. I'd found her unconscious in our spare bedroom. She had taken an overdose and was brought to hospital but I wasn't allowed to see her.

I did visit her later in a large Epsom asylum. The spartan isolation room along the hallway spooked me on the way to find her waiting in the dining room. Her worn bloodhound expression, drugs pulling down her features to reveal bloodshot, watery eyes, nicotine yellowing and roughening her skin in lines and crevices, a cigarette defiantly cupped in her mouth, a cup of tea shaking in her hand. She always had a carrier bag waiting for me full of fruit pastilles and Mars bars. We made each other laugh, me mimicking Frank Spencer and Brian Clough, her playfully supporting Arsenal against my team Chelsea, repeatedly shouting 'arse n' all' to all and sundry, releasing a wheezy cauldron of sound from deep inside her chest.

'Don't get too close,' she said, pointing at an old lady walking in circles by the door, wringing and tearing at her hands. Later, I had to squeeze past her to open the door. Her mouth was open wide as if she were screaming. Nothing came out, but I could sense this high frequency hum vibrating through her body. 'Is my son coming, is my son coming?' she pleaded. I could only shake my head and say, 'I don't know.' She pinched me hard on the arm and said, 'You do know, I know you do.'

After a few months of working at Saint Francis, I was joined there by my best friend, Mark. Our friendship had grown away from the rigid confines of the town's grammar school, and the mock liberation of sixth form, where if you weren't going round with a fixed grin all the time and having 'a fantastic experience' then there was something wrong with you. And they were right: there was something wrong with us.

I took every chance to blot out the all-too-real madness invading my family, and, together, we welcomed any distraction from the late teenage sadness suffocating us both. We liked to escape with our packs and sleeping bags onto the Sussex Downs. From the highest point of the Beacon, looking north, rows of flat fields, skirted by newly planted woodland, joined the grounds of Saint Francis. We usually walked east along the highest ridge towards Lewes or Newhaven and Seaford, long stretches of bumbling hills and shallow ravines, ancient copses and stony bridleways. We would talk excitedly, sharing our outsider angst, excitement and belief that books and music mattered more than almost anything else. We both loved Jack Kerouac, The Velvet Underground, JD Salinger, Hermann Hesse and Sylvia Plath. Mark aligned himself with teenage outsider narrators Holden Caulfield and Esther Greenwood—the latter a thinly veiled disguise for Sylvia Plath—a curl to his lips as he viewed life through their young, world-weary eyes.

Mark cut a fine figure in those days, a siren for both women and men with his tousled dark hair and delicate, poetic looks. Sometimes he was Keats and other times, in his tight red motorbike jacket, he was Jules, the charismatic young postman from the French film, *Diva*.

Mrs Nettles saved certain jobs for polite middle-class boys, and on weekdays Mark would often be sent to work as a theatre porter in the adjoining neurological hospital. Maybe I was harder to fathom and seen as more of a risk, as she kept me at Saint Francis. At weekends we had the chance to work together, driving the rickety hospital laundry van, with its wretched, stinking load of soiled bedding, the necessary distraction of a cigarette permanently in our mouths. Sometimes we took the van for a spin outside the grounds and rested up in a nearby field, chatting, sharing a joint, taking in the sun's rays climbing up over the Downs.

We liked to lose ourselves in other people's lives and stories whenever we could. One character's life particularly touched us. Biddy was born in 1900 and had been at Saint Francis since she was fifteen, when her father had deposited her at the gates for lewd behaviour: kissing a neighbour's boy. A farmer's daughter still, she got up at the crack of dawn and spent her days busy and bent over, a willing helper, fetching and carrying for the nurses and tending the less able patients. Mid-morning and mid-afternoon she'd settle into her chair with her own teacup and saucer.

'My cup, see, it's got a picture of the Queen, lovely.'

Proud, a quiet voice with no hint of rancour, apart from maybe a tinge when she talked about her father.

'I told him I only kissed the boy but his mind was made, and I told him not to bring me but he wouldn't listen. He had a temper, see.'

Biddy's eyes blinked out from tight skin creases, her pupils shiny and bulbous, damaged by the lack of light from prolonged incarceration.

'Love my tea, I do.'

Tipping the pot repeatedly into her cup and smiling. A smile of the contented; Zen and vacant.

We admired Biddy's spirit and enduring stoicism. Sometimes I also saw my gran in Biddy, and, in turn, a glimpse of how Mum could become, the shuffling slippers and institutionalised pallor of tranquillising medication. But in truth Mum and Gran were already defeated, finding ways to give up the ghost; Biddy had a spirit that sought to get away. On Sundays, she busied herself handing out hymns and prayer books for the patients' morning service. As the asylum organ groaned and struck up, she closed her eyes and her voice escaped wild and shrill, like a scalded cat let loose amongst the congregation.

Under the Downs, in the long shadow of Saint Francis Hospital, is a nunnery where Mark's friends and family met, a decade after we'd worked at Saint Francis, to commemorate his life and unexpected death. I gave a talk and the wind blew and chucked like a madman. The steeple wavered, and the building groaned and slammed, the choir's voices trilling and booming like banshees (Biddy surely joining in!) and hanging in the rafters, before dropping like mist amongst us, touching us with a sense of togetherness, otherness, in shared dismay at his life torn away.

Mark's body was never found after his last lone mountain hike in the foothills of Pakistan. When I think of him now I remember his weary smile and soft voice, and find myself laughing about the time we shared magic mushrooms under the Beacon.

All October I'd been picking them in the hospital farm's sheep fields. Other porters had shown me how to wipe and dry them with paper, how to make tea with them, how many to eat to make things tingle, how many to scramble the brain. Tingle was for the afternoon shift at work—I'd need maybe ten— so that the harsh lights along the hospital corridors would slowly blur into gorgeous pinks and purples, and the newly buffed floors would sparkle and glimmer like an ice rink on a star-filled night. The soles of my shoes sliding and skating along, my arms out wide, my mouth slipping into a wide, beatific smile when I met the patients.

I had a knapsack full from a recent mushroom harvest when I met Mark at Hassocks Station, close to his home. We shared them out on the long footpath out to the Downs, eating a small handful at a time. Within minutes the stomach cramps and swirling waves of nausea started, but we were on a mission and knew to ride it out. We waited and then took more, and by the time we climbed over a stile to Wolstonbury Hill, we were sweating, in the grip of a tumultuous tsunami, senses all churned up and at odds with each other, excitement beset with anxiety, struggling to keep a lid on the madness, the horizon moving like a seesaw, the soft Sussex Down ahead taking on the shrouded outline of an Anglo-Saxon burial mound.

I'd learned from experience that angst and sadness usually passed and so I trusted somehow that this derangement would pass too; I knew to breathe slower and let things happen. Time jumped forward and back, and then slowed, so that we seemed to be there a lifetime, with my gaze fixed on the top of the hill where sheep moved and shimmied against the clouds, marching one minute with iron masks ready for war, dancing in brown *cage-aux-folles* knee-stockings the next, the clouds behind massing, re-forming, the orange mouth of the sun grinning in between.

Rain seeped from the sky to caress my cheeks. I lay down and drank it in. Mark was near, moaning (or was it a cow in a nearby field?), crawling on all fours to examine a patch of grass, wearing a small brown felt hat, that, with his protruding black curls, made him look less like Keats and more like Chico Marx. Then I was Harpo, squeezing my imaginary horn, looking like a cherub, cheep, cheep, cheep, a wig of sheep wool, no judgement necessary… so that's why the sheep were marching: to cover my head.

Mark and I looked at each other and started laughing. Big teeth monkey laughs (that's where we originated from, then!), the sun erupting out of the clouds and the sky suddenly going Van Gogh blue.

'I'm going to be sick,' said Mark.

'No, you won't,' said I, the warmth of the sun calming, healing, making me talk as if I were Jesus. The thought of me as Jesus set us off laughing again. But I wanted the laughter to stop, for that bigger connected feeling to return, and then we were lying next to each other, long rays reaching down and baking the earth and our skin, everything chiming, the scattering clouds making patterns on our eyelids, the ancient past buried in the earth, revitalised and reaching out, new grass rising, a bird passing above, our breathing slow and in unison, all one, all one big united world. At that moment we were closer than ever, love pouring out for each other, for everyone, for everything.

Mum and Gran carried through with their threats and are long gone, and Saint Francis was turned into luxury flats soon after Mark died, but its memories linger, ghostly expressions at the windows infiltrating my thoughts and dreams.

Mark had a relationship with my sister and died when their son, Den, was eight. I've kept Den close ever since, unconsciously inculcating him into the spirit of my relationship with his father, taking him travelling and eating out from a young age (ticking off a list of thirty different ethnic restaurants on his visits to stay with me before he was sixteen), pulling him leftward and buying him music and books Mark and I had enjoyed. He's his own person, but sometimes I can see Mark clearly in him: the humane intelligence, the ever-present dry humour, the juxtaposition of steely independence and moments of vulnerability, a gentle, understated communication that cuts to the core. Den is thirty-six, three years older than Mark when he died. We're close friends, and it's he who recommends the restaurants, books and records now.

Somehow, I managed to keep a pictorial record of my trip with his father: shots taken from weird angles, sunlight bleaching out colours, hats endlessly swapped, our faces distorted and gurning, eyes smiling, so that the camera seemed like it was tripping with us. The pictures sit in their own album (how could they go with any others?) and when I look at them that feeling of trepidation overcome by a tidal wave of understanding and love still floods over me.

I recently stayed with Den and showed him one of the photos. It's a miraculous close-up of me and his father, a selfie before the term even existed: we've come down from the mushrooms and are sitting next to each other on the grass. We're both smiling, and there, behind us, is the blurred, outstretched outline of Saint Francis.

Call Centre

On my first day I heard something musical
crinkle its way across an unfenced field,

and typed out the smell of soap-drowned fish.
It shouldn't be like that, I say, though there's nothing

I can do to change it. The ones who call
don't know that. I'm essential, invisible. Maghaberry.

Magilligan. A farmer in Magherafelt
has destroyed evidence of negligence. A cow

is listed as male when it's not. I can't
change it. Is God like this—not wizard

but tinman summoning smoke from behind
a curtain, near crying at those who think him

greater than he is? So far-off they could be
ants. However they call, I answer. I follow

the script. I have learned to take notes
on how, across the blades of wind turbines,

a gull's wing bones splinter.

Tanvi Roberts

In Belfast City Centre A Woman Follows Me Down the Street, Barking Like a Dog

so I close my eyes and throw my head back,
like I'm tap dancing across Holywood
with two Ls. The stars unclench
their brightness. I think instead

of what I'll order when the restaurant door
opens and washes me with light: full-fat
mash and sausages crisp, salty,
so local you couldn't trace them. I bless

the cheer of Belfast waiters: their unconditional
praise of every choice, their unswerving
devotion to the sticky toffee. How they fill glasses
and pretend not to hear. My white friend

tells me it was random, leads me away
with talk of the new bridge to Belvoir.
The part of me that pays £2 for a kaccha
mango believes her. Past the window

new buses glide purple through streets
flashing with rain. But they are late, as they
always have been. When we walk home
I think of dogs and their secret language.

How one, passing another on the street,
will call out in a bark foreign and strange.
How impossible it is to know what they mean.

Tanvi Roberts

Fire Island

James Ward

It was a hot Sunday in July when I heard he was dead.

It was coming on evening, and I was pulled in for petrol at the pumps outside Rigney's and had the front windows of the mother's old Cortina rolled down with the closeness.

A shadow darkened the driver's side, and Pat Rigney's big hand tapped me on the elbow. 'Good man, young Kerrigan,' he said. 'Home to see the mother.'

'Well, Pat,' I said.

'You're doing it big beyond in New York,' he said.

I mustered a smile. 'Ah, you know yourself, Pat.'

'Sure, no better man,' he said, and he reached for the petrol pump handle: 'Will we fill her up?'

'Might as well,' I said.

'Your mother's out of the hospital anyway,' he said. 'How's the cratur?'

'Coming on, Pat,' I said.

'The aul' cancer's a hoor,' he said. 'Gives no fuck.'

I nudged the sunglasses down my nose and caught sight of my face in the wing mirror. In the ambered light my beard seemed almost red, giving me the look of some Viking marauder, and I thought about the first time I'd come home bearded from college and how the mother hadn't even let me out to Mass on account of what people might think.

The pump clicked to a finish. Pat Rigney put the pump handle back in its cradle and leaned an elbow on the roof of the car. He brought his face down to meet me.

'Jaysus,' he said, 'but isn't it horrid sad about young Quinlan?' He shook his head. 'Ah, but you're surely feeling it, gosson,' he said, 'and he a great buddy of your own.'

I stared into Pat Rigney's eyes. I found myself considering the bloodshot whites around his milky pupils. But all the same, I understood at once what he was telling me.

'Tadhg.' I heard myself say his name.

Pat Rigney retracted his face a little, and he made a gummy grimace.

'You hadn't got word?' he said.

I looked away through the windscreen to where a bleeding sun was coming to set above the lake, and I shook my head.

Pat Rigney sucked back the air. 'Arrah, no,' he said, 'but sure the news is fresh still. I only have it 'cause Christy Quinlan was in here not an hour ago to use the coin box. Ringing London to get news of Tadhg, he was. Wouldn't use the phone at home on account of the cost. That'd be him, like. You know yourself.'

Dense strands of sunlight crossed the tarmac in front of Rigney's shop. My sunglasses softened the evening glare, and I was glad now to have them hide my eyes.

In the days since I'd come home, I'd kept the sunglasses hidden under the driver's seat of the Cortina and only wore them when driving alone on the country roads, which spared the mother from grizzling over the offence that the unmanly wearing of sunglasses would surely cause to anyone who saw me.

The sunglasses were tan-tinted aviators and had come from a store on West 8th Street, and it seemed strange now that just a fortnight had passed since I'd picked them up, since Jeff and I went shopping ahead of a weekend at the beach. Jeff had been boyishly playful as we tried on sunglasses and appraised ourselves in the row of vintage mirrors. His vest top had riffed on the muscularity of his frame, which made me picture the proverbial bull in the china shop.

We paid for our sunglasses and caught a train for the coast and Fire Island.

At Ron Altman's beach house in The Pines, our friends gathered, a dozen or more of us, and we drank as night closed in over the ocean. The talk turned again to plague, deaths on two coasts, and funerals in the city. But soon we said less, and we laughed less, and lastly, we listened as Ron's sage voice came to scratch with warning, to pitch to something like pleading.

Jeff rose then and went to the ocean's edge. I followed but stopped at a distance and sat on the sand, and I watched as he cast his clothes aside and waded knee-high into the black, lapping water.

Jeff turned his face back to me, and he smiled. Then he was gone beneath the dark swell, and Tadhg had taken his place. Tadhg of a summer's evening, when he and I would come from football training and alone together in the Cortina, we'd park up on the far side of the lake, and he'd be first out always and into the bright Shannon water.

I knew then, on the dark beach on Fire Island, that I was going home. Almost three years in New York and I hadn't once been home. But the mother wanted to see me now. It would be a comfort to her, the family said.

The mother said I should go over to Quinlan's place and sympathise straight away. She said I should go and press my help on Tadhg's brother Christy. I shouldn't delay, she said, what with the whole country knowing I was home, and poor Tadhg being so great with me always.

It's too late now, I told the mother. I'll go over to Quinlan's first thing.

I went to bed, but sleep wouldn't come. I lay awake until I heard the cows coming in for milking. I got up, made coffee, and drank it sitting at the kitchen table. I decided then to walk over the fields to Quinlan's farm.

I set out across the shorn meadow, and the land rose before me. From the brow of the hill, I saw the lie of the lake, low and silver, and on the nearshore, the spread of the cemetery beneath speckled monastery walls.

And there, just beyond, lay Quinlan's farm.

The sunlight glinted off the corrugated sheds in the farmyard and the sash windows of the house where Tadhg was reared. The yard was empty and silent but for the hollow creak of sheet metal in the breeze.

I crossed the yard to make for the house. Ahead of me, Pat Rigney was standing by the open back door, his ear cocked like a dog listening to the wind. The sounds of raised voices were coming from inside.

Pat Rigney turned his head and clocked me. Then he spun and took the few steps to the yard gate and out onto the lane.

The lane was scarcely wider than a car, and the only approach to Quinlan's place by road. The tarmac pocked with potholes, the lane ran for a mile or more from the village junction to a dead end at the lakeshore.

Pat Rigney beckoned for me to follow him. Away from the house, he turned to me.

'For shame,' he said, 'but aren't they only fighting adin.'

'Who's fighting, Pat?' I asked.

'Arrah, a clatter of the Quinlans,' he said. 'Christy and Mick and Colm, and the eldest wan, Mary, that's married in Longford. They can't agree on who'll bury Tadhg. Who'll foot the bill, like.'

'No way, Pat,' I said.

'Dirty looking eejits!' he said. 'And Tadhg a medical man. Sure, wouldn't a doctor have a few bob to bury himself?'

'No doubt,' I said.

'But isn't the bold Christy adin barking,' he said. 'Says he can't bury his brother on account of being married now and building the new bungalow.'

Pat Rigney pointed along the lane to where a bungalow stood on a raised site. I pictured the likely views of the lake from the bungalow's front rooms.

'It's Christy's woman's paying for that house,' he said, and he winked. 'Sure, isn't she a teacher below in the National School in Kill.'

He began to move away. 'Here,' he said, 'will you take a lift?'

'You're alright, Pat,' I said. 'I'll go down as far as the lake.'

I watched Pat Rigney walk away, and the worn-hipped motion of his uneven gait. He hadn't driven into Quinlan's yard. His HiAce, I saw, was parked up the lane, out of earshot, in the gateway to a field.

I turned and saw a young woman coming out from the bungalow and onto the lane. She had the 'Shy Di' hairstyle that was in fashion. A Jack Russell Terrier trotted at her heels. She didn't turn in my direction but went away along the lane towards the lake.

I took my time going down the lane. When I reached the lake, the terrier was rutting among stones on the shore. The woman was standing nearby, looking out at the water. But she turned then and saw me, and she smiled, and when I came close, she opened her arms and embraced me.

I hadn't once been held by another since I'd left New York, and I felt myself slipping towards helplessness in her arms.

After a moment, she pulled away and looked up at me. She had large eyes which were dappled hazel, and I thought about what Pat Rigney had said, and about the National School in Kill, and I searched her gaze for that old teacherly malice.

But she smiled softly. She was older than me, into her thirties, and had a dewy, country prettiness that was already coarsening into something else.

She put her hand to her belly, and beneath the loose fall of her cotton shirt, she cupped the curve of a bump.

'I didn't realise,' I said. 'Congratulations. When are you due?'

She laughed. 'You're all right,' she said. 'The second week of September. Please God.'

'Is it your first?' I asked.

She nodded. 'I'm not long married,' she said.

I smiled and looked over her shoulder and out across the lake.

'But don't you know me, Dermot?' she asked. 'I'm Sarah Brady. Well, I'm Quinlan now. Christy Quinlan's wife. But I was at school with your sister Ruth. We were boarders together at Saint Dymphna's. I was always very fond of Ruth. She was gas! How is she?'

'She's married in Melbourne,' I said.

'She went far enough,' said Sarah.

'She did,' I said.

Sarah turned to check on the little dog. He had moved away along the shore, his snout to the ground, towards the cemetery and the ruined monastery which stood above the lake. The morning sun had bleached the monastery walls, the chapels and the towers, and the Celtic crosses over the graves.

I saw the monastery now with a stranger's eye. It stood as a citadel amid the coarse grasses of the fields. It was something transcendent in the mirroring waters of the lake.

Sarah watched me.

'Did you know that the monastery ground was once an island?' she asked.

'I think I remember that from national school,' I said.

'Part of the lake silted up and joined the island to the mainland,' she said. 'But an old name for the area around here is Inishtin.'

'Inishtin,' I said. 'Fire Island.'

Sarah nodded. And I glimpsed the measured teacher her pupils must have known.

'Some say the name derives from the fire of faith that brought the first monks here,' she said. 'Those monks could hardly have been more than boys, but they saw God in the beauty of this place. Or maybe the place saw the beauty in them. I like to think they're here still in the clay of the island.'

Then Sarah turned her face towards the water, and she said, 'Tadhg talked about those monks during his last weeks. He told me he was looking forward to resting here among them. He made me promise to scatter his ashes on the lake beneath the monastery.'

'You knew,' I said. 'You knew Tadhg was sick. But the rest of the Quinlans knew nothing.'

Sarah turned back, and she looked me in the eye. 'Tadhg was on duty at the hospital when he collapsed,' she said. 'He never regained consciousness. It was a brain haemorrhage. A blameless thing in one so young. That's all the family need to know. It's all they want to know.'

I hesitated for a moment, but then I reached out and put my arm around her. She came close again and pressed her cheek against my shoulder.

When next she spoke, Sarah's voice was scarcely more than a whisper. 'He used to talk about you, Dermot,' she said. 'Towards the end, Tadhg talked about you every day.'

My Name is Raven, and I am 12 Years Old

Margaret Gillies

3

I had a dream once. I saw a person in a hood with no face. I woke up. He was still there, standing at the end of my bed. I couldn't move. There was roaring in my ears. It was so loud I thought I'd lose my hearing. Then I had tinnitus, not calming post-gig tinnitus, hellish tinnitus, like the kind soldiers hear that makes their heads explode and robs them of silence and every other sound, the kind that makes some people kill themselves. The hooded figure faded away after about 30 seconds. I went downstairs for a glass of water. I was thinking of death. I drank my water. I went back to bed. None of this made any sense to me until 53 minutes 8 hours and 17 days later.

4

Nitor used to live with his older brother Bello on my housing estate. My own older brother Huey used to live in the back of Bello's SEAT Ronda. The SEAT Ronda was battered, navy and uninsured. Callum Ryan once rode his bike off the roof of his house and landed on it. The bike went through the windscreen and Callum was in hospital for nearly three weeks afterwards. I knew Bello. He was Huey's friend. Was. Not anymore.

8

I remember when once I accidentally made eye contact with Nitor. I was looking out of my bedroom window, which is on the first floor. He was walking past my house on the other side of the road. He looked up. I looked away, and seconds later I heard stones bouncing off the glass. I remember this well because Mr Parry from school was driving past the estate on his way to a funeral, saw what Nitor was doing and phoned the police. Nitor was still there, hurling stones at our house right up to the very second the Hyundai Sonata with two police officers in it was pulling into the drive. They took Nitor away. After that I finished the Radical Train level in *Sonic 06* on the Xbox. I saw Mr Parry in school approximately 12 minutes 4 hours and 2 days following this incident. We were walking past each other in the corridor. Mr Parry said hello. He didn't say anything else.

6.1

39 minutes 3 hours and 15 days ago I went to Stockport with Cairbre and a few others. Curled up in the boot of his Toyota Aristo wasn't very nice, especially as we were pulled over by the police twice during the journey. I was concerned at one point that one of the coppers was going to walk around the car, swing open the boot and find me looking back at him, but he didn't.

Apart from that, we all made it to Stockport without much incident. Cairbre parked the car in a multi-storey and we all piled out. I felt like I was stepping out of a grave as I climbed out of the boot. I threw up against the wall while Cairbre and the others argued about who had what credit card and where we were going to go for lunch.

1

It's all coming back to me now. My brother Huey—and I can barely picture his face—had dated this girl, Thalassa, for a while. That's how I'd became friendly with Cairbre. That's what I believe anyway. Or what I think. Cairbre was her brother. They'd lived in Stockport before. I remember Thalassa. Only vaguely. I remember the first time I'd met her. I'd come into Huey's room because he'd asked for a lighter and Thalassa was there. Huey's room was misty and smelt of McDonalds, cigarettes and changing room. Thalassa had long, orangey hair with curls. I don't know if she'd put them in with curlers or not. She had foundation on that looked more orange than skin-colour and wore dungarees that looked a bit stupid. Huey had asked me how my day was. I'd told him about what had happened with Mrs Harding and Kelly Stewart at lunch time and Thalassa had laughed like an excited cat and said to Huey that I was fucking hilarious. Then she'd asked Huey if I was good at maths like Sheldon or Rain Man and Huey had laughed in that way he did, which wasn't really a laugh at all but a kind of spluttering noise he did when he was smiling, and he said to Thalassa that I was a complete weapon. Then they'd started talking to each other and not to me. So I'd walked away.

9.1

I feel sad when I think about Huey. I hated him sometimes. I hated him a lot of the time. I feel sad when I think about Thalassa which is even stranger. There is a pain in my chest. My arm is tingling. I feel like I'm floating. I'm concerned about this even though it is statistically unlikely for me to have a heart attack at my age. I'm falling asleep but I'm not quite sleeping and my brain is doing this thing it does when I'm nearly asleep but not quite sleeping where it imagines shapes that get bigger and smaller and I feel like I'm getting bigger and smaller myself but I'm not.

6.2

While we were in Stockport, I could tell people were eyeing us in the streets, wondering what we were all up to. We walked past shops that were playing music from speakers so loudly the songs were just noise. It was strange because I'd never seen Cairbre look so happy. Conrad was giving Red a piggy-back and the rest of us were laughing at them, but Cairbre was just smiling. He was so calm, the cigarette that was hanging from the side of his mouth hung there for several hours. He was at peace. I realise that now.

We hung round in Mill Lane cemetery for a bit. When he was leaning against his favourite headstone, Cairbre shoved his fist into his jacket pocket and then pushed an old BlackBerry into the palm of my hand. I asked him why he was giving me his old phone. He just smiled weakly and lit up another cigarette.

We went to the shopping centre. Alvah bought a can of Sprite. Conrad bought three family-sized bags of sweets. Cairbre bought a bracelet for Thalassa. I bought myself a new lighter. I had a strange feeling someone was following me. I dismissed it.

9.2

My chest is hurting. I can hear a song playing in the background. I think it's 'Jealous Guy' by John Lennon. I don't know if I'm actually hearing it or if it's playing in my head. I'm breathing in water or maybe it's gas. I'm blind. I don't know I don't know I don't know

6.3

While we were on our way back to the car park, Red said something about Thalassa and Bello that he found very funny. He laughed a bit too long and a bit too loud. Cairbre didn't find it very funny. He punched Red in the face. The blood spatter on the pavement looked like a grim pointillism artwork. Alvah pulled Red away. Conrad and I grabbed the back of Cairbre's jacket. I wasn't looking around, but I knew people were staring. Cairbre was shouting things at Red and flailing his arms about. Red was shouting back. It wasn't fair. Cairbre had just been to visit his mother. It was hard to keep holding on to him. He broke free from our grip. He stormed away across the road, right in front of a silver Citroën Axel that came so close to killing him it almost did. The noise of the horn was so loud I felt sick. And then Cairbre punched the bonnet of the car with a loud slamming noise. He ran. So Alvah and I ran after him. Red stayed where he was. He was shouting after us that we could all get fucked. The driver opened the door of the Citroën and hollered after us as well. He asked what the fuck that was about and that he had a good mind to call the police on us for damaging his car, even though I didn't think it was that damaged.

5

Nothing that happens in the world ever really makes any sense. I also know lots of people who don't make sense. Like Angus Rafferty in the year above me, who spits in my direction whenever I walk past him in the corridor and finds people dropping things by accident really funny or Logan McKenna who ties his short hair into a tiny ponytail and thinks it looks good. I wish they were dead. And Mr Parry too. Fuck Mr Parry. I overheard him in the corridor one time talking to Mrs Reed about Cairbre after he'd been sent home for calling her a word when she'd told him off for having a lip piercing. Mrs Reed said he'd amount to nothing in the world and Mr Parry had nodded because Mr Parry is stupid.

6.4

We caught up with Cairbre. He was breathing heavily. We went back into the multi-storey and into the car. We left Red behind. We decided he could catch the bus. I sat with the others this time. I wished I'd gone back into the boot. Nobody was talking. Cairbre was driving. He was still angry. He beeped a car in front of him when he thought they were moving too slowly and went over the speed limit six times.

7.1

13 minutes and 10 hours later I decided I wanted to go to Cairbre's house to give his BlackBerry back to him. Bello's SEAT Ronda and my brother Huey would both go missing that night, but I wasn't to know that yet. I don't know why I wanted to give Cairbre his phone back. I suppose I thought he might have regretted giving it to me.

2

Oh shit. That SEAT.

Why did Mum have to throw Huey out of the house?

I know he hit me and I hated that. That was bad.

But it didn't have to be the last straw.

I was annoying him.

I regret many things.

Oh Thalassa. Why did you have to go? I'm crying now.

7.2

When I was on the road to where his house was, I could see there was a Vauxhall Astra police car parked next to his dad's silver Citroën C5 in the driveway and a Fiat Ducato ambulance with the back doors open parked on the pavement at an angle of approximately 10 degrees. The house was a mint green bungalow. The sky was white. It was drizzling. The damp concrete made the air smell of playground and memories. There was a bus shelter a few yards away from the house with an advertisement at the side. The ad was of scarecrows wearing brightly coloured clothes in a field. The glass over the ad was spotted with raindrops so the scarecrows looked like they were crying. The ad said:

You'll be 10% better off at Asda. Let's go disco.

As I got closer to the house I could hear people shouting inside. After I knocked on the door, a policeman opened it. He said that now really wasn't a good time. I heard Cairbre's dad inside. Screaming who the fuck was that.

When I was walking out of the gate, I looked up and saw a person who had travelled with us to Stockport the day before. Nobody had invited him and yet he'd been there. He still had a black hood pulled over his head. I didn't know who it was. I didn't know his name. I had never in my life seen his face. He suddenly became twenty feet tall in front of my eyes. His black cloak stretched backwards into forever and billowed gently behind him. The sky turned black. I knew somehow he would follow me forever.

9.3

Huey. Huey. Huey. I miss him. Where is he? I am sleeping now, I think. I see him. Huey. He smells of smoke and a cheap dodgy aftershave. He is on the phone, slamming the door, shouting at Mum, being an idiot. He is by my side when we're walking through Primark and there's women with buggies all round us and older kids pushing people around. There is so much going on I can't see or hear anything. Huey's hand is on my shoulder. It stays on my shoulder. Not holding too tightly but not letting go either. I'm not looking at him, but I know he is there.

Bello.
Bello.
Bello.
Why doesn't someone
just
kill him?

I went home and watched television.

No Name

The river has no name
starts from a trickle
high up in the mountain
this mountain with no name

looks down over the valley
valley with no name
fish with no name carried
on a bed reaching out to sea

to an ocean with no name
caresses land with no name
from pole to pole

birds fly over sea and land
birds with no name
look down on man with no name.

Bernadette Gallagher

Black Cat Prowling on a Harbour Wall

Lauren Mackenzie

Every day around four I watch the fishermen return, their painted boats panting like thirsty dogs. I will tell Joe this. Painted boats. Panting. And he will say, Alliteration. Very good. Very good. On the quarter hour, the ferry gives up its passengers, then grumbles and fumes as it reverses out. I will say, Even the boats find it hard to leave. Yes, he will say, it's almost impossible.

I sit at my table in the corner of Niko's terrace where I can see everyone coming and going. The villagers ignore me. The tourists don't know what to make of me. I don't look Greek, but neither do I look like them, all pale and soft from long winters inside. The tourists give me hives; there are more tourists now than the island can bear.

It's the youngsters, yellowed paperbacks in hand, that I wait for. They plant their two feet on the island, scan the harbour, and grin like maniacs when they spot Niko's Bar and the orange tiles of the church tower behind. Look. The stopped clock. The half door. The hipped ridge. The diving rock. Ohmygodlook. *That* is cerulean blue. Some stop in front of Niko's and scan the harbour wall, waiting for the black cat to prowl just as he had in the poem they'd memorised for their final exams. The cat's been dead ten years, but I don't tell them that. I say, Sit here, wait, he'll come eventually, hungry. Always hungry.

I prefer the young men.

If they are smokers, I look for a light. If it is windy, I let my hat fly. Sometimes, all I need to do is smile and they come to me. Sit. Sit, I say. Take some shade while you take in the view, smoke your cigarette, rest your weary legs. Have some water. So sweet of you to return my hat. It may be a ratty ruin like me, but it would break my heart to lose it. There is a story for the hat. A story for the brass zippo I use to light their cigarettes. A story about the bar and why Niko is no longer talking to me. These are people who like a story, who can work the metaphors.

Richard Blake didn't smoke. Didn't see my hat fly away. I saw him look at the view and look back at me several times. I pointed at the hat, and eventually he brought it to me. He was slow, plump, his hair dull brown and silky. His face, shiny with heat, was as round and pure as a baby's. I feared he was going to make me do all the work.

Thank you. How kind. I held my hand out for him to shake. Anna.

Richard.

His hand, limp and damp, didn't surprise me. Joe always said no matter where we run to, there's no escaping ourselves.

You look like a writer, I said. Are you a writer?

No. No. Richard's gaze immediately dropped, cutting short what I imagined was a further denial of any ability or ambition. They all did it, they all lied. Deep down they believed they were geniuses answering the call.

I dabble, he said.

Very good. We need more writers in this world. Is it poetry or prose?

Poetry, he whispered.

I leaned in. Wonderful! What a coincidence. My partner writes poetry.

I know, he said.

I knew he knew. I wear my long hair the same way I always have, same as in the black and white photo on the cover of *Ghost Apple – Collected Works*. London, 1998. A single, long plait down my back, once bleached white by the sun, now white with age. There's very little difference in it.

Are you hungry? I asked.

Richard stopped to think. He looked at the sea for the answer. And to the clouds. Then to his sandaled feet.

I was sick on the boat. I haven't eaten since yesterday.

Sit, I told him.

I called for Niko, ordered souvlaki and wine. Niko brought the meat, bread, and a carafe, poured two glasses. I had a piece of bread in my hand, had barely touched it to my lips when I saw the boy place the skewer down, stripped clean, his mouth shiny with grease. The grilled red peppers on the side, untouched.

I love a man with appetites, I told him. More? He dipped his head. Niko brought another plate of souvlaki, and took the first plate, peppers and all, away with him. I made myself smile. Richard got to work. Sated, he leaned back in his chair. Again, he left the sweet red peppers. I could taste their smoky saltiness. My dry bread longed for them, needed the oil's basting. By now my new young friends would usually ask if I wasn't getting something for myself? I would say, I'm sorry, that's so rude of me to leave you eating on your own, and I would order my kokkinisto and another carafe of wine.

Have you visited Greece before?

No.

This was the first and only word he'd uttered since the food arrived. He was better at answering questions. He lived in Dublin. Graduated a year ago. English. First Class Honours. Worked in a phone shop. He was considering moving to Berlin, somewhere more affordable where he might be able to work little and write more. When he said his mother was on her own, worked in a supermarket, I excused myself and headed for the toilet.

Niko was smoking in the kitchen, muttering to himself. I thought I could slip out the back door without being seen but he moved quickly, took my upper arm in his meaty fist.

Niko! You're hurting me.

Anna. Anna. Where you go? You leave money? He peered around the corner, checking Richard was still at the table.

Niko, this is not kind.

He squeezed harder. Strong as he ever was. I leaned into him, let my breast brush against his hand.

Please. I only came back to ask you for my kokkinisto.

Will you pay?

He will pay. He is my friend.

Niko gave me that look. Filthy swine. He released his fingers, leaving a red outline around my arm.

You are a good man, Niko.

Niko returned to the kitchen and clattered among the pots to remind me of the power still left in him.

Richard had finished all the bread and all the wine. He wanted to meet Mister Gallagher.

Of course, but I'm afraid he's not well.

The boy's expression appeared to melt. How is he not well?

There's madness in this kind of love. It used to frighten Joe; he knew it was blind and deaf and had nothing at all to do with him. I took the boy's hand in mine. Ah pet, it's the flu. Just the flu. It's left Joe completely wrung out. A shell of a man.

I must see him. He's why I came.

You and everyone else. Did you not see the queue?

Richard glanced behind him.

He was simply too much, this boy. My laughter made him bristle.

A poor joke, I'm sorry. It's just everyone wants a piece of him. He's been picked clean. Picked clean. Skin and bones.

The boy looked askance at me, as if I was suggesting he was like all the others, which of course he was. Niko was taking far too long with my kokkinisto.

What can I do to see him? I leave at four tomorrow.

Niko's wife arrived, flip flops slapping, fat little boys in tow. She stopped to shoot me daggers then headed into the kitchen, yelling. I was not going to get my kokkinisto today. I sat my hat upon my head and took my leave.

Adio!

Richard's mouth fell open like a carnival clown's.

I hurried past the church and up the steep, cobbled hill. At the edge of the village, Lexi's tomatoes hung fat and heavy in his yard, trailing in the dirt. I leaned over his wooden fence and plucked two. They filled each hand, still warm with sun. Obscenities erupted from the cottage. So kind, I shouted, thank you! At the top of the hill, well beyond the cobbles, I stopped to catch my breath. That hill was getting steeper by the day. Goat shit littered the track to our cottage. One day I will catch one, cut its throat and roast it over an open fire.

Joe was at his desk under the window, a finger of sunlight left to illuminate his crossword, his pencil dulled by the crossings out. Every day he woke and sat at the desk. Three hours. Then food and a nap. Another two hours in the afternoon. When the sun went down, he would stop. Our home, once a shelter for shepherds, was built into the side of the mountain to stay cool. One door, one window. Joe had done marvellous things with it: a stove and chimney, a rainwater tank with a tap. I leaned in close and rested my cheek next to his.

Seven across. 'Hydra'. Many-headed beast.

He howled with outrage. Every time. It still amuses me.

I sliced the tomatoes, chopped herbs I'd foraged along the path, and crumbled the last of Niko's crusts into a bowl. When I heard a squeal, then a slap of skin, I knew Richard was close. It had been years since any villagers had climbed the hill, which was why I never closed the door behind me.

Richard's face was a pink balloon and his shirt, framed by backpack straps, stuck to his girlish chest. He squinted at me from the doorway. What's biting me? Is it ants? Little bastards. Sorry.

I stayed in the cool of the doorway and waited for him to catch his breath. He shaded his eyes as he looked inside. Wrinkled his nose. Rude.

Does he live here?

No.

Joe called out, Anna? Who's at the door?

Nobody, I told him.

The boy raised his eyebrows at that. Arrogant pup.

Is that Mister Gallagher?

He's working. Come back tomorrow.

When?

If you have your book, I can get him to sign it?

No, I—

As I moved to close the door, Richard jammed his foot against it.

You didn't pay, he said.

What he expected me to say to that, I had no idea. I didn't eat anything.

I mean when you ordered for me, I thought, I assumed you were paying. And he brought out a dish for you, Niko, he said it was for you, that you ordered it. He wanted to charge me for it even though I didn't ask for it. The boy wheezed. The hill and speaking so many words had taken all the air from him. I know I shouldn't have assumed anything, he said.

Did you enjoy your meal?

That confused him. I was hungry, he said.

Niko's is Joe's favourite place, I told him. He often writes there in the morning before it gets hot. He says the coffee has balls.

The boy cocked his head and considered this. He seemed to take some comfort from the thought.

He took all the money I had. He said this without rancour.

Sounds like the beginning of a story, I said. Go now. Follow the adventure. Let the cards fall where they may. That is the writer's life.

Joe peeked over my shoulder. Who's this?

The boy, who had been wearing the face of a lost child, suddenly pulled himself to attention and gave Joe a smile to launch a thousand ships.

I am Richard Blake, sir, and stuck his hand out. Forthright. Friendly.

I did not like Richard Blake.

Joe's eyes passed right over Richard and came back to me. Anna, what is there to eat?

The boy said his own name again, louder, sharper, as if we should know who he was. I am. Richard. Blake. His right hand hovered in the air, unloved. My mother's name was Rebecca Blake. Is. IS. She's still. Here. In Dublin. Alive. Well.

This time I didn't let Richard Blake know I was shutting the door on him.

Fuck you, Joe. Another one?

Joe stood at the table, spooning tomato salad straight into his mouth. There was a time he would have set the table outside under the shade of the bougainvillea and scattered cerise petals over an embroidered tablecloth.

Rebecca Blake? Any bells, Joe? A woman in Dublin?

There are a lot of women in Dublin, he said. Tomato seeds peppered his beard. His boxers gaped above his brown, scabrous legs.

Richard Blake knocked at the door.

Could you not have deposited your seed in a rich girl, Joe? It would've made life so much easier.

Knock. Knock. Knock.

Joe opened the door before I could stop him.

Fuck off, yelled Joe. But this time the boy was ready. He held a bottle of duty-free vodka. Hello there, said Joe as he took the bottle and let him in. Anna, look, we have a visitor. This is—

Richard Blake, said Richard, without complaint.

I couldn't be sure if Joe was failing to remember Richard Blake's first attempt to ingratiate himself. Or whether this was an amusing play for all of us. Richard Blake asked for tonic for his vodka, then settled for ice before he understood we had no fridge. The village's power didn't make it this far up the hill.

We prefer candlelight, I told him. It is a little darker than usual but only because I haven't had a chance to whitewash the walls.

I lit the candles. Candlelight flattered Richard Blake's bone structure. And there, underneath his beans-on-toast face, I caught a glimpse of Joe's high cheekbones and sharp chin. I had to turn away, my heart. My heart.

Joe helped himself to another shot and offered the salad to Richard Blake in exchange.

I ate already. Is that mould? On the bread? There was an edge of panic in Richard's voice.

It's herbs, I said. Joe downed his third or fourth shot. I prised the bottle from his hands and supped.

So, Richard Blake, I said. Tell us about your mother, Rebecca Blake. Was she very pretty?

Rebecca Blake saw Joe read in Dublin on a wet Wednesday night in a bookshop, the one in the city centre with the crooked stairs. I knew it well. In the eighties we were there every Sunday afternoon, reading, or more often, listening to others read. This was 1998. She lived in a basement flat near the Phoenix Park.

Joe didn't even pretend to remember. He brandished the empty vodka bottle. D'you have any more, Richard?

The boy said no.

This won't do at all, at all, said Joe and darted out the door. Richard Blake looked at me as if awaiting instructions. Go, I said. GO! He ran after Joe and I ran after him, but Joe was already at the bottom of the hill, as light and nimble as his goat friends. Richard Blake inched his way down in many tiny steps. I yelled for Niko. Last time Joe got out, he drank from Dimitri's kerosene lamp.

Niko grabbed Joe as he turned the corner, swung him into the bar and put him in a chair. Joe greeted him as if he'd made a reservation. It'll be three tonight, Nikolaos. Richard and I fell into the chairs beside Joe. He demanded wine. There was no point in my objecting: no one ever said no to Joe. With a glass of yellow house wine in front of him, and the promise of more to come, Joe relaxed into his charming old self. His voice boomed up and down the quay, his accent verging on song, fuelled by vodka and a childlike excitement at his escape. Tourists slowed outside the bar, eavesdropping, certain he must be someone. Some wandered in, said hello, others hung back, waiting for a clue. Niko steered them all to a table.

Joe fully committed to whomever he was talking to. Under his light, people sat up straighter, imagined themselves erudite and astute. It was no different for Richard Blake. He fell in love, fast and sure. I think you're a genius, said Richard Blake.

Joe exhaled slowly as he always did at compliments, a gesture that melded grandiosity and humility, as if to say, that's quite a claim, but who am I to question your judgement?

I excused myself.

A benign neglect, combined with years of smoke, sea salt, and piss, had turned the walls of Niko's toilet verdigris. The effort it took to avoid touching the walls while squatting was nothing compared to avoiding the mottled mirror over the sink. The island was not kind to us northerners; the endless sun made us coarse and left us blind. We drank and danced and fucked ourselves stupid. Like infants who learn to either walk or talk, never the two at once, our minds shrivelled like nuts in their shells. There was no joy for me in the mirror.

I was so very tired.

I could hear Niko out on the terrace, bantering with the tourists. On the counter in the kitchen, I found the bowl of kokkinisto, cold with orange fat solidifying on the edges. It didn't matter. The meat melted in my mouth. The slow-roasted tomato yielded like a velvet pillow. Niko hadn't a clue about love, but he was tender with food. An old tabby watched from the open window, a progeny of the black cat, living off fish guts in exchange for keeping the rats at bay. I lifted the empty bowl to the window ledge. She dipped her head and licked it clean, winding her tail around my hand in thanks. Such grace.

No more, no more, roared Niko. Joe squared up to him, fists forward, but Niko planted his feet and stood tall, a wondrous colossus of a man, Joe a blade of grass next to him.

The boy helped me push and pull Joe back up the hill to the cottage. We lit the candles and watched as Joe tore into every cupboard, reached into every nook looking for more drink. He opened the filing boxes, scattered papers and notebooks. He tipped up Richard's backpack and rooted around. And when he couldn't find anything, Joe roared at me. I must've taken it, his treasure. I'd leached him dry. Stolen his joy. He had a sacred duty to create. Who was I to deny him anything?

The boy looked on, his back to the door, no expression on his pale moon of a face.

Who am I, Joe? I asked him. I'll find the bottle if you can tell me.

Joe used to joke to others he found me in the bog, a lonely, cold thing until he gifted me the sun. And I would laugh because it was true.

Joe stared at me. As blank as a page. Then he hit me.

I hit him back.

With surprising speed, Richard Blake planted himself between us. I underestimated him. Joe fell back on the bed in a heap of bones and faded cotton and was asleep in seconds. Richard Blake asked if I was all right. I was, in the way I was always all right. We crawled on our hands and knees to gather the notebooks, the papers, years and years of them. When Richard Blake came across a scribbled poem or line he recognised, he sunk back on his haunches and sighed.

You should sell the notebooks, he said. People would pay a fortune.

I felt my teeth grind.

Something's eating them. He held up a notebook with a missing corner.

Mice. Book lice. Whatever you fancy yourself.

The boy leaned towards me with the same conviction he used to attack the souvlaki. You need to take better care of them. And Joe. You must look after Joe. Joe's a national treasure. He gathered up his belongings and returned them to his backpack.

Have you anything for me to look at?

He looked like I'd just propositioned him.

A poem?

In his hand was a school copybook folded in half. He glanced at the bed as if considering waking Joe to read. I snatched the book off him. The boy's writing was tiny, and in pencil. I had to bring the candle close to decipher anything. Much of it was free verse, with an overreliance on enjambment.

Why the line break after 'denim sky'?

Richard shrugged. Instinct?

Oh pet, I thought. Instinct gets you into the river but won't save you from drowning. I picked up a pen. The boy grabbed the copybook out of my hands.

I was going to sign it for you.

The face on him.

Child, I have signed thousands of Joe's books. A dealer wouldn't be able to tell the difference. Besides, I wrote half of them. Including your beloved *Black Cat Prowling*.

Richard Blake's eyes opened wide but then his mouth curled up on one side. Scepticism was easy. Recognising an awkward truth took courage.

He tucked his unblemished copybook away and stood, swinging his backpack up over his shoulder.

Where are you going?

The beach. I have a sleeping bag.

As you wish, I said.

His parting words were something about how I should really try and publish under my own name. As if, somehow, I was stealing Joe's. And the notebooks blah blah blah.

I listened to his mincing steps descending the hill.

Niko was cleaning up, smashing bottles.

I thought of the boy's lines about a sky of sequined denim.

Of the Roscommon bog and how the night sky was so much darker there.

Of the black cat prowling.

And how long I'd been waiting for Joe to die. And now the boy, that raw, moon-faced boy, would seek his share of the notebooks. My notebooks. Joe's notebooks. How it didn't used to matter whose.

It's ten minutes after four, and the ferry is rounding the headland. The fishermen stretch their nets out on the pier to dry. Niko inspects the catch for the restaurant, looking for clear eyes and shiny scales. He stops when he sees me pass. His hand shades the sun.

Anna?

I put my basket down by my feet and blow him a kiss with both hands.

The tourists perch on wooden piles or sit cross-legged on the silver pier, waiting for the ferry. Backpacks and wheeled suitcases lie in tiny islands, draped with jackets, topped with hats. When the ferry grumbles into port, they lift their luggage, and form a line. Richard Blake, in a yellow bucket hat, is near the front, rooting through his backpack. He looks up, his face polka dotted with sweat. There's relief in his expression.

I've lost my ticket, he says. I don't have any money to buy another one.

I'm sorry. I would help you if I could.

It must be in the cottage? When Joe—

Perhaps.

He looks back to the ferry. People are boarding. Would they wait for me, d'ya think?

I shrug, helplessly. Your father will be happy to see you again. I told him about your poems. The denim sky. He said it was genius.

The boy looks behind me, up the hill, past the church tower, as if he could see Joe in the doorway of the cottage waiting for him. But Joe is at his desk with the crossword, yesterday erased, the day begun anew, a kiss on the crown of his newborn head.

I kiss Richard Blake on the cheek, left then right. Thank you.

What? What?

I have reached the top of the queue. I hand the ticket to the ferryman. Leaving the island only seems impossible if you forget that the sky and the sea never meet, that the horizon is an illusion.

I don't look back.

I

I am a metaphor,
says the poem.

Expanding itself, reaching far across the page with its script, overtaking both page
and attention.

Yet to be figured out.

If text could smirk it would,
but instead
      the
         poem
            struts
               about
            the
        page
    back
      and
         forth
           while
        it
      is
   studied,

        then
stops.

It looks up.

Get it?

Niamh O'Connell

Dino Matcha

Shane Tivenan

EVERYTHING THAT LEAVES COMES BACK

Dino Matcha's box flat is on the Westside of Town.

Dino Matcha's Town is peopled by friend, family, foe.

Dino Matcha says the Town never got over that missed penalty against Milan in 1975. Heads dropped that day and never came back up.

Dino claims it's the want makes us weak.

Claims the government has a lot to answer for.

Claims governmental rent allowance for his one-bed box by the Shannon and to the woman in the dole office he explains on a week-in week-out basis that work of that description is for other sorts, the steady-as-you-goers, the 9-to-fucken-5ers, the three square meals and decide what's what, aged early, with hand-me-down opinions and plain sailing from childhood to confirmation to sweetheart marriage to 2.1 kids and fixed monthly payments and no questions asked and that's just not Dino. The woman looks blankly at her screen, week-in, week-out, tap tap tap tap tap, printout, hands Dino another Career Navigation appointment for the following week and says, Next. Dino Matcha leans, whispers, Some days I don't know what to make of meself either, Mrs Killian, but I assure you this handout is a temporary measure, all I need is time to…

Next!

Dino Matcha puts it down to vested interests.

Says the flash floods of the mid-2000s when the Town's sewers disembowelled and entered front doors and floated out leather cushions from hire purchase L-shaped sofas and remote controls for plasma TV screens and instruction manuals for jacuzzis, fucken jacuzzis! and carried all off down the street were no more than karmic bailiffs bringing warnings from somewhere deep that all was not well with the way we were living. The way we are living.

Dino Matcha, head in hands, says no, no, no, there's enough mouths to feed in the world as it is, love. And off she goes.

Dino pushes his forehead again the cold bedroom wall and repeats, over and over, Everything that leaves comes back.

Dino's box flat is close enough to the River Shannon to hear its waters gushing through the sluices. He gapes daily at the water's flow. Says everyone from the Town knows people down there, such is the draw, such is the draw.

THE UNWANTED GAME

Charlie Clarence is of Scottish extraction, temper and complexion. He is Dundee United not Dundee. Says it is Godly grace what moves the legs of our most gifted strikers. Says if it wasn't for Ralph Milne's left peg, he'd never have had a son, and no cunt will ever tell him that it's not the Lord himself who orchestrates such events.

Charlie Clarence swears that fatherhood whipped him into shape. Blesses himself every time he passes the door of a boozer. Reckons that a club like Dundee United need not be winning more than one Scottish Premier League title in his lifetime, not after what happened in 1983. That the thought of the flower-in-the-wind-like movement of the crowd that day in the packed open stand behind the goal still goosebumps his skin. That he does not remember the one-night stand that cost him his marriage and gained him his son. That all he remembers of the day is this: four minutes gone, I mean four fucking minutes and we are mortal, pie-eyed from the night before. A few swallies and lines of whizz for breakfast. I lose the crew in a haze approaching Dens Park but at kick-off, the tangerine dream becomes alive, combines, grows fucken legs and wings and arses and tits and it takes off and flies. Every fan of The Terrors, and I mean every last one of us warrior bastards and bastardettes, there and not there and all over the city and those dead and those alive and those unborn and those somewhere in-between, all we for that 90-odd minutes stand as one. Dens Park only 200 yards away from our home turf in Tannadice, but everyone in Dundee knows it's light years what separates our two clubs. And it's only four minutes on the clock and off he goes. Ralphie Milne. Acquires the ball near the centre of the park. Dribbles. Shimmies. Dundee come and attempt to slay him on his approach as they recognise danger when they see it but Ralphie, he's a dancer. Doesn't even look up as he nears the box. He's studied the form of Colin Kelly between Dundee's sticks. Fancies himself as a big man does Col. Likes to stand that extra metre off his line and whisper a few sweet rough ones into the ears of the opposition's strikers. Shake them up a wee bit. And Ralphie, number 8, just a little nick, a perfectly weighted chip with his left peg and over the keepers hands and under the crossbar. A masterly opener. Four minutes later and we're two up. Twelve months later and there's an Irish lass at my door talking to the missus. This is Roy, she says, and nods my direction. It's his.

Dino Matcha calls it the unwanted game.

Charlie Clarence says we all get our comeuppance in the end.

SEE THE WANT

Charlie Clarence moves to Ireland in late 1984 to be close to his son. He has little money and no career but a taste for the page convinces him a night-time certificate in local journalism is the way to go.

Dino Matcha receives his calling loud and clear, aged young: pick up the paint can and spray words onto depressed-looking walls, harmless embankments, buildings reclaimed by nature, tree stumps, barriers, ramparts, burnt-out vehicles, felled fences, torn clothes.

Charlie Clarence is headbutted on the streets of the Town in 1989 and told to fuck back off across the water. His second meeting in St Mary's Hall on Northgate Street breaks him. On all fours he says all I want to do is rear me son. I just want to rear me son like. At the fifth meeting he declares himself an alcoholic. Begins the work. Takes a cup of tea. Feels home. Is told he is at home.

Dino Matcha, everywhere he goes, sees the want.

Charlie Clarence lets on he doesn't see his teenage son crushing up prescription Tramadol and rolling up a note. He reverses out the bedroom door and shouts in, Cup of tea son? Aye, Da, go on. Sound Son.

Dino Matcha says if you put your ear to the surface of the river and listen, eyes closed, you'll hear the swan songs of those swallowed by her over the years. But don't stay too close for too long. She's charismatic, is the Shannon. She'll charm you in.

Dino Matcha is heavily armed against such charms. Graffiti can in hand. Montana. Ozo orange. Water based. Quick drying as the rain's never far away. Molotow markers. SoySolv. Krink K42s. Sprayer. Stencilled lettering in copperplate font. Dust mask. Latex gloves. And all weapons concealable inside his neon blue mack.

Charlie Clarence sits in the pub with his son. His hands never lost the shakes and he the guts of a decade off the gargle. Young Roy gets a taste for it nice and young. Pint and a small one son? Aye Da, go on. Charlie assures his son that their blood is tangerine even though they live on the green isle. That he's going to up-skill himself. Make enough money to fly them both to Dundee at the drop of a hat to watch games, and with fucken regularity at that, are you with me son? Aye, Da. Listen, I'll be back in a sec, I just need me meds. Giving you gip son? Aye, Da. Charlie Clarence orders a pint and a small one for the wee man, and a coffee and a toasted sandwich for himself. He watches his son's gimped gait enter the jacks and turns to the barmen and says, Funny, isn't it Bill? What's that Charlie? How in the end, we all get our comeuppance.

ALL OUR HATE
COMES HOME TO ROOST

Dino Matcha shows great promise as a young striker for St Peter's FC, and makes the Under 10's number 10 jersey his own at a mere 8 years, 8 weeks old. Give him a ball and a yard of grass, writes Charlie Clarence for the local rag after witnessing a stellar performance at the Regional and District Schoolboy League Final of 1994, and this kid will do damage.

Dino Matcha's lifetime ban from participating in any regional sporting event seems harsh at first for a 15-year-old, but not to the people who are at the match. The two-footed high-studded tackle on the Willow Park defender, long after the ball had left his feet, ended up being a career ender. There was no getting that cracked kneecap back near working order, nor any way to give the victim of the tackle a chance of pulling on his boots again. Your son has suffered extensive compound fractures to the tibia, fibula and patella of his left leg, the patella and quadricep tendons have also been severely ruptured. I'd prefer be given it straight like, doc. If this was in my grandfather's day Charlie, we'd be amputating the lower part of that leg. But with time and rehabilitation and medication, young Roy will walk again, even run again, but chances are he'll do so with a limp.

WE MUST NOT HATE
WE MUST NOT HATE
WE MUST NOT HATE

The state developmental psychologist asks 16-year-old Donal McGowan why he doesn't fill in his CBT forms correctly. Cognitive behavioural therapy is not complicated, Donal. Dino. Sorry, Dino, it's literally ABC. A, you write your activating event. B, your belief as to how this event will unfold. Then C, the key, you note the actual consequence of that event and how it aligns with your belief in B, and what we find time and time again is that B and C do not match up, therefore making A completely redundant as an activating event. What? We imagine things worse than they are, Donal. Dino. Dino, sorry, okay, so, imagine, A, you try to ring your friend and they don't answer. B, you believe your friend no longer likes you. C, a few days later they ring and say their phone was not working. How do we know that's the truth? What's that Donal? Dino. What's that, Dino? People say what they want you to hear but it's often not what they really mean.

Charlie Clarence receives his 10-year bronze sobriety medallion. Cups of tea and Toffeepops and whispers in his ear: Sobriety is no small feat Chaz. Well done Charlie. The wee man is proud, no doubt, Chazzer. We're all so proud of you here, Charlie.

Dino Matcha stops going to his appointments and throws his medication in the bin. Says he's too young for therapy. Too young to be lying in bed all day listening to the sound of grinding teeth.

Charlie Clarence takes on shifts as a night cleaner in the Regional College to pay for his Masters. Writes for the local rag during the day. Blesses himself every time he passes the door of a boozer.

Dino Matcha, no grub, low funds, gives in. Sits in the local job centre. Sickly grey ticket in hand. Six before him. Corporate slogans on the wall. Infinite. Linear. Growth.

Dino Matcha comes to his senses. Stands up. Leaves.
Shakes. Sprays. Seethes.

WANTED FOR CRIMES AGAINST HUMANITY: RONALD MACDONALD, MICKEY MOUSE, ET AL.

Dino Matcha figures that if the true laws that govern us all are anything to go by, then linear growth can never exist: If you throw a stone in a straight line into space, throw it with enough force, and wait enough time, that stone will come back to that exact hand. Fact. All movement happens in circles. Everything that leaves comes back. Zoom in on any circle in the world and you'll eventually hit straight lines. This information has always been hidden in plain sight: the pagan spirals, the snake eating its own arse. Everything we do comes back to visit us, tap tap tap on the shoulder, hello there, remember me?

Roy Clarence survives another unintentional overdose. A combination of prescription meds and potent alcohol. He awakes in A&E but is told he's being transferred to the drug and alcohol abuse section in the psychiatric ward.

Charlie Clarence smiles down at his son as he is trollied by orderlies through hospital corridors. I've just got me Masters, son. Distinction. We can branch out now. Some freelance job offers coming in already. Bills sorted on time from now on and I'm getting you that private healthcare. We can even try one of those new clinics, you know, one of the fancy ones what takes in all the celebs?

Aye, Da.

Even Ralph Milne had trouble with the gargle and pills, son. It's nought to be ashamed of. But the drink made a mess of him. It was the drink what took Ralphie in the end. Are you with me son?

. . .

Dino Matcha, ear to the water, listens. Stays too close for too long and on him the Shannon works her charm.

Charlie Clarence gets young Roy on the Back-to-Work scheme as part of his social reintegration programme.

Dino Matcha takes off his shoes and socks. Places in a circle by the water's edge his phone, wallet, keys to the flat, spray-paint, stencils, accoutrements, a picture of her, a picture of him and her, a wildflower, and drops his blue mack to the ground as he stands.

Roy Clarence limps off to his first day of paid work. His father fills up, chest out, whispers, if it wasn't for Ralph Milne's left peg.

Dino Matcha places his bare foot into the cold black body of the Shannon.

Roy Clarence places his hand on Dino Matcha's shoulder. Says, Sorry, pal, eh, like, your work is bang on and that but I've got to re-paint all these walls. New government scheme. Can't say I'm in complete agreement but powers that be and all that. Work is work. Need the money. Listen pal, come out and I'll explain more. Take me hand there. The thing is, I know all the spots not on me list here. If you come out, I'll tell you where they are. I'll take you there. Come on. It's all right. Take me hand, pal.

Dino Matcha shivers and rocks back and forth on the banks of the River Shannon. Has his feet dried by young Roy Clarence. Has his socks and shoes pulled on as he tries to pull himself together.

Roy Clarence asks why?

Dino Matcha says, Such is the draw, such is the draw.

Roy Clarence says aye.

responsorial psalm: would you die for Ireland? (i'm very sorry, i can't)

The economic structure is not an accident, it is precisely related to what is
being said

What if I said the island was a tax haven
but
hemmed on all sides with the most exquisite
       Wild Swimming

the young in one another's DMs
fish flesh fine girl y'are

If St Patrick banished all the snakes, does that make FF/FG/G *slow worms;*
why do the other boys in school keep calling *me* a rat
(a question of debt translation)

no one can tell you why it's called the forty foot
there is no firm consensus on the details
of the 2011 NAMA report to the government
the theme is: all quiet on
      keep dad on   keep sins of auxiliary father, son

and FYI they call them 'coffin ships' because they are all shaped like coffins
      that's literally it
educated *somewhat* privately
        just *which* bloody Sunday?

(until you have watched the bonus episode of
RTÉ's Reeling in the Years
you will never know how sinister
the singing priests, etc.)

pre-Crash
the High Chief paid from petty cash to have my braces removed;
joke's on him—I was always already éire anew:
all gums no teeth

I unravelled the scroll and read with aplomb
'I felt loss when I could not floss'
overleaf, regret:
'thy rent, alack, is dueth'

—a crushed bullet against the amazing wishlist in my breast pocket—

on this United Ireland-shaped rock
~father's *Four Green Field sites*~
we don't know enough about historical materialism yet to fully
appreciate vaping
e-scoot   authoritarian-dryrobe
but
          I, too, dislike it.

Will Fleming

The Dance

The invitation came hand-written
on ebony paper and black ink,
sealed with red wax.
It read *six in the evening*
a reception at the Manor House:
The Wellingtons request the pleasure of your company.

The workers stood by the side entries
peeking from the long drawn curtains.
Good evening, madam.
Evening, gentlemen.
Echoing through the gilded wallpaper,
red carpet, and gold candle holders.

The great painting of the Boer War in the hallway,
the opulence of the fresh orchids
by the window,
and the dazzling chandeliers
play tricks on the eye.
The fireplace
almost sets the tone.

When Lady Wellington entered
wrapped in diamonds
we all stood in awe.

Let's dance! the Lord exclaimed
followed by a trumpet call.
Foreign fruits
on ivory plates,
gold goblets,
silver cutlery.

Nandi Jola

The Settlement

Joanne Touhey

My mam's voice would quaver when she asked me for money. Her voice mimicked vulnerability, almost magnetic, drawing my pity as she asked for a loan until the following week. Often, I'd never see the money again, and if she did pay me back, she would ask for it again within a few days. It was a role reversal. I never asked her for money, because if I did, she would tell me she was broke. Money slid out of her hand as soon as she got it. It would be fifty to a hundred euros every week or two. She would tell me it was for food, for my siblings, or to pay a bill. Sometimes, she would tell me the truth: that it was, in fact, to play a poker tournament. Mam hadn't worked in years—not after a terrible fall she had while working as a waitress when pregnant with my second-youngest sister. Mam was now a single mother, caring for five children, because she chose gambling over her marriage.

It was Mam's mood that got to me the most when she ran out of money. There'd be a lingering sadness in her eyes, and it was clear she was criticising herself as she slouched into the couch with her laptop on her knee, ignoring us all. We'd never get more than a grunt from her. So when Mam asked me for money, I was happy to give it to her because it would cheer her up. She'd hug me, thank me and tell me she loved me, which often made me feel uncomfortable rather than pleased.

I'd try to avoid her on days she had no money, but she would call me:

'Joanne?' she'd say, in a high-pitched voice.

'Yes?'

'How much can you give me until next Wednesday or Thursday?'

'I only have my rent money here.'

'How much is that?'

'I only have two weeks' rent there but it has to be paid on the 30th.'

'Ok, that will do. I'll get Granny to put it back into your account on the 28th.'

'You better, Mam, because I can't be late with it. I'll transfer it now.'

It was impossible to say no to Mam, partly because she was relentless, but more than that again: we knew how hard her life had been, because she took every chance to remind us. And so, when opportunities arose to help her, to ease those burdens, I felt obligated.

Most of the time she wouldn't pay my rent money back, and I'd have to ask my stepdad for the money or borrow it from a friend. Every time I saw an incoming call or a text message from Mam pop up on my notification screen, I'd know it was for money. When I moved out at seventeen, she never came to visit me at my apartment or even texted me to see how I was doing. Our only conversations were about money and asking me to babysit my youngest three sisters. I was just a pool she could dip into.

At eighteen, with a lump sum on its way into my account, that pool deepened. It was 2011, and I had been awarded a settlement of €48,000 from a car crash my mam, my three sisters and I were in five years earlier.

I felt I was set up for life. I had worked out what I was going to do with it: a deposit for a house, money to fund college, a holiday or two, a new laptop, phone and a car. I had, of course, planned to give a small sum to my close family. But if I'm being honest, I knew. I knew this money would leave my account as quickly as it had come in. I knew that my mam and grandmother had made their own plans, and I knew I had no strength or will to stop them.

It started a few weeks before this life-changing amount of money was due. My mam made her first visit to my apartment. Well, she parked outside it and beeped for me to come out. She and my grandmother had come to collect me.

'Hi darling, how are you?' my grandmother said, her round face framed by the open car window as I got into the back seat of the car.

'I'm fine,' I replied, wiping my sweaty hands into my jeans.

'I'll do most of the talking. You just tell them about your hearing problem, that you want me to speak on your behalf,' my grandmother said.

It was true that I had a hearing problem, but in a one-to-one conversation, I was fine. I knew that I would go along with my grandmother's plan, but it didn't stop me from feeling ashamed. I didn't want to live my life like my mother and grandmother; I didn't want to deceive people. I felt as though I was waist-deep in the ocean, trying to stand against waves of powerful emotion. The wave that knocked me to the bottom was fear: the fear of saying no to them. Families are strange. They encourage us to say no to lots of things, but never to them. In my family, this was ingrained through guilt, the insinuation that you were letting everyone down, and silence then, showing you the misery you'd created.

I nodded to my grandmother and looked out the car window.

'I've no doubt in my mind that Joanne will be approved for the loan,' my grandmother said, looking at Mam.

'I hope so. I owe the landlord two months' rent and Sky is threatening to cut me off,' Mam replied.

I sat there.

At the counter in the credit union, I turned off my hearing aids; it made the lie about my hearing more plausible. My grandmother stood to my left, telling the woman behind the counter how badly I needed an €8,000 loan to buy a car. I wondered if she would ask for a driving licence to prove it; I hadn't even passed my theory test. Maybe then we'd be refused the loan. The woman slid a couple of forms towards me. I was about to read the papers when my grandmother said to just sign my name wherever there was an X.

I felt a familiar powerlessness. I could never have a conversation with my grandmother. I could never even have one in front of her. She made me feel small, nervous, stupid and even afraid. It was the same fear some experience in the schoolyard, the fear of that one person who holds the power to turn everyone against you, the one you must pacify, side with or else suffer their wrath. It was a horrible feeling, a shaking sickness from my stomach up. I always did what I was told to end the interaction as quickly as possible. Now, at the Credit Union, I did as my grandmother asked. I quickly signed the forms, and slid them back across the counter, my heart beating hard against my chest.

The woman looked at the forms and then looked at my grandmother and told her I would definitely get approved for the loan based on the strength of the €48,000 coming in a couple of weeks. I didn't understand this fully. How did that have anything to do with this loan, particularly when Mam said she'd pay it back and not me?

I asked my grandmother about it outside the credit union.

'Your mam is going to pay it over the next five years, honey,' she replied, putting on her leather gloves.

'But I thought you both said she was paying it back within a year when she gets her claim?' My mam had been awarded €72,000 in the same settlement.

'Your mammy wouldn't be able to, honey. Her claim is accounted for with debts, but she can afford to pay €100 a month out of her domiciliary or children's allowance. I'll make sure she does. I collect her domiciliary every month, so I'll put that into your credit union myself,' she said, linking her arm with mine as we walked towards Mam's car. There was confidence in her voice, and I wanted to believe her. So I did.

The loan was approved.

When the day arrived that I would receive my €48,000, I logged in to my account. My mam and grandmother were there with me, over my shoulder, watching. I didn't want to look. I was afraid of it not showing up and seeing the familiar zero in my balance. When I tapped 'Overview,' it said Current Account: €40,000.

I frowned. The €8,000 promised to the credit union had already left my account.

Mam and my grandmother discussed where my money would be going: €5,000 to my grandmother, €5,000 to my mam, €3,000 to my stepdad, €2,000 to my grandmother's boyfriend, €100 to each of four out five of my siblings, €500 to the fifth sibling, €2000 for my holiday and €10,000 to my secured savings account.

'That leaves Joanne with €12,100,' my grandmother said to Mam, holding a list in her hand.

'You wanted money for a laptop and a phone, didn't you?' Mam said.

'Yeah.' My mouth was dry.

'How much will you need for that? €1,500?' my grandmother asked.

'I think so,' I said.

I wondered why the credit union took €8,000 from my bank account when Mam was meant to be paying it back over the next five years. It was only then it clicked with me. I understood what the woman meant when she said I was getting this loan on the strength of my claim coming. How could I be so stupid? There was no way Mam was going to pay back €8,000 when there was no loan outstanding.

'What about the loan in the credit union?' I blurted.

'Oh, that's cleared now. Don't worry, I'll still be taking a €100 a month off your mammy until it's paid,' my grandmother replied.

I raised my chin and cupped the back of my head with my hands.

In the days following, Mam was buzzing. I'd never seen her so happy. Instead of me waking her up in the mornings, as I always had to when I lived at home, she now woke me, ringing the phone, ringing the bell—her energy was abundant. The motivation for this behaviour change was quite simple.

She wanted to pick up my grandmother and be outside the bank for when it opened at 10 a.m. She treated us to breakfast after I made each withdrawal for them.

Each night I rehearsed a dramatic 'No', but the only word I had in the mornings was 'Yes'. A yes that stemmed from a misplaced sense of guilt, and obligation—a longing that made me desperate to buy love and affection.

On one of these mornings, after we'd been to the bank, Mam dropped me at my grandmother's while she went grocery shopping. My grandmother said she wanted to confirm that list she had made detailing where my money went, and to see what plans I had for the rest. We went to her bedroom, where she kept the list, and where she had gathered around twenty plastic bags filled with pennies. Lined up along the bed, the bags filled with her coppers ran five-wide across the bottom of the pillows and four rows down, creating a strange patchwork over the floral duvet cover. Before I even saw my grandmother's list, I was staring at the bags of copper coins, thinking: this is what I'll have left.

I sat at the bottom of the bed while she sat at the top of it. She produced a piece of paper and a pen.

'This is the list,' she said, putting it down on the bed.

The list made a dividing line on the bed; I sat one side and my grandmother on the other. I glanced at the list of names with amounts written beside them. Oblivious or indifferent to my discomfort, my grandmother began:

'What do you plan to do with the remaining €10,600?'

'I don't know,' I replied. I wanted to leave it in my account for a rainy day. But deep down, I knew if I left it there, Mam would get her hands on it.

'Perhaps build your credit rating by getting another secured loan?' my grandmother said.

'I'm not sure,' I said, shrugging at the paper.

'You and me both know if you leave it idle, your mammy will ask for a loan of it,' she said, with a wry smile.

Her phone rang. I liked the sound of the landline ringing; it brought the room to life, unlike a mobile which just seemed intrusive when it rang. It was her brother, Paddy—my godfather—on the phone. I recognised his voice.

I got up to leave and give my grandmother privacy, but she gestured for me to stay.

I couldn't hear the conversation, so my thoughts drifted back to the list, and how I might talk to my grandmother and say that I wasn't happy with this.

After the call, her eyes were downcast. She focused on the list.

'What's wrong?' I asked.

'Paddy was supposed to go to the Philippines to meet his girlfriend, Glenda,' she said.

'Why can't he go?'

'Oh, that ex-wife of his is bringing him to court again for more money. She wants Paddy to buy her out of the house. He can't afford to go now.' My grandmother's face reddened.

'How much was it going to cost?'

'€3,000 for his flight and spending money.'

I thought: what's €3,000 out of €10,600? I knew what was expected of me. I was required to jump in to save the day with some money. I felt it was what was expected—mixed with my own misplaced sense of obligation, and already, if I'm honest, the money was becoming a burden. As my grandmother rooted through her bedside locker for something, I googled what to do in Davao City in the Philippines. I'd never been abroad before and thought maybe I could go with Paddy. I read an article listing the top ten things to do. The crocodile park and turquoise waters sold it to me.

'I could give him the €3,000 to go, and, if he didn't mind, I could go with him?' I said.

'Aw Joanne! He'd be over the moon. Of course, Glenda's family would be delighted to have you. Are you sure? You would love it there.' My grandmother's face lit up in the way that only greedy people's do. I'd seen this expression on Mam's face too. The expression reminded me of a cartoon villain, the one who had all the pies around them, face scrunching as they rubbed their hands together celebrating their spoils, but still empty and alone.

'Yeah, I wanted to go somewhere on holiday. I don't mind once it's out of Ireland.'

'Aw, honey. Will I ring him now and tell him?'

I nodded, my stomach a ball of knots. I thought about the place I wanted to go on holiday—the Heathman Hotel in Portland, Oregon—and I worried I wouldn't have enough money to go there too. After reading *Fifty Shades of Grey*, I'd googled to see if the hotel mentioned in the novel was real. When I'd discovered it existed, and that they offered Fifty Shades of Oregon packages, I had decided the chocolate and wine-tasting package was the one I'd go for.

After my grandmother rang Paddy, she hugged and thanked me. She looked at me and said, 'Joanne, are you sure? Because you will need about

€5,000 in total for both flights and spending money. I don't want Paddy to get his hopes up. It wouldn't be fair on him.'

'Yeah. It'd be nice to go somewhere different,' I replied.

'God is good,' she smiled. 'Let's look at this list again. We must put down money for a car and those driving lessons you wanted.'

'Okay.'

'That leaves you with €5,600 to spend on a car, lessons, or whatever you want. You also have the €10,000 we're going to lock into your savings. You can't touch it for five years. By doing that, you'll get interest each year,' my grandmother said. 'When your mother is back, we'll go to the bank, get Paddy's money out and put the €10,000 into a savings account.'

I was happy to lock away the €10,000 because I didn't want Mam to guilt-trip me into taking out any of that money for her. This was the money I planned to use as a deposit on a house. I looked at the list again, and noticed now that my stepdad's name wasn't on it—the man who raised me for over fourteen years and treated me as his own daughter.

'Did Mam give Darren his €3,000?' I asked.

'Your mammy has it put aside for him. There's no point in giving him it yet, not with him being in rehab. He's an alcoholic, Joanne. If you give someone like that that much money, what do you think'll be the first thing they'll do with it?'

'Well, I want him to have it now, or as soon as he is out of rehab. I don't want him to think I'm not giving him anything.' I wanted to add, *It's up to him how he spends it. I don't care if it goes on drink,* but it was as if my throat sealed up any time I wanted to put my foot down.

'Okay. I'll say it to your mam. Hopefully, after his time in rehab, he will have gotten the help he needed and he won't drink it all,' my grandmother said, sourly.

I didn't understand how my stepdad's alcoholism was any different to my mam's gambling addiction.

'I'll save the €5,600 in the credit union for now until I can choose a car and get the lessons,' I said. This was a diversion; I did not want to justify my decision to give Darren the money.

'If you're sure, honey. I think that's your mother pulling up now.'

In the car, my grandmother told Mam all about me accompanying Paddy on his trip to the Philippines. Mam seemed a bit jealous—I'm not sure if it was the exotic holiday or the thoughts of Paddy getting money. She nodded and half-heartedly said, 'That'll be nice.'

At the bank, I felt sick and yet relieved not to have to deal with the money. My grandmother did all the talking with the banker. It puzzled me how they never asked me anything and just looked at my grandmother as she spoke. They only acknowledged me when I had to sign something. I felt small and child-like.

The banker, in a navy suit, beard neatly trimmed, divided money into different envelopes and handed them to my grandmother.

Mam was sitting in the car outside the bank, smoking a cigarette. My grandmother handed me €1,500 for my laptop and phone and walked to the driver's side window and handed Mam some money.

'I've to lodge €5,600 into Joanne's credit union account for her car and stuff and head to work,' my grandmother said, and waved us goodbye.

I was annoyed my grandmother told Mam about lodging my €5,600. It would only be a matter of time before she'd ask for some of it.

'Thanks for the money. Not that I'm left with much of it, trying to catch up on rent and my car loan ,' Mam said, as I sat in the passenger seat.

I changed the subject.

'I don't want to go to the Philippines anymore,' I said.

'What? Joanne, Jesus you can't let Paddy down now. Granny has already transferred the money to him.'

'But she only took out the money for him now?

'She transferred her own money to him, so she's paying herself back from what she gave Paddy.'

'I just don't want to go anymore.'

'You can't ask for the money back. He'll just have to go on his own,' Mam replied.

'Can I not just give him €3,000 to go instead of €5,000? Two of that was for me?' A lump formed in my throat.

'Sort it with Granny.'

We drove in silence for a while.

'Stop here,' I said, as the car approached the shopping centre. 'I'm going to buy my laptop. I'll walk home.'

I walked to Click, thinking of how I could ask for the €2,000 back now that I wasn't going to the Philippines, but I knew it was gone. Even if it wasn't, I would never have the courage to ask for it. Instead of looking for the cheapest laptops, I looked at the more expensive ones. I handed €700 to the cashier; it felt strange, a little funny, and there was even a touch of guilt at handing the money to someone other than my mam. I had one thing to show for my settlement. I wanted to believe I had nothing left, not even savings, but I had and the voice in my head told me that somehow Mam would find a way of getting it.

Two weeks later, I moved back to Mam's because I could no longer pay for rent and fund her as well. Though my settlement was almost gone, I was still topping up Mam's income to the detriment of my own life. My bills mounted as we tried in vain to clear hers. My rent went into arrears as we caught up on hers. The circle of financial ignorance continued. My bedroom had been taken over by one of my sisters, so I kitted out the shed, which was attached to the house on the ground level. I put down carpet, boarded up the shed door and painted the block walls. Since there was no heating in the shed, I bought a paraffin heater.

Midweek, my mam usually went out to play poker, but one Wednesday she decided to play in an online tournament with her new boyfriend, Jimmy, instead. They got settled in the sitting room, while my sisters binged on a takeaway. Relieved from babysitting duties, I decided to head to the cinema with my boyfriend. I opened the safe, a purchase I had made when my little shed renovation project commenced. In a way, a very unfortunate purchase. It sat on the bottom of my bedside locker, the top of which was covered in toiletries, perfumes and other bits and bobs. That safe, that heavy, dull grey metal, seemed to look me square in the face any time I reached for toothpaste or some other mundane item from the locker. It was a box of distrust, a very real representation of my relationship with my family.

I took out a brown envelope of money: €820, all I had left. I took twenty, then left the envelope on my bed while I grabbed my handbag. Someone knocked on my door. I quickly slid the envelope underneath a bunch of teddy bears at the bottom of my bed.

'Come in,' I said, locking the safe.

It was my sister, Katie, telling me my boyfriend was outside to collect me. I smiled and took a deep breath. My head started to pound, the hills of pressure that had been building swiftly becoming mountain ranges. I regretted suggesting going to the cinema.

When I got home, I could hear Mam and Jimmy talking and laughing in the sitting room. I shouted 'Hello', but I got no response, which wasn't unusual. I went into my room, where the loud squeak of my door irritated my headache. I opened the safe to put back the twenty because Anto had paid for us into the cinema.

The brown envelope was gone.

My heart galloped until I remembered I had put it under my teddies. I jumped up and moved my hand around underneath the teddies, but I couldn't feel it. I moved them, one by one, to the floor, but the envelope wasn't there. I pulled back the duvet and looked down the side of my bed. I checked my coat, my jeans and my bag. It was nowhere to be seen.

I marched into the sitting room.

'Did you see an envelope with money in it?' I asked Mam.

She was on the couch with her laptop on her knee. I turned to look at Jimmy, who also had his laptop on his knee. Neither responded. Mam glanced up from her screen for a split second as she often did, but without any acknowledgement of me or my question.

'Did you hear me?' I raised my voice. I felt my temples pulsate.

'What is it, Joanne?' Mam said.

'I left eight hundred in my room, and now it's missing.'

'How could it go missing, Joanne?'

'I don't know! I left it on my bed in my room before going to the cinema, and now it's gone.'

I couldn't stop myself from crying. I wasn't upset; I was angry. I hoped that somehow it was a stranger who broke in and stole the money.

'Joanne, you must have misplaced it somewhere.'

'I didn't!'

'I'll help you look,' Mam said.

She shouted up the stairs for my sister Ally to come down to help. I stood in the doorway of my room, watching the two of them search in the same places I'd already searched.

'You're right, it's not here,' Mam said, shaking her head. I tried to suss her out. Did she look guilty? Would she have taken it? Would Jimmy have taken it? I didn't know what to think. My head hurt so much. My eyes were heavy, and I felt drained.

As though Mam read my mind, she said, 'Joanne, you've been so tired. You've had to deal with a lot of money over the last few weeks. You could have left it anywhere.' She rubbed the back of her neck, looking around the room, and then directly at the corner of the bed where I had left the money. I frowned. But I couldn't understand why she would take the money when she could have just asked me for it, like she did so many times before, like she always did.

'Majella, your game is starting,' Jimmy shouted from the sitting room.

'Look, it might show up tomorrow when you've gotten a rest,' she said, leaving my room.

'Okay. Perhaps,' I whispered. What was the point?

The missing €800 was never spoken of again. I used to hear people use the old saying 'money doesn't buy happiness'. Well, I could attest to that; it brought me only division, distrust and exhaustion. I was glad it was gone. I didn't want any of it anymore.

Ten years later, I sit with my two children and listen to them talk about being rich one day. They argue about who will have the biggest house, what cars they'll buy and the countries they'll visit. I ask them, 'Why is money so important?'

'I can buy a big toy shop!' my three-year-old says.

'Do you think it's important to have lots of money?' I ask.

'Well, you need money to live,' my nine-year-old replies.

I smile, knowing in a way that he is right. I have nothing to show for the €48,000 I received. I gave it all away to my family, even the €10,000 savings. It's as though it never existed.

Sometimes I wonder what I could have done with that money, where I could have gone and how different my life might be now, but then I hear my children laugh, see my partner smile, and it doesn't matter about the money because I feel true wealth all around me. That money could have blown me on a different course, and I'm glad it didn't because I am where I should be. And some good did come from it: Paddy went to the Philippines, he and Glenda got married, and now live in Ireland with their two children.

But only some.

I can't help but remember how it was that I noticed Mam's quaver returning. I began to hear it again in her conversations with my next eldest sibling, Ally, who had been in the same car accident, and was awaiting her settlement; one that was very substantial indeed. Not long after my pool dried up, Ally was being brought off for breakfast with our grandmother. The lists were about to be drawn up.

Ugolino's Last Son

The ice is melting, my father.
Chromatic scratches and guano
streak this coop; I'm half-chicken, I'm bony,
turning blue. Remember among the asters
as a little boy you played black bear
to my salmon in that leafy river;
caught me on your big head, you bore
me dizzy, drunk as a lord on your shoulders.
I feel your eyes like a generation
fall on me, such tremendous admiration.
No, it's not too much to ask
in our mutual darkness.
So, my head to yours I incline:
your want is greater than mine.

Karl O'Hanlon

White Worm

I piece you together—
a composite of pale blue
eyes and crooked teeth.
A broad northern brogue,
discernible now, only through
stories told by others.
Aloof and wryly amused, you wore
an air of nothing left to prove.
I have survived you.

You are survived by is a curious
phrase. A wife survives you.
Two daughters. Three sons.
I pick a striped, green fig. Slice it in two.
Inside, white worms wriggle.
I hoped it would be ripe and sweet
but the red flesh was already swallowed.
Their soft pinheads wave to me,
tell me I am outliving you.

Lucy Holme

Tell Someone

Conner Habib

In the photo we're in the back yard. Adam is at the top of the plastic blue slide, apprehensive in his orange bathing suit. I'm at the bottom, waiting for him. I'm sure as he came sliding down to me, I splashed him and he screamed, the way children scream when they mean to laugh.

I'm in the midst of Adam's things now. Ruins.

He's been dead for three weeks. After the police came and the paramedics came and the body was removed, the stain of him was revealed on the grey cushions of the couch. I had opened all the windows, but the air was humid and wouldn't carry away the smell—wilt and cumin—so it's still here with me.

In the other rooms are the clothes and the shoes and baseball caps that went into black plastic bags, a Tom Clancy paperback with an unbroken spine, a used up AA Big Book filled with underlines, some old psychology textbooks from before he dropped out. There's the furniture to get rid of, mostly old and cheap, though some of the kitchenware—the knives, the cutting board, the plates and bowls—was brand new. He must have thought he was going to cook more, and invite friends over.

Another photo, three of us together on the couch. Adam, Dad, me. The carpet was red, Dad had his shirt off and Adam had his head against Dad's chest, just above his heart. Looking at Adam's face, you can see the man he'll become. You can see how growth and age will push his features out and deepen him. The photo is on top of a pile of photos in a box in his bedroom closet, which had his phone in it. The phone made what he did so decisive. He must have known what he was going to do and known, also, that I would come.

I'd made a deal with Adam four years ago after Dad's funeral. Dad, who had an embolism, then a fever, then that was it. Dad had seemed so invincible, never small, until the ashes were delivered in a plastic urn.

'Do we scatter his ashes with Mom?' I asked. Mom hadn't come to the service. 'She used to love him. So did we, I guess.'

'We still fucking love him,' Adam said.

'Yes,' I admitted quietly.

'Sorry,' he said. 'But she's not here, so why would we?'

'It's fine. It's okay to have whatever feelings you need to have.' By this time he'd been sober for a year, so I was used to this sort of flare up. It'd come and go almost instantly, but the feeling would linger in me, like a shot. My therapist said to just witness it as something that was happening in him, not at me. I held my hand out for the urn. I wanted to hold the remains.

'We need to talk about something,' Adam said, then.

I waited, but he needed to be asked.

'What?'

'When I die, promise me you'll clean out my place.'

'Oh, planning on dying soon?' I said, and smiled. He smiled back a little, but then he closed his eyes in a wince. 'Not Dahlia, not Mom either. Just you.' I tried to not think about the implications; Adam was my brother.

'Bury me,' he said 'I want my body. But burn my things.'

It was two weeks before I came to find him. Just a little while with no returned calls. You'd think, he's busy or depressed or went on a trip and didn't tell any of us. Sometimes when Adam would stop answering his phone, he'd be fighting with Mom or Dahlia, Mom's girlfriend. He'd emerge a few days later and say something like, 'There's enough in life to deal with.' I knew what he meant.

But this time, none of us had been fighting with him, so I drove to Stroudsburg and pulled the key hidden in the light by the door. I called Saoirse first, before the police. 'Is our baby okay?' I asked, frantically, as I saw the foot turned in a strange direction off the couch and then flies racing past my head into the house. They must have desperately wanted to get in, to crawl into his mouth, crusted at the edges with puke; onto his eyes, across him. 'Is our baby okay?'

'Yes! Luke, what is it, Luke? What?' I heard her say as I dropped the phone. Three empty bottles of pills were on the stand next to the couch: two prescription, one white and red Tylenol bottle. My brother's body. As I leaned down to pick up the phone, I avoided his face and thought of Saoirse's belly.

I'd told her not to tell me if it was a girl or a boy because I wanted to be surprised, to not have any preconceived notions. That's what I'd said.

There came, then, the invading thought. It slid past the narrowest passage of me, like a knife finding its way into masonry. *What if it's a boy?*

He knew I'd come. He trusted me.

In the closet, there's no note with the code for his phone. I'll smash his phone and take out the card and break that, too. Underneath that, there's a magazine. It's on top of other things. I don't want to lift it.

What if it's a boy?

A set of eyes look up at me from the cover. It's a teenage girls' magazine, a boy who I vaguely remember from a movie; the awkward kid in family dramas. He's smiling against a magenta background. The cover is rippled with age and use, but the colours are still bright, the boy still young and smiling.

Beneath it, a VHS tape. And now, yes, photos.

A stack of them almost as thick as playing cards, held together with a rubber band. They aren't of our family. Young boys in bathing suits, their flesh pale or dark with tan. At the playground, turning around each other, in the motion of shouting or laughing. On stage at a school play, the auditorium dark. They must be as young as seven and as old as twelve. 'Why would you keep these?' I hear myself say out loud. I know why he had them, but why keep them, why not just use his phone to take photos and then delete them or… I don't know why I'm trying to help him.

Then I realise that he probably didn't take any of these: they're too varied in the kind of picture and the eras they're taken from. And that doesn't make me feel better. If someone gave these to him. If he bought these. He's dead. He's dead now.

I sort through hurriedly, hoping that none will be naked or—

There's one.

A brown-haired boy sitting on the edge of a bed, laughing. No one else in the photo, and it's night time. There's a T-shirt and a pair of little trousers on the unmade bed. It's an innocent photo. In the bottom right corner, a time stamp in a font that looks like a digital clock.

Under the stack of photos, there's a folded up piece of notebook paper with something in it. A small pendant, a small silver disk with a loop for a chain on top. SAINT NICHOLAS it says, the name arching across the top of the medal in embossed letters. There's a man surrounded by children. He has a beard, and they're all looking up to him. He has the middle and index finger of his right hand pointing upward. He has a pointed hat and a halo surrounding his head. SAINT NICHOLAS. There's writing on the paper in pen, across its folds, in blue pen. I know It's Adam's handwriting.

Loving Saint Nicholas,
May I strive to imitate you.
Give me courage, love and strength.
And where I cannot be brave or strong,
Please protect the children.
Amen.

I run to the bathroom to vomit, expecting my insides to burn their way out of me, across the sink and across the floor. But nothing happens except me kneeling, coughing and waiting for it.

When I was seven, my room was at the top of the stairs. There was a gate in front of the steps because Adam was still small and could totter down them. Dad and Mom's room was to the left of the stairs, Adam's to the right. I'd fallen down those stairs once, but didn't remember it well; Mom said I was playing chase with the babysitter and I'd tumbled forward. My body remembered, though. I reached for the rail every time I went down those stairs. Still, now, I hold the rail on stairways, and Saoirse calls me 'old man' to tease me. Memory finds its way to stay with us, in our bodies, in our behaviours.

The first time with me, Dad was saying goodnight. He put his hand on my chest and told me to take my shirt off. The event is absolutely certain, but the details are dark at the edges. It's the words I remember vividly, with their thick outlines. He told me he never slept with his shirt on. 'Let me see you,' he said, as he pulled the covers slow off my body. 'Let me see you.' Then there were the sensations. Not pleasant, not unpleasant, not warm or cold, but like he'd poured water over me that rushed against gravity, from my legs up to my head. It was a feeling that I'd grow to think I wanted. It was something we did together.

Three years, each night, coming into my room. Then he stopped.

Those first weeks, when I was left to fall asleep on my own, I'd fitfully wait for him to arrive, to see his form in the glow of my nightlight with the bulb shaped like a candle flame. I'd stare at the ceiling, I'd hold the pillow. I'd think, 'Why did my dad leave me?'

That was the year Adam turned seven. One night, I heard the sound of breathing by the open door. Dad walked past my room and down the hall. Adam's door opened.

When I leave Adam's house, Saoirse calls.

'How was it?' she asked.

'How was it? What, like I just went to a movie or something?'

She breathes in to calm herself. She has a temper, but she knows and I know that we've both started this conversation the wrong way.

'I'm sorry,' I say, though I'm angry that I'm apologising first. Then she apologises too and everything lifts and I start to cry.

'Was there anything you want to keep of his?' she asks. I hadn't even thought about taking anything; I was looking through his things for him, not for me.

'I don't think so,' I say.

'Nothing? He was your brother.'

I hang up on her. 'He *is* my brother!' I shout, and hit the steering wheel. The horn honks, and the sound is stupid enough to relieve me of my anger.

I drive away from Adam's complex and towards home. The bags and the phone are in the trunk; when I make a turn, there's a knocking sound from the inside.

There's a 7-Eleven on the way and a dumpster on the side. I slow but see the cameras there. What if I'm caught throwing these things away: a bag full of pictures of children, whatever is on the VHS tape and the phone? If someone saw me, I'd be arrested. So I keep driving till I get to Conaught's Hardware and I pull into the back parking lot, go to the trunk and find everything turned over on itself. I bring it to the front. First I drop the phone on the floor and push on it with my foot till it cracks. Then I stomp on it until it starts to chip away, till the little card, huddled inside, is exposed. I tear the photos and the magazines up. I pull the faces in half, the tiny bodies. I pull the shiny black ribbon of VHS tape out of its plastic and tear it in half.

I get out quickly and open the lid of the dumpster and push the bag in between the other garbage bags. It's not a cremation of his desires, like he asked for, but it'll be burned soon enough. Or the torn young faces will disintegrate over time, in a landfill, strewn through other people's things. I close my eyes tight when I walk away. Blot the edges of the thing. Non-existence.

When I get home, I yell at Saoirse. I tell her I love her, and that sometimes I don't think she knows how to be a normal human being. 'Please tell me the exact way you think I should grieve,' I say.

She doesn't let herself be yelled at. She never does. She shouldn't.

'Well, why don't you tell me the exact way to talk to you, so that I don't hurt your feelings every time I open my mouth?'

'A good start would be, "I'm sorry",' I say. '"Your brother is dead, your *brother is fucking dead I am so sorry.*' And then I'm shaking and crying and she puts her arms around me. She leans in so that the baby doesn't keep us too far apart.

'I was just thinking, I was… I don't know, I wasn't judging you at all. I just worry. I thought, is there something of Adam's that would help you through?'

'Through?' I ask.

That night, as Saoirse gets into bed, I go to the bathroom to brush my teeth. When I'm done I take my shirt off and fold it, and before I take my pants off I empty the pockets. My wallet, my keys. A piece of paper. And a photograph.

I unfold the paper, but I don't need to. I know what I'll see. *Loving Saint Nicholas…* The prayer without the pendant.

And the photo, also folded twice into itself.

The boy on the edge of a bed. When I look at him now, I think, *He looks just like us.* He isn't one of us, but he could be our brother. Or a son.

I try to remember when I saved these. In the house? In the car? There's nothing there. A clipped-out hole in the day when I slid these into my pocket. Now I put them back in my pocket. I have to remember they're there. I have to remember and not let Saoirse wash my pants. I'll wear these tomorrow, I'll throw these things away.

The bedroom is already dark and I put my clothes on the floor, folded squares like the squares in my pocket.

In bed, I say, 'I'm sorry.' But she's asleep already. For a month now, in her pregnancy, she is awake one moment, asleep the next, like a blown-out flame.

I put my arm around her and say the prayer of Saint Nicholas to myself.

There is no through, this is it.

We're already through, and this is what it feels like.

'Dad,' Adam would call out at night. 'Dad.'

The year his teeth started to change, the year he finished first grade. What would have happened if I'd called, too? A chorus of two boys, calling for their father? What was Mom doing? I want to think that the Ativan addiction had started way back then, that she was all but unconscious, dealing with her own troubles. But wouldn't that be just as bad—my mother, drugged out while my father went into my room at night, then my little brother's?

Sometimes my father would poke his head in my door and ask if I was okay, and I would nod, and lie awake and stare at the ceiling and wonder what I'd done wrong.

When I was in my twenties, just before Dad died, I started to talk about it in therapy. My therapist asked where my mother was during all of that, and it was the first time I broke down crying.

'Sometimes we focus so much on what one parent did that we don't look at what the other parent didn't do,' she said.

When I told the therapist that I had felt abandoned, I was terrified. I felt implicated. But she explained that this was how things normally go. That kids aren't held down and forcibly violated.

'Your body responded the way bodies respond. But you were too young to understand what was happening. It's hard for a child to know how damaging the abuse can be until it stops,' she said. 'Then they're left wondering why the thing that happened with their abuser over a period of time suddenly ceased.'

She was full of perspectives like this that provided a great relief to me.

A few sessions later, she asked me if my brother was seeking help, too.

Not as far as I knew. She asked me what I thought of that, and I said I didn't know.

It felt as if we were still in different rooms. Adam down the hall, me in the darkness. Like someone passing through me to get where he wanted to be now, parting me on the way.

But I didn't tell her that.

Saoirse is on the phone in the other room; she's talking about the baby. She's careful, even when talking to others, to not say the gender. I can hear her wavering as she speaks.

I open my laptop and go to the Megan's Law page on the state website.

There's a picture of police helicopters and text telling me that people are safer if this information is online. Under that, there's a green button I must click to agree I can't use the information to harass the people listed, or their families. I click it, and a side bar with MOST WANTED OFFENDERS pops up. I type in Adam's zip code, and a small list of people appears. All men. Their photos. Their addresses. What they've done. I click on one; he's 20.

The page states in capital letters that there's a tattoo on his leg of a jester. This man is an 'SVP' which stands for Sexually Violent Predator. As far as Pennsylvania law is concerned, he falls under an abbreviation.

I click on another, this time a man who has abused a child. He looks young, too.

TATTOO: BACK, MYSTIC SHOOTING STAR.

There are a few pictures, taken across a few years, I guess so the offender becomes recognisable. So that people can keep their neighbourhood safe. It's not their neighbourhoods they need to keep safe. It's their own families. It's whatever they ignored in the middle of the night, just down the hall.

I have a strange fear, scrolling down, scrolling through, that I'll see my own face. A little square, Luke Edmonton, in row with the others.

I click on another zip code. I'm not there, either. Of course I'm not, I haven't done anything, of course I don't see my own face.

There's a woman in this county, she's in her 60s, she looks like anyone's grandmother or aunt or a family friend. I wonder what she's done? I'm about to open up her file when Saoirse walks by, and I close the laptop, but she catches me. She probably just thinks I'm looking at porn, and doesn't say anything, smiles as she passes the doorway.

And I realise that I was looking through the site for Adam.

Saoirse's voice, from down the hall, comes as a jab. 'Are you done,' she asks, 'looking at other women?' Then she's in the room. 'Feel,' she says. I put my hand on her belly. There's the knock from the inside, and I remember the sound the bags made in the trunk. She looks down. 'Just a couple more weeks till you meet Mommy and Daddy,' she says.

But what if it's a boy?

'I was in high school, and we had a group field trip,' I told the therapist. 'They also brought some of the middle school boys along. And the high school boys... we relentlessly teased the younger kids, throwing wads of paper at them, stealing their bags. And there was this one kid, he was... I don't remember his name. He was little, though. Hadn't even grown into being eleven or twelve yet. And even though I joined in teasing the other boys, I thought, if anyone goes *near* him, I'll break their nose. And so to protect him, I got up and sat next to him.'

'Was there any physical contact between you?' the therapist asked.

'Listen, I know if I say anything like that, you have to report me, you have to tell the police' I said. 'So I know why you're asking, but no, nothing, I just sat next to him. I was protecting him. But I felt... something. And I'm not even gay or anything, but there was... a feeling. Nothing happened. I'm not just saying that.'

'Luke,' she said, and her saying my name pulled me out of it. 'You were a child then.'

'But not like he was,' I said.

'No, not like he was. But you were still a child. You know, most abused children do not become abusers?'

'Why did it happen to my Dad, then?' I asked.

'I don't know,' she said. 'There are lots of reasons it could have, but I don't know.' She shifted in her seat. 'There's a group,' she said. 'Would you consider going? It's a therapy group for survivors.'

She wrote the information down.

The therapist had probably saved my life. But after that, I stopped seeing her.

And I didn't go to the group right away. I should have. But I didn't until Adam was gone.

There are twelve of us in metal chairs.

This is the second time in a week that I'm here. I told Saoirse that I was driving around to clear my head.

One of us stands.

'It was my aunt and uncle,' she says. 'I was eight. My mom was a drunk. She's okay now, I talk to her and she's sober, and I don't know why I'm defending her. I just... Anyway. Back then. My mom's sister... They took me on after Mom was arrested for the second time for a DUI and had to go to jail. So suddenly I was living with them, and the first night, my uncle...'

Gilbert, who runs the group, says, 'Take a deep breath, and if you can keep going, keep going. But don't feel you have to.'

'I can,' she says. 'I can, I can. My uncle sat me down on the couch and put his hand on my leg, and my aunt was standing right there, and she said, "Don't worry, that's just what we do in this house."'

'How long were you there?' a man to my right asks.

'Five years,' she said. 'I didn't realise it wasn't normal until I told my friend at school about it.'

There are meetings like this everywhere. There are public service announcements when you're a kid. There are books about it. There are sites on the internet devoted to it. There are laws around it. No, it's not normal, but it's everywhere, so what is it instead? It's happening all the time, happening right now. And still we only talk about it, really talk about it, in these little rooms, where it looks like an AA meeting, where we're confessing, or reviewing it.

'Does anyone want to add anything?' Gilbert says.

I'm about to stand and ask:

Do any of you feel afraid it will follow you?

Do you feel afraid it will trace its way through you, hunt you down, make you become it?

Did you wonder if it happened to the adults when they were kids?

Do you wonder if that means it will come through you too, like you're a marionette and you can't help it; just a current, a bend of history, a tide, an invader?

Do you feel like you've escaped?

And if not, how can we escape?

How can we get out?

My wife is pregnant. My wife is pregnant, I need to know.

What if it's a boy?

But before I can speak, I recognise a face across from me. And that face can answer those questions.

Mystic shooting star.

There was an ad on TV when I was a boy, a PSA. It had a child actor in it, although actually the child actor had a rare genetic disorder or something, something that kept him looking like a kid most of his life. So this adult, who looked like a child, was talking to the viewer; talking to me, talking to Adam.

'If someone touches you in a way you don't like, say NO then GO and TELL someone you trust!' He ran in front of giant plastic letters that spelled NO and GO and TELL.

And at school the guidance counsellor came into our classes with a puppet shaped like a dolphin and the dolphin on her hand told us that only doctors were allowed to touch us under where we wore our bathing suits, and that that was a 'good touch', but otherwise it was a bad touch, and if it was a bad touch, we should tell Mommy and Daddy. The dolphin nodded, and we nodded. Especially if they forced us to be touched. That was the worst, the dolphin said. No one should force you to be touched.

Tell someone we trust, but we trusted Dad. We trusted Mom. Don't let anyone force you. But we weren't forced.

'Dad,' Adam called from down the hall.

After the meeting, I follow the man with the mystic shooting star tattoo to the parking lot.

'Hey!' I say, as he reaches his car, and he gets in and closes the door and opens the window just a crack.

'What?' he says.

'I just...' I'm not sure how to go on. 'I just wanted to talk to you. I'm new, this is my second time here. I'm trying to make friends.'

I think he notices my wedding ring, because he says, 'Are you married?'

'I used to be,' I lie, as though my normal life will be too much for him. He rolls down the window all the way, and I think, suddenly, of the bag sitting by the door at home, filled with Saoirse's things, ready to go as soon as she feels the baby coming. Then I feel him holding my hand.

'I'm Bryce,' he says.

I look around. Everyone else is going their separate ways or lingering just past the entrance of the VFW, illuminated by the orange lights inside, being there for one another. When he touches me, it's like the truth shows in a flash. His name is Jeremy Silver. The mystic star tattoo shoots from shoulder to skull. Not Bryce.

Is he allowed to lie about his name? He has to tell everyone in his neighbourhood that he lives there and that he's a sex offender. He's also not supposed to be where children gather. Every move he makes could be a potential crime. I think about him accidentally walking past a playground on his way to a grocery store and someone seeing him, recognising him, calling the police.

'What's your name?' he asks.

'Luke,' I say, though again I have this urge to lie, have the urge to say: *Adam.*

'I just want to be a father,' I said to the therapist once.

'Is there a reason you think you can't be?'

I wanted to yell at her, but I sat in silence until the feeling either went away or was just driven deeper into me. Who can tell the difference?

'Not like mine,' I finally said.

'What would it mean to be a father?' she asked, after a time. 'Are there images?'

'Holding my kid up in the backyard,' I said. 'Against the sun. We're smiling.'

'A boy?' she asked.

Two days later, I go to a restaurant in the mall with Jeremy Silver. He's still calling himself Bryce. The restaurant has memorabilia on the walls. Old newspapers above the urinal in the bathroom, a kid's red wagon hanging from the ceiling. Every booth has a different glass lampshade.

'I'd like to kill the fucks that do that to kids,' Bryce, or Jeremy, says. He's talking about the woman from the other night. Her uncle and aunt. The waiter comes over and leaves a plate of fries for us to share. Jeremy has a drink ordered from the restaurant's klutzy cocktail menu; it's a pale orange and has Swedish Fish floating in it, soaking up the alcohol. 'Her own family,' he goes on. 'Maniacs.'

'What happened to you?' I ask. 'You don't have to tell me. But, if you want to.'

'What happened to *you*?' he counters, quickly.

'My father,' I say.

'I'm sorry.' He eats a French fry.

'And my brother.'

'Your brother? Which side was he on?'

Side?

'He was like me,' I say. But maybe one day he wasn't anymore. Maybe one day he was like my dad.

Jeremy eats the Swedish fish and, chewing, says, 'There are a hundred ways to hurt kids. Even when we're born. Circumcision. Genital mutilation. Do you know that sometimes they botch that and cut off the head of the dick? Or the penis... I guess that's a better word for it when you're a kid. That should be against the law.'

'Did that happen to you?'

He gives me a look. 'What the fuck? No, I have everything intact. My physical body, anyway.'

He turns to look around before he speaks again, and I can see the mystic star shooting just past the collar of his shirt, seized in the mid-air of his flesh. It's mystic because one of the points has Sanskrit on it. I want to ask him what the words say, but I don't want him to know I noticed it. He turns back to me and says, 'Do you know there's stuff like, all the time, just going on? That right now, some kids are getting abused?'

'What do you think is going on with the people who do it?' I ask.

He eats a little more, then says, 'Satan.'

He doesn't continue, and I'm not sure what to say, so I sit, stunned, until the silence lingers too long and he elaborates. 'All that stuff in the 80s, you know? The day-care stuff, butcher knives up the ass, skin hung on trees. People just worshipping something. I don't know. Power or what.'

'But my Dad wasn't like that—'

'Sure, sure, there are lots of people that are just fucked up. But like what that woman at the meeting said. Where they just sat her down and said, "this is how it is, you're going to get raped", or whatever. That's devil stuff. Child porn. That sort of thing.'

'Don't you think it's because it happened to the person, the abuser, when he was a kid or that it can, you know follow through. Like, It's an impulse, or…'

'How do you think the devil works?' he says quickly, like it was the stupidest question I could have asked. 'He jumps from abuser and into the kid and then the kid grows up, and then that's it.'

I want to ask if that's what happened to him. I want to ask if it ever ends, or if there's always a lingering threat. *Will it happen to your kids?* I want to know. *Would you ever have kids?* I start formulating a question that will reveal something, that will help me understand, but before it comes together, he says something.

'It's like the devil walking through high grass. *Wsssh*, you can hear it. *Wsssh*, the grass parting, a path opening up, and everything just making way until he gets to the fingertips and touches the boy, or the girl. *Wsssh*, and suddenly, he's in the next person, and that sound is inside him. That breath of the devil parting the high grass.'

Adam called me once.

Said he'd been going through it. Could I come by?

'I don't know what to do,' he said, when I arrived. 'I got fired.'

'From the church group? We can find you another job. Want me to ask—'

'It's not about the job,' he said.

I sat down next to him.

Before he told me the story, he said please, please don't tell anyone.

He was twenty, I was twenty-three. That summer, he'd gotten a job with a church group, though he wasn't sure he believed in God. He was aimless, but they liked him. They didn't care that he didn't talk much. He told me he sang a lot, and that surprised me: my brother singing revival songs. He was assigned to be a residential director at Youth Fest In Christ, a week-long camp that took place on a college campus, with middle school students staying in the dorms, paired up with roommates they didn't know. The supervisors wanted him to make sure the kids didn't drink or smoke or fuck or swear. They were supposed to have fun, but with the Lord in mind.

At night, Adam was to stay up until 11:00 to make sure everyone was asleep or at least quiet enough that they might be. He would walk up and down the halls, and in his own dorm room try to read the Bible and take notes. It was alien to both of us; we hadn't had any religion beyond a half-hearted trip to the Lutheran church down the street when we were kids. All around us, Catholic kids and Protestant kids, a whole world we weren't a part of.

Just after 11, there was a knock on his door.

In the doorway, a boy named Micah, smaller than the rest of the boys his age.

'I asked him what was up,' Adam said. 'And then he came in and asked if he could tell me something, and asked me to not say anything to anyone else.'

Micah's roommate had been using swear words all weekend, had said that he was just there because his parents forced him to come, that the InFaith worksheets were a waste of time, and worst of all, was going up two floors to the girls' rooms. Micah had begged Adam not to tell anyone.

Adam paused. 'The rooms,' he said, finally, 'they were… tiny. It was just a desk and then a foot or two between that and the bed. So. We were. He was. Sitting on the edge of the bed next to me when he told me.'

'What happened?' I asked, quietly.

'Nothing,' Adam said.

The boy was wearing shorts and a T-shirt, and when Adam talked to him, he put his hand on the boy's thigh.

'I sort of, I don't know, I felt something, I—'

I stood up.

'Why the fuck are you telling me this?' I shouted. 'Why?'

Adam put his face in his hands and started to cry.

'Adam. *What happened?*'

'Nothing!' he said through the muffle of his hands. He pulled them away but wouldn't look up. 'Nothing, nothing, I just… But… He was gone the next day, and he'd told the camp director that I made him feel weird. They asked how, they asked if I'd done anything, and he said no, nothing, but that I wouldn't stop the kid's roommate from getting drunk, that I wouldn't help him, and that he didn't feel like he had anyone to turn to. Or, well, his parents... his parents said that he told them that. I was fired the next day. I've just been... waiting for something to happen.'

'Adam, you need to fucking get help,' I said.

'That's what I was doing when I called you.'

'Not me,' I demanded. 'Someone. It can't be me, it can't.' I walked to the door and when I opened it, I turned and saw my brother, his eyes now puffy with the crying.

'Who else would listen?' he said, alone at the table.

When I get home from the restaurant, I sit in my car in the driveway and I call the therapist. I haven't spoken with her in two years, but she answers after a few rings.

'It's Luke Edmonton,' I say.

'I know, hi Luke. Is this an emergency?'

'No, It's not an emergency, but I have to ask you something, and I have to ask right now.'

'Go ahead.'

'If you found out that someone had those... feelings, about kids, what should you do?'

She's quiet for a second. Then she asks, 'Is this person a clear danger to children? Is the urge overwhelming?'

'I don't know.' I realise that she might be asking me a different question. 'There's this guy,' I say, quickly. 'And he was on the sex offender registry and I met him at a group, the survivors group? You told me to go to? And he's lying about his name, and I just don't know why he's there.'

There's a moment. Then, 'Is this about someone at the group, or about someone else?'

My brother Adam had magazines in a shoe box in his closet.

My brother Adam used to tell me his whole life he thought about what our father had done and couldn't forget it at all, like it was a mark on him.

My brother Adam put his hand on a boy's leg.

My brother Adam had a prayer for children and a pendant to protect them.

My brother Adam had a photo of a naked boy.

Each possible statement rolls through my head.

'I'm sorry about your brother,' she says, and my thoughts stop so abruptly that my head hurts.

'My brother Adam… '

'I saw the notice. In the paper.'

I hesitate. I didn't think she'd remember. Or that if she saw that Adam had died, that she'd make the connection that it was *that* Adam.

'Listen, you should really make—' she says, but a light goes on in the house and I hang up on her.

I go in, and Saoirse is sitting on the edge of the bed.

'Hi, sorry, I just needed to drive longer tonight. Just to clear my head.'

'Luke,' she says. 'What is this?'

She's holding the photo of the boy. It's divided by a scar of white cross made from the folds.

The first time Adam hurt himself, he was twelve. He sliced the top of his arm open with a pair of scissors, three lines across the top, Holy Spirit, Son and Father. We were in his room and he pulled up the top of his sleeve.

'Did it hurt?' I asked, blankly.

'That's the point,' he said.

We were sitting on the edge of his bed, and the lines were still red, and punctuated by scabs.

'Do you want to do it?' he asked.

'I think it would hurt,' I said. I felt like his little brother instead of his older brother. 'And I don't care if that's the point.'

Adam stabbed the top of my arm with the tip of the scissors.

'Fuck!' I shouted. It was like a dog biting in play, an unpleasant surprise from someone you trust.

I got up and left the room. I didn't know what to do, so, stupidly, I told on him. Mom was at the kitchen table, Dad was looking in the fridge. 'Adam cut his arm up,' I said. 'And look.' I pulled my sleeve up to where a pearl of blood clung at the puncture.

My dad walked past me and up the stairs.

'You shouldn't have said anything,' my mom said.

It wasn't until we were older and Mom was sober that I could think of her holding us as babies, cradling us. Even though I'd seen photos of us just out of the hospital, helpless and tucked close to her body, it never seemed like the woman in the photos could have been her.

'Do you even care?' I spat at her.

I went back up the stairs. I saw my father through the open door to Adam's room. The scissors were on the carpet, and Adam was under Dad's arm with his head against Dad's chest. Dad had tears coming from his eyes.

'Why would you do this?' he said. He rocked back and forth, holding my brother. 'Don't ever do this again, you understand?'

My brother swayed with him, crying too, scarred up the arm.

The rain is falling as I leave the house the next day. The sound of the devil in the grass. I'm going to Jeremy Silver's apartment, to the address on Pennsylvania's sex offenders' website.

I told Saoirse it was a photo of a childhood friend of Adam's and mine.

I could tell she didn't totally believe me, maybe because the photo looked more recent than photos of our childhoods should have, but the cross in the folds had ruined the picture just enough.

'So what's his name?' she asked.

'Bryce,' I said.

Jeremy's apartment is in a building called Forest Village. The brick is tan; concrete balconies, beige railings, green awning over the entrance. At some point, a police officer walked through this building with flyers of Jeremy's face, sliding them under each door. 'This Notice Is Provided For Advisory Purposes Only', it would have read. 'This Is Not A Wanted Person'.

Were his neighbours kind to him? Did they ever talk? Did they look at him with fear as they walked down the hall? What happened if one of his neighbours had kids over? Or had a kid?

What if it's a boy?

Someone walks up to the door and I get out of the car and walk up quickly behind. She gives me a quizzical look, but doesn't question me as I walk in behind her.

Jeremy's front door is brown with a brass knocker. He opens the door in a college sweatshirt and shorts.

'How did you know where I live?'

I don't say anything, and I feel then that he must know how. He asks me in.

The apartment is clean, nondescript. It looks like Adam's. There's a book on the kitchen counter with a baby on the cover. Jeremy pulls two plastic bottles of water from his fridge and hands me one.

I find myself making sure it makes the sound of the lid cracking as I open it. I take a drink and look at the book on the counter.

'Oh,' Jeremy says, and holds it up. *The Circumcision Trauma: Ending An Ancient Atrocity.* 'I just can't believe they would do this to a baby. It's barbaric, if you think about it. I joined a group a while ago that does protests, online petitions and stuff.' He offers me the book.

'No, that's all right.'

'Are you?' he asks.

'Am I?'

'Sometimes they accidentally cut off the glans. You know, the head? For what? So they can keep worshipping some Jewish God?'

I steady myself. 'It's not just Jewish kids,' I say.

'Oh, I know, of course, but still.' He tosses the book back on the counter and sits down on the couch. I think about his activism group. How would they feel if they knew what he'd done? They'd probably shun him, no matter what he did. The only way he could make the world better at this point would be to not try to help.

'Who's Bryce?' I ask.

He looks at his hand, holding the water. Outside, someone shouts across the street as the rain picks up.

'It's not like you're not the first person who's just showed up at my door,' he says. 'But look, I'm *trying*. I've been trying.'

'Trying to what?'

'Are we friends?' he asks.

I don't say anything.

'Hold on,' he says. He walks out of the room, and I hear him shuffling around.

'I came to ask you something,' I say, but he doesn't respond. My phone vibrates again and again in my pocket and I look at it. Saoirse.

Jeremy comes back into the room.

'I have to—'

'Hold on,' he says. 'I have to show you something.' He's holding a VHS tape. 'Just… promise you won't say anything.'

Jeremy goes up to the TV and kneels in front. 'Promise,' he says. But I don't answer.

The phone vibrates again in my pocket. *It's happening!* A text reads.

He reaches behind and hooks up the VCR; a relic, a machine from childhood.

He puts the tape in and turns the TV on, presses play and moves to the side.

On it, a little boy is sitting at the edge of a bed. The film is shaky.

A flash comes across the little boy. Photos. The little boy laughs. There's the sound of breathing near the camera.

'Do you like this game?' A man's voice behind the camera, so close to the mic that it fuzzes in the TV speakers at the edge of each word. It's not Jeremy's voice.

'Yeah,' the little boy says.

My phone vibrates.

'Jeremy,' I say.

'Now jump up and down on the bed!' the voice says, and more flashes illuminate the room, the arrival of a force of light. The boy gets up and starts jumping and laughs more. A woman's voice, then. 'Now we want you to take your shirt off, okay, honey?'

'I'm dizzy!' the little boy says.

My phone vibrates.

The boy takes his shirt off. His skin looks soft and muted white against the room, almost translucent when the camera flashes cut across him. He looks familiar. He looks like someone I know.

I stand up. 'I have to call the police,' I say. 'Jeremy, I have to—'

'No!' he shouts. 'No, you don't understand!'

The boy is laughing on the TV. The man's voice comes again, pushing on the boundaries of the speakers. My phone vibrates.

'Look,' Jeremy says. '*Look!*'

I pull my phone out.

Saoirse: *Where are you.*

Saoirse: *You're supposed to have your phone.*

Saoirse: *I'm calling an ambulance.*

'Please, put your phone away!' Jeremy presses pause as the boy is leaning back to lie down and a flash has just started to invade the room again.

'That's *me.*' Jeremy touches the TV screen. '*Look*, that's *me.* The boy... That's me. *Me.*'

He's sitting on the floor in front of the TV, looking up at me. The star is frozen on his skin, paused like a flash, seized in the air.

'Jeremy, why do you still have this?'

He closes his eyes and starts to cry. I kneel in front of him. My phone is ringing, but I ignore it. I reach into my other pocket and pull out the tiny sheet of paper.

'Here,' I say.

He opens it.

'Read it.'

'Loving Saint Nicholas,' he says,

'May I strive to imitate you.

'Give me courage, love and strength.

'And where...'

He takes a deep breath.

'And where I cannot be brave or strong, please protect the children.'

'Amen,' I say.

'Amen,' he says. And like a photo, for a moment, everything is still.

At the hospital, time moves forward, the baby is being born. I rush to the desk, soaked through by the rain. 'Saoirse Edmonton,' I say.

'Finally,' the receptionist says.

I put on a gown and run down the hallway.

A doctor is about to usher me in, but I pause. I close my eyes. I say a different prayer.

Please Dad.

Please let the devil die.

And I see my brother's face. A boy, in a backyard pool, the sun falling on him, my father standing behind me, watching.

Please let the devil have died in Adam.

Amen.

I walk into the room, where the baby is already in the nurse's arms, smeared with blood and fluid from my wife's body. And it's screaming, screaming itself into life.

Saoirse looks up at me, not in anger or relief, but confusion.

And the doctor turns to me to say, with beaming pride and innocence, 'It's a

STINGING FLY PATRONS

Many thanks to:

Susan Armstrong
Maria Behan
Valerie Bistany
Jacqueline Brown
Angela Bourke
Trish Byrne
Edmond Condon
Evelyn Conlon
Claire Connolly
Kris Deffenbacher
Enrico Del Prete
Vicky Dillon
Andrew Donovan
Elaine Feeney
Stephen Grant
Brendan Hackett
Huang Haisu
Sean Hanrahan
James Harrold
Teresa Harte
Christine Dwyer Hickey
Dennis & Mimi Houlihan
Garry Hynes
Nuala Jackson
Charles Julienne
Jeremy Kavanagh
Jerry Kelleher
Margaret Kelleher
Claire Keogh
Joe Lawlor
Ilana Lifshitz

Lucy Luck
Jon McGregor
John McInerney
Maureen McLaughlin
Niall MacMonagle
Finbar McLoughlin
Maggie McLoughlin
Ama, Grace & Fraoch MacSweeney
Moira MacSweeney
Lucius Moser
Michael O'Connor
Ed O'Loughlin
Maria Pierce
Peter J. Pitkin
George & Joan Preble
John Putt
Fiona Ruff
Anne Ryan
Linda Ryan
Ann Seery
Attique Shafiq
Eileen Sheridan
Helena Texier
Olive Towey
John Vaughan
Debbi Voisey
Therese Walsh
Ruth Webster
The Moderate Review
Museum of Literature Ireland
Solas Nua

*We would also like to thank those individuals who have expressed the preference
to remain anonymous.*

BECOME A PATRON ONLINE AT STINGINGFLY.ORG

Kate Caoimhe Arthur lives in County Down. She was selected for Poetry Ireland Introductions (2018) and New Irish Writing (2020). She has published poetry in *The Tangerine, Abridged* and *Blackbox Manifold*, and reviews in *PN Review*.

Bebe Ashley lives in County Down. Her current writing charts her progress towards qualifying as a British Sign Language interpreter. *Gold Light Shining*, her first collection, was published by Banshee Press. www.bebe-ashley.com

Tríona Bromwell is a disabled person living in Dublin with her husband, two daughters and miniature schnauzer, Ozzy. An occupational therapist in a previous life, chronic illness has thrown some curveballs. Reading is an old friend, writing a new companion.

Edel Brosnan has worked as an ESB cashier, youth hostel cleaner, screenwriter, radio playwright, script editor and grant funding consultant. Originally from Tralee, she was based in London for over two decades, and has recently relocated to Dublin.

Ríbh Brownlee is from Belfast. She is the founder of *Catatonic Daughters* magazine.

Gonchigkhand Byambaa is a social worker and writer from Mongolia. She is proud of her nomadic heritage and passionate about improving minorities' rights in Ireland. Gonchigkhand wishes to contribute positively to Irish society, which she deeply admires.

P Kearney Byrne is working on a novel in short stories, assisted by funding from the Arts Council. Her work has appeared in *The Dublin Review, The White Review, Banshee, Per Contra* and elsewhere. She lives in County Clare.

Sara Chudzik was born in Poland and moved to Limerick when she was 12 years old. She is a graduate of the University of Galway and a recipient of the Play It Forward Fellowship. Sara currently works and lives in Dublin.

Polina Cosgrave is a bilingual poet based in Ireland. Dedalus Press published her debut collection, *My Name Is*. Polina features in *The Forward Book of Poetry 2022*.

Aoife Esmonde lives in Dublin and is writing a novel. Her first short story, 'Overspill', was published in the anthology *The Last Five Minutes of a Storm*.

Sarah Fitzgerald, from Tullamore, has been writing for eight years. Her work has included articles, blogs and monologues. Interested in amplifying the rights narrative for disabled people, she is working on her first novel, about a headstrong protagonist called Rachel.

Will Fleming is a PhD candidate and teaching assistant in the English department at University College London. He researches contemporary Irish experimental poetry. He was born in Limerick and raised in Wicklow.

Bernadette Gallagher is a poet from Donegal living in County Cork. She is a recipient of an Arts Council Agility Award 2021. bernadettegallagher. blogspot.ie

Margaret Gillies completed the Creative Writing MA at University College Cork in 2021. Her work has featured in *Dodging the Rain, The Echo, The Sunday Independent* and *Quarryman*. She is currently working on a novel.

Neo Florence Gilson is a Cork-based poet, singer, writer, and storyteller from South Africa. Neo is a recipient of the Play It Forward Fellowship and an artist-in-residence at Sample-Studios, in conjunction with the Radical Institute Studios of Sanctuary. She is also developing new work as an artist-in-residence with Corcadorca Theatre Company.

Eva Griffin lives in Dublin. Her pamphlets *Fake Hands / Real Flowers* (2020) and *one last spin around the sun* (2021) are published by Broken Sleep Books.

Conner Habib is the author of the novel *Hawk Mountain* and the host of the culture, occult, and philosophy podcast, *Against Everyone with Conner Habib*. He lives in Ireland.

Lucy Holme is studying on the Creative Writing MA at University College Cork. Her poems feature in *Southword, Wild Court, Poetry Birmingham* and *New Irish Writing* among others. Her chapbook, *Temporary Stasis*, is published by Broken Sleep Books.

Liz Houchin lives in Dublin. In 2021, she was awarded a Literature Bursary from the Arts Council and her chapbook, *Anatomy of a Honey girl—poems for tired women*, was published by Southword Editions.

Nandi Jola is an MA student at the Seamus Heaney Centre, Queen's University Belfast. She is a commissioned poet for AMBIGUITIES on Poetry Jukebox, supported by the Arts Council of Northern Ireland and Poetry Ireland, as part of the centenary James Joyce programme of Centre Culturel Irlandais. Her debut poetry collection, *Home is Neither Here Nor There*, is published by Doire Press.

Francis Jones is an Irish poet based in Glasgow. Their debut pamphlet *sacrificial fabric* was published by SPAM in 2021.

Fiachra Kelleher is a writer from Cork. He is working on a novel.

Viv Kemp is a writer from Dublin. They have edited *Icarus Magazine* and their poetry has appeared in *Notes, New Writing*, and *The UEA MA Poetry Anthology 2021*.

William Keohane is a writer from Limerick. His essays have been published in *British GQ, Banshee,* and *The Tangerine*. He is currently writer-in-residence at Ormston House.

Chris Kitson grew up in County Down and lives in Scotland. His work has appeared in *Poetry Proper* and *The Tangerine*.

Lauren Mackenzie has published short stories, flash fiction and poetry in the *Irish Times*, *The Moth*, *Banshee* and *The Lonely Crowd*, among others. *The Couples*, her first novel, will be published by John Murray Press in 2023.

Maija Sofia Mäkelä is a musician and poet from the west of Ireland. Her debut album, *Bath Time*, was nominated for the RTÉ Choice Music Prize. Her writing has appeared in *Banshee*, *The Thin Air* and elsewhere.

Alan McCormick lives in Wicklow. His first story collection, *Dogsbodies and Scumsters*, was longlisted for the Edge Hill Short Story Prize. He's recently completed a second collection and is working on a memoir. His story, 'Firestarter', was first runner-up in the 2022 RTÉ Short Story Competition in honour of Francis MacManus. www.alanmccormickwriting.wordpress.com

David McGovern is an interdisciplinary, socially engaged artist. He works with moving image, audio, performance and text to create space for self-enquiry, reflection and speculation. David is currently developing new work entitled HARDCARE, a participatory artwork exploring unconventional care experiences.

David McGrath is currently mentored by Colin Barrett thanks to the IWC National Mentoring Programme and Wicklow Arts Office. He won the Bare Fiction Prize with a story entitled 'Ger Sheen and the Satanists', also set in the universe of 'The Untameable Donkey.'

Majed Mujed is a multi award-winning Iraqi poet currently residing in Dublin. He has published five poetry books, is a 2022 recipient of an Agility Award from the Arts Council, and a recipient of the Play It Forward fellowship.

Chandrika Narayanan-Mohan is writer, performer, and cultural consultant from India living in Dublin. Her work has been published by Dedalus Press, UCD Press, Lifeboat Press, *Banshee*, Poetry Ireland and others.

Niamh O'Connell holds an MA in creative writing from Newcastle University. Her work has appeared in *Quarryman*, *Bind Collective*, *Banshee* and elsewhere.

Karl O'Hanlon lives outside Maynooth. His poetry has appeared in *Bad Lilies*, *Poetry*, *The Hopkins Review*, and elsewhere. His pamphlet *And Now They Range* was published by Guillemot Press.

Shane O'Neill's creative writing appears in various journals including *Púca*, *Sonder Magazine* and *Paper Lanterns*. He was the recipient of an Agility Award for non-fiction from the Arts Council in both 2021 and 2022. He recently completed his doctoral thesis.

Leopold O'Shea is from Dublin. This is his first work of fiction. He would prefer not to.

Cait Phenix is a recent graduate of the Poetry MA at Queen's University Belfast and was a recipient of the Ireland Chair of Poetry 2021 Student Award.

Tanvi Roberts lives in Belfast. Her poems have appeared or are forthcoming in *Rattle, Poetry Ireland Review,* and *The Moth*. She was longlisted for the 2021 National Poetry Competition.

Brenda Romero is a game designer and writer in Galway. She has written four trade books and published game-like pieces in *The Dublin Review* and *Tolka*. A PhD English student at Trinity College, Dublin, she is working on a memoir.

Tom Roseingrave (he/him) is a writer and performer living in Dublin. He writes short fiction and essays, and runs the Frustrated Writers' Group.

Sree Sen is from India and currently based in Dublin. Her work appears in *Poetry Ireland Review, Banshee, Honest Ulsterman,* and elsewhere. Her debut poetry chapbook, *Cracked Asphalt*, was published in August.

Rosa Thomas is an actor and writer based in Dublin. A graduate of The Gaiety School of Acting, her poetry has been shortlisted for The Bridport Prize and The Hot Press National Poetry Competition.

Shane Tivenan's work has appeared in *The London Magazine* and been broadcast on RTÉ Radio 1. In 2020, he won the RTÉ Short Story Competition in honour of Francis MacManus. He is currently writing a collection of short fiction, supported by the Arts Council.

Eoghan Totten is a Longley scholar in poetry (Seamus Heaney Centre, Queen's University Belfast) and Ireland Chair of Poetry student awardee, with poems in *Magma* (forthcoming), *Romance Options* (Dedalus Press) and elsewhere.

Joanne Touhey is a writer based in Roscommon. Her prose and poetry have appeared in literary journals *Tír na nÓg* and *Olney Magazine*. Joanne is pursuing a PhD in English at Trinity College, Dublin, and is working on a memoir.

Jennifer Walshe is a composer and artist whose works often focus on technology, the internet, invented histories and text. She is professor of composition at the University of Oxford. Her most recent album, *A Late Anthology of Early Music Vol. 1: Ancient to Renaissance*, uses AI to rewrite the early history of Western music.

James Ward is from Westmeath. He holds an MA in Creative Writing and Education from Goldsmiths, University of London. He is currently working on his first novel. He lives in London. You can follow him on Twitter at @jamesfward

Anam Zafar is a UK-based translator working from Arabic and French into English. She was awarded our inaugural New Translator's Bursary in 2021. Her translations have been published in various places. She runs translation workshops for young people and volunteers for World Kid Lit.